The Struggle for
the Ottoman Empire
1717—1740

The Struggle for
the Ottoman Empire

1717–1740

✣

LAVENDER CASSELS

THOMAS Y. CROWELL COMPANY
New York · Established 1834

To
R. and P.
who endured the vicissitudes
of the struggle

First published in the United States of America in 1967

Printed in the United States of America

L.C. Card 67–26100

Contents

Preface   ix

Acknowledgements   xi

Prologue: The Pivot of the Struggle   1
The Fortress of Belgrade, 1717

Part One

THE PROTAGONISTS

I.   The Emperor and his Ministers   13
Vienna, 1718–1726

II.   The Czarina and her Advisers   29
St. Petersburg, 1727–1730

III.   The Cardinal and his Ambassador   44
Paris–Constantinople, 1726–1728

IV.   The Sultan, the Porte and the Foreign Envoys   54
Constantinople, 1728–1729

Part Two

PRELUDE TO THE STRUGGLE

V.   Diplomatic Stalemate   73
Constantinople, 1730–1732

VI.   The Discomfiture of the French Ambassador   86
Constantinople, 1733–summer 1735

VII.   Russia Attacks   97
St. Petersburg–Azov and the Crimea–Constantinople,
Autumn 1735–1739

Part Three

TRIAL OF STRENGTH

VIII.   Austria goes to War   115
Vienna–Hungary–Serbia, January–July 1737

IX.   An Abortive Peace Congress   127
Nemirow, July–October 1737

Contents

X. The Second Round
Vienna–St. Petersburg–Paris–the Battlefields–
Constantinople, October 1737–December 1738
138

XI. A Mediator is Appointed
Paris–Constantinople–Belgrade, January–August 1739
156

XII. Deadlock
Belgrade, July–August 1739
171

XIII. 'This Thorny Negotiation'
Belgrade, August–September 1739
182

XIV. The *Fait Accompli*
October 1739–May 1740
197

Note on Currency
208

Notes
209

Bibliography
217

Index
223

Illustrations

Equestrian portrait of Prince Eugen of Savoy. *Reproduced by kind permission of the Heeresgeschichtliches Museum, Vienna* Facing page   18

The Battle of Belgrade, 1717, from an engraving after a contemporary picture by van Huchtenburgh. *Reproduced by courtesy of the Trustees of the British Museum*   19

Emperor Charles VI, from a portrait in Schönbrunn by an unknown artist. *Reproduced by kind permission of the Bildarchiv der Österreichischen Nationalbibliothek*   34

Czarina Anne I, from an engraving by Joseph Wagner after a painting by Jacopo Amigoni. *Reproduced by kind permission of the Bildarchiv der Österreichischen Nationalbibliothek*   35

Field-Marshal Münnich, from an engraving by Bornigoroth after a painting by an unknown artist. *Reproduced by kind permission of the Bildarchiv der Österreichischen Nationalbibliothek*   66

Cardinal Fleury, from an engraving by François Chereau after a painting by Rigaud. *Reproduced by kind permission of the Bildarchiv der Österreichischen Nationalbibliothek*   67

The Sultan and two court officials, from a contemporary painting by J. B. Vanmour. *Reproduced by kind permission of the Rijksmuseum, Amsterdam*   82

View of Constantinople and the Serail, *c.* 1730, from a painting by J. B. Vanmour. *Reproduced by kind permission of the Rijksmuseum, Amsterdam*   83

Illustrations

The Emperor's Chancellor, Count Sinzendorf, from an engraving by Claude Drevet after a painting by Rigaud. *Reproduced by kind permission of the Bildarchiv der Österreichischen National-bibliothek* 130

The Grand Vizier, from a painting by J. B. Vanmour. *Reproduced by kind permission of the Rijksmuseum, Amsterdam* 131

An Austrian Infantryman, from a coloured print. *Reproduced by kind permission of the Heeresgeschichtliches Museum, Vienna* 146

A Janissary, from a drawing by Weigel in the author's possession 146

An Ambassador, possibly the Marquis de Villeneuve, received in audience by the Sultan, from a painting by J. B. Vanmour. *Reproduced by kind permission of the Rijksmuseum, Amsterdam* 147

Field-Marshal Oliver Wallis, from an engraving in the Exercitium des löblichen General Graf Wallischer Regiments zu Fuss. *Reproduced by kind permission of the Heeresgeschichtliches Museum, Vienna* 178

Count Neipperg, from a portrait by an unknown artist. *Reproduced by kind permission of the Kriegsarchiv, Vienna* 179

Belgrade in 1739, from a painting by F. N. Sparr. *Reproduced by kind permission of the Kriegsarchiv, Vienna* 194

Ground plan of the Fortress of Belgrade, 1739, from a drawing by F. N. Sparr. *Reproduced by kind permission of the Kriegsarchiv, Vienna* 195

Sketch map of Eastern Europe and Turkey, 1699–1740
Between pages 75 and 76

Preface

At the beginning of the eighteenth century Constantinople, the capital of the Ottoman Empire, was regarded by Christendom as a remote and barbarous city. The post of Ambassador at the Sublime Porte therefore lacked both prestige and glamour, and was considered to afford few opportunities for the exercise of diplomacy. The Porte had no conception of the refinements of negotiation as practised by Western countries; the Sultan it seemed could only be impressed by force of arms.

In 1739 this assumption was shattered. The Ambassador in Constantinople of a European country which had never defeated the Ottoman army in battle achieved one of the most brilliant diplomatic coups of the century. The struggle which was the prelude to this coup; the patience, the stamina, and above all the intelligence which prevailed in it are the theme of this book.

Acknowledgements

Many people helped and advised me while I was writing this book. I am most grateful to them all, and especially to Baron Ernst Gudenus who, by generously making available to me a privately printed copy of his ancestor's diary, first aroused my interest in this struggle for the Ottoman Empire; Professor Otto Demus for his help with introductions; Professor Holzmair of the Kunsthistorisches Museum in Vienna, who was so kind as to give me the benefit of his great knowledge of eighteenth-century currency; Hofrat Dr. Hans Pauer and Dr. J. C. Allmayer-Beck, the Directors respectively of the Bildarchiv der Österreichischen Nationalbibliothek and the Heeresgeschichtliches Museum, for the help which they personally gave me in my search for illustrations.

The assistance which the staff of the London Library gave me in my researches was invaluable: I acknowledge with gratitude similar help from, in London, the staff of the Public Record Office and the British Museum and, in Vienna, from the staff of the Nationalbibliothek, the Heeresgeschichtliches Museum and the Kriegsarchiv. I thank the staff of the Austrian Institute in London for their unfailing readiness to answer my many requests for information.

I am indebted to the Controller of Her Majesty's Stationery Office for permission to reproduce material that is Crown copyright.

Amongst the authors whose works are listed in the bibliography I wish especially to record my debt to the late M. Albert Vandal. His account, written in 1887, of the Marquis de Villeneuve's achievements while he was French Ambassador in Constantinople, provided much valuable material for this book.

Finally I thank my husband for many helpful suggestions and the utmost patience with the throes of authorship and Mrs. William Younger, who read and commented on every stage of the typescript, for her unique blend of encouragement and astringent criticism. To both of them I owe a very great deal.

PROLOGUE

ๆๆๆๆๆๆๆๆๆๆๆๆๆๆๆๆๆๆๆๆๆๆๆๆๆๆๆๆๆๆๆๆๆๆๆๆๆ

The Pivot of the Struggle

The Fortress of Belgrade 1717

At seven o'clock on the evening of the 19th of August 1717 Count
Hamilton, an emissary from the army, covered with dust and grey
with fatigue, preceded by six postillions sounding their horns rode
into the courtyard of the Favorita Palace in Vienna. The Imperial
family were amusing themselves with target shooting. Hamilton
dismounted and knelt to kiss the Emperor's hand. As he rose he
stumbled with exhaustion. According to the Empress's mother
Charles VI, assisting him, asked 'What good news do you bring?'
Hamilton replied 'The best news of all. The enemy has been
utterly defeated.'[1]

Hamilton had every reason to be exhausted; in three days he
had ridden over 400 miles from the battlefield to Vienna. The
cheering crowds through whom he forced his way when he
reached the capital had every reason for rejoicing. Since May
prayers had been offered throughout the Empire for the victory
which he came to announce; for the past few weeks it had seemed
that those prayers would be unavailing and the whole Imperial
army annihilated. But the miraculous had happened. In place
of the Turkish crescent the Imperial double eagle now flew over
Belgrade.

The fortress of Belgrade, standing on the rocky promontory
dominating the junction of the Save and the Danube was sited on
a position of great natural strength. From it cliffs fell steeply down
to the two rivers; an assault could only be attempted from the
landward side across the base of the triangle two sides of which

they formed, but where the fortifications had the reputation of being amongst the strongest in Europe. It was the key to Hungary, the strongpoint from which the Turks not only menaced the Emperor's newly acquired and precariously stabilised possessions in south-eastern Europe, but also from which, as in 1683, they could advance on Vienna. Apart from a brief interval of two years they had held it for nearly two centuries.

Belgrade was considered to be virtually impregnable. The Imperial directive for the 1717 campaign therefore designated its main objective as being to bring the Turkish army to battle, with the proviso that if this could not be done, Belgrade was to be invested and contained while an advance was made on Nish. Only one man in the Empire—perhaps in all Europe—thought differently; a small man with a pronounced stoop, unostentatiously dressed, the ugliness of his upturned nose and short upper lip redeemed only by the extreme intelligence of his eyes. On May 15th, accompanied by a small body of attendants, he rode out of the eastern gate of the city of Vienna along the road to the Leopoldstadt where a ship was waiting to carry him down the Danube. That such an unimpressive figure should be treated with such extraordinary deference might well have surprised an uninformed onlooker—until he learnt that the centre of this attention was none other than Prince Eugen of Savoy, Field-Marshal of the Holy Roman Empire, Knight of the Golden Fleece, the fame of whose victories resounded from end to end of Europe, on his way to assume command of the Imperial army in Hungary.

According to one of his contemporaries Prince Eugen was 'reserved and sparing of words'.[2] During the following week, as he sailed down the Danube, he was even more silent than usual. The landscape on either bank was all too familiar to him. He had travelled through it many times. As a young officer to take part in the capture of Budapest, the battle of Mohács, and Max Emmanuel of Bavaria's attack on Belgrade. Again ten years later when, at the age of thirty-four, he had for the first time commanded the Imperial army against the Turks, and had driven his men on in that desperate forced march which ended with the victory of Zenta, and lastly a year ago when he had once more defeated the Sultan's forces at Peterwardein. Years of experience had given him a unique knowledge of the terrain, and of the difficulties of campaigning in an area of marshland and trackless steppe, so thinly inhabited that it was impossible to live off the country; where dysentery and malaria combined with the exhaustion of marching in the blazing sun could reduce the fighting strength of an army by a third in a matter of weeks. Above all it had given him a unique knowledge of the Turks.

The Prince who in the Low Countries, on the Rhine and in Italy, had confronted and defeated the greatest Marshals of France, had no doubt of his ability to out-general any of the Sultan's commanders, but he was also well aware that there was an element of hazard and unpredictability in warfare against them to be encountered nowhere else in Europe. Their appearance, weapons and methods of fighting were alien to anything to be found in the West. A Christian commander joining battle with them, as Eugen had done so often, was confronted not by an army drawn up in neat formations according to the prevailing rules of warfare, but by a vast barbaric horde assembled from all parts of the Ottoman Empire—Bosnia, Thrace, Moldavia and Wallachia; from the shores of the Black Sea and far into Asia. This was reflected in its appearance. In place of the three cornered hat, surcoat with coloured facings and cuffs, breeches and boots which were the standard uniform of other armies of the day, the Turks wore turbans, baggy trousers, fur hats, Saracen helmets and armour of the pattern of 500 years ago, and were equipped with an assortment of weapons—muskets, pistols, sabres, pikes, maces, scimitars, bows and arrows. Their mobility, the impact of their massed charges and their fanaticism made them redoubtable opponents. Each Turk went into battle with the assurance of an immediate earthly reward for the head of every infidel he killed, and of an eternal sojourn in Paradise should he fall in the conflict, a prospect calculated to stiffen the morale of any army. They were savage fighters, and the hope of survival of any Christian whom they captured was slight.

Eugen from his long experience by no means underrated the

belligerent qualities of the Turks, but that experience had also taught him one indisputable fact about them which dominated all other considerations. They might be dispersed and driven back, but they had never been finally defeated. Always they reformed and returned, and always the base from which they mounted their next attack was Belgrade. The Prince was convinced that there was only one way of ending this recurrent menace to the security of the Habsburg territories, and he therefore proposed to interpret the Imperial directive for the forthcoming campaign in his own manner. He would bring the Sultan's army to battle, but at the place of his own choosing, outside Belgrade. He hoped that he would first be able to capture the fortress, but if he failed to do this the defeat of the main army beneath its walls would compel its surrender; in any event and whatever the risks he must take Belgrade.

The risks were formidable. The steepness of the cliffs on those sides of the fortress facing the water and the presence of a strong fleet of Turkish warships on the Danube ruled out, even for a commander of Eugen's audacity and skill, any possibility of investing it from the north. The only course was to bridge one of the rivers, cross it, and cut off Belgrade from the landward side. The crossing might be opposed by the Turkish garrison in the fortress—over 30,000 of the *élite* of the Janissaries under a determined commander—assisted by their warships, and there was always the risk that a storm might carry the bridge away.

In Vienna throughout the previous winter the Prince had worked ceaselessly to prepare for this hazardous operation, using all his authority as President of the Hofkriegsrat—the Imperial War Council—to speed up recruitment for the army, assemble supplies and organise the building not only of the necessary ships to carry them down the Danube, but most important of all, of small ships for a bridge of boats and of warships to protect them. He had done everything possible in the time available and had issued instructions for the completion of the task, but he left the capital with little confidence that they would be carried out to his satisfaction. His colleagues, as he knew only too well, were far too apt to agree a proposal and then to find innumerable reasons for doing nothing about it. Neither could he hope that the Emperor would urge them on. Concerned though Charles VI might be about the fate of his army or his Empire, he was temperamentally incapable of initiating decisive or immediate action. Eugen had every reason to be preoccupied as he journeyed downstream through Hungary. He was aware that he was inadequately supported in Vienna as he embarked on the biggest gamble of his career, in which the stakes were not merely his own reputation but the survival of the army and perhaps of the Habsburg dynasty. But he had coldly calculated and accepted the risk and that was final. Sustained only by his confidence in his own ability and his conviction that nothing less than the ultimate prize was worth striving for, he was determined that he must capture Belgrade for the Emperor.

The Prince reached his headquarters on May 21st to be greeted with the disagreeable news that the Turks were assembling an immense body of men at Adrianople. The intentions of the Grand Vizier were still unknown, but it could only be assumed that he proposed to join battle with the Imperial forces, and to do this he must march on Belgrade. Slow though his advance must be he could scarcely fail to arrive before the end of July. This meant that Eugen had under two months in which to lead his army over either the Save or Danube and besiege and capture the fortress. If it did not surrender within this time there was every likelihood that he would be trapped between it and the main Turkish army. The heavy siege guns had not yet arrived and time was running out. At this stage it would still have been possible for him to have remained on the north bank of the Danube, hoping that the Grand Vizier would cross to attack him there, and that if the Turks were defeated in the ensuing battle Belgrade would surrender. The Prince does not appear to have contemplated any such revision of his original plan. It has been suggested[3] that while he was nearly always controlled by his intellect, balanced judgement and sense of perspective, there was a reckless element in his character which occasionally took over, and when it did, he left his command post and flung himself into the mêlée in the midst of the battle, driving straight for his objective, regardless of the consequences or risks involved. This element may have been uppermost at the end of May 1717. In his mind Eugen had already joined battle with the Turks, in the manner which he had long planned, for the ultimate prize—Belgrade. Nothing could now deflect him from his appointed course. He proceeded calmly with his preparations and, after a careful reconnaissance, built a bridge of boats across the Danube at a point a few miles to the east of the fortress where the river was about 800 paces wide. On June 15th the entire Imperial army 80,000 strong, a priest holding high the diamond-studded crucifix which the Emperor had given Eugen at his final audience, began to cross with drums and fifes playing.

On the same day the Prince wrote to the Hofkriegsrat and to the Emperor. He reported that the crossing was by God's mercy proceeding successfully and had taken the Turks by surprise, but stressed that this was no more than a beginning, and that it remained to be seen how far the enemy would permit the operations to proceed against Belgrade. He urged the Hofkriegsrat to hasten the dispatch of supplies, pointing out that before his siege guns arrived he could make no attempt to storm the fortress. Then, once the army was across the river, he deployed it so that with one flank resting on the Save and the other on the Danube, he had cut off Belgrade from the landward side. He next set his men to work to construct defence lines to his rear against an attack by a relieving army and waited for his artillery and supplies.

The following six weeks were arduous. Sorties by the garrison of the fortress gave the troops no rest. In mid-July a storm sank many of the supply ships, and for a time put out of action the two bridges of boats which were Eugen's only lines of communication. More and more men went sick. Before there was any possibility of attempting to storm the fortress the Grand Vizier Khalil arrived. Towards the end of July the vanguard of his army was sighted. A few days later his main force of over 150,000 men was encamped on some low hills about half a mile to the rear of the Imperial lines. The maze of coloured tents and standards was a visible proof to the Prince that he was no longer the besieger but the besieged; boxed in between the Grand

Vizier's army and the fortress; menaced both from the front and the rear by an enemy whose strength by now outnumbered his own by nearly five to one.

During the next fortnight the position of the Imperial forces steadily deteriorated. Their lines were under continual fire and supplies began to run short. In the merciless heat of the August sun the sickness rate rose sharply. Men died from fever, dysentery, malaria, while every day the Turks inched their way forward. Prince Eugen shared the hardships of his troops. His tent damaged by enemy bombardment had to be moved to a safer position and he had a severe bout of fever. The circumstances were such as to break the nerve and cloud the judgement of a younger and stronger man. Eugen was fifty-three and had never been robust, but he still retained that extraordinary nervous energy which had enabled him to remain in the saddle throughout the night before Oudenarde, and then to play his full part in winning the battle in the morning. Now he calmly held on, waiting for the Grand Vizier to advance out of his camp to the attack, convinced that this would be the best chance which he would have of routing the Turks. It did not come.

By the middle of the month two things were clear to the Prince. Firstly, Khalil had no intention of risking an early battle and proposed to wait until his opponents were so weak that they could offer little or no resistance; secondly that he could hold on no longer, for if he did the Imperial army would cease to exist as a fighting force. It was impossible to assault and capture Belgrade. An attempt to retreat across the river was both too hazardous and too ignominious to be contemplated. There was only one course, and it was the only one which he could in honour entertain. Late on the evening of August 15th he summoned his generals and announced his decision. He would attack early on the following morning, and the object of his attack would be nothing less than the total defeat of the Grand Vizier's army. He issued his orders, which were as clear and precise as if they had been drafted at leisure in Vienna for a parade ground exercise. They conveyed to all ranks not only their exact duties, but also their Commander-in-Chief's conviction that they would perform them successfully. If any of the generals urged, as they may well have done, that a retreat by night across the bridges offered a better chance of saving at least a remnant of the army. Eugen brushed their arguments aside—it was never his habit to permit comment on his orders. His closing words made his position clear: 'Either I shall take Belgrade, or the Turks will take me.'[4]

The advance began shortly after midnight. After an hour or so a thick mist rose from the Danube and, unable to see more than a few yards ahead, the leading detachment of the Imperial cavalry lost their way and blundered into the enemy lines. The advantage of a co-ordinated surprise attack was lost, and the Turks immediately gave battle. As it was impossible for individual units to keep in touch with each other as Eugen had planned, each attacked the enemy wherever and whenever they could see him and a period of savage hand-to-hand fighting followed. When the dawn wind blew away the mist the Prince saw that a powerful force had penetrated his lines, cut off his right wing, and unless they were checked would annihilate it. Without hesitation he put himself at the head of the reserve cavalry, rode straight at the advancing Turks, scattered them and closed the gap. He then pulled back to his command post, surveyed the battlefield as calmly as if he had never left it, and ordered the infantry to advance. With colours flying and drums beating they went steadily forward through a murderous fire, and in a devastating charge shattered the enemy. It was the turning point of the battle, and within an hour the Turks were in full retreat leaving over 10,000 dead on the field. The booty captured by the Imperial army included 60 standards and 150 guns. Two days later Prince Eugen had the final satisfaction of accepting the surrender of the fortress of Belgrade.

Nine days after the battle he wrote his report on it to the Emperor. He described it as 'this hard-fought action', and praised the conduct of all ranks in terms which can seldom have been exceeded by any general about the men under his command. Their unshakeable courage and almost unequalled valour in the face of overwhelming odds rendered them, he wrote, worthy of undying fame throughout Christendom. One of his few references to his own part in the victory is contained in a short paragraph which reads almost as an aside. It was, he explained, necessary for him when the battle was at its height to go forward to the advanced positions, and while there he received a slight wound. In consequence, and much against his will, he had been confined to his quarters, but hoped to be able to get out again in a few days. Finally he permitted himself a short evaluation of the significance of his triumph. When the fortifications of Belgrade were so strengthened as to render it absolutely impregnable (he was about to give orders that this should be done), it would stand for all time as an outer rampart not only for Hungary and the Habsburg hereditary lands, but for the whole of Christendom.[5]

PART ONE

The Protagonists

꧁꧁꧁꧁꧁꧁꧁꧁꧁꧁꧁꧁꧁꧁꧁꧁꧁꧁꧁꧁꧁꧁꧁꧁꧁꧁꧁

CHAPTER I

The Emperor and his Ministers

Vienna, 1718–1726

In October 1717 after the capture of Belgrade, Prince Eugen of Savoy returned in triumph to Vienna. The gate through which he entered the city bore an inscription in letters of gold, 'Happy Austria (for whom God always doth wonders against the Turks and the French)'.[1] It seemed appropriate. Certainly at that time the Prince had no reason to foresee any decrease in the support of the Almighty for the Habsburg dynasty. From the site of his new summer palace, the Belvedere, where Lukas von Hildebrandt was building for him one of the greatest masterpieces of baroque architecture, he had an unparalleled view across the spires and domes of the Imperial capital to the heights of the Kahlenberg and the Leopoldsberg. It was from the Kahlenberg that Eugen had first seen Vienna when the sun rose on that historic morning of September 12th, 1683, to reveal a beleaguered town surrounded by 200,000 Turks. A few hours later he had taken part in the battle which saved the citadel of the Holy Roman Empire from the infidel. Now at Belgrade he had slammed home the bolt in its outer postern gate and sealed that victory for all time. He was entitled to feel assured of the lasting approval of God for the cause for which he had fought so superbly.

Charles VI was in no doubt whatsoever about the matter. He was a fervent adherent of the *Pietas Austriaca*, that special Habsburg brand of Catholicism which closely associated many of the central observances of the Christian faith with the traditions of his House.[2] If, when he met a priest carrying the Host to a dying

man, he dismounted and knelt as it passed by, he was following
the practice of Rudolf the Founder of the dynasty who was said
to have dismounted in similar circumstances and given his horse
to the priest, for which act he had been rewarded with a prophecy
that he would win a great empire. His veneration of the Cross
and belief that it would protect him and further his cause was
also in the family tradition. Another legend of the Founder
related that, lacking a sceptre, he had held out a wooden crucifix
on which his vassals swore their oath of allegiance to him. The
Founder, it was said, had always invoked the help of the Blessed
Virgin in times of peril. Charles throughout his life regarded
her as the source of the advancement of his dynasty. The Habsburgs, he was convinced, had a close working arrangement with
God, and the victory of Belgrade demonstrated that it was
functioning admirably.

The Peace Treaty which was concluded with Turkey at
Passarowitz a year later confirmed this belief to the Emperor.
By it he acquired the Bánát and Temesvár together with parts of
Serbia and Wallachia, and obtained advantageous terms for
trading with Turkey. The security of Hungary was assured by
the retention of Belgrade; Bosnia was deprived of her natural
frontiers. He was now free to colonise and develop his newly
conquered territories, to expand trade with the East and to devote
his full resources to the struggle with the French in the West.

Charles had not only secured substantial material advantages
and added to his possessions, he had also fulfilled the sacred
mission entrusted by the Almighty to the Habsburgs to defend
the eastern marches of Christendom against the infidel hordes.
By a happy coincidence his interests and those of God were
identical. Having accomplished a great deal for their mutual
cause, he was certain that continuing Divine favour would
sustain his efforts and support his arms when the time came to
advance from Belgrade on Constantinople and to crown his
achievements by the final destruction of the infidel. But for the
time being he contemplated no such advance. The resources
of the Empire had been severely taxed by the war, and Prince
Eugen insisted that some years of peace were necessary to rebuild

the army and replenish the treasury. The Imperial Resident in Constantinople reported that the Turks, shattered by their defeat, no longer constituted a threat to the Empire. The Emperor, confident that his south-eastern frontier was secure, felt free to turn his attention to other problems, and to enjoy the dignities and prerogatives of his exalted position which had been so brilliantly enhanced by the capture of Belgrade.

By the grace of God Holy Roman Emperor, King of the two Sicilies, of Hungary, Bohemia, Dalmatia, Croatia, Slavonia, Jerusalem, Archduke of Austria, Duke of Athens, Burgundy, Steyr, Carinthia, Krain and Württemberg, Markgraf of Moravia, Count of Flanders, Tyrol. . . . The titles of Charles VI at the height of his reign were appropriate to the head of a family which had ruled since the end of the thirteenth century, and had held the Crown of the Holy Roman Empire in unbroken succession for over 300 years. The area owing him allegiance appeared on the map as a great slab of territory extending across the heart of the Continent, from the North Sea to Siebenburgen deep in the Balkans, from Brussels to Naples, and was inhabited by some 20,000,000 people. His capital, Vienna, on the eastern glacis of these great possessions was both a mirror of their diversity and their focal point. People from all parts of his lands jostled together in its narrow streets, from there the highways radiated to Bohemia and Italy, to Hungary, to the Principalities of the Empire and the Rhine. Vienna was the seat of government, the administrative nerve centre of the whole. In Vienna were the Chancelleries of the Empire and the Habsburg hereditary lands, the Imperial Privy Council, the Treasury and Council of War.

Before 1683 Vienna lacked the magnificence fitting to an Imperial capital, for the recurrent Turkish threat had precluded any significant building outside the city walls. When the Turks were routed and driven back far into Hungary a new spirit of security and confidence swept the land. The nobles vied with each other in erecting splendid town and country palaces and the abbots of the great monasteries followed their example.

When Charles VI came to the throne in 1711 he successively commissioned the building of the Karlskirche, the Imperial

Riding School and the Imperial Library. These, like the palaces of the nobles and the new monasteries, are baroque buildings proclaiming the optimism of a victorious and upsurging age and a belief in the basic underlying harmony of the universe. Throughout Europe it was a time of grandeur, of renewed interest in the exploits of classical heroes. Its slogans were fame and glory. Baroque with its colour, its *trompe l'œil*, its capacity to lift the eye of the beholder upwards and outwards, to make the fact into a dream and to metamorphose the dream into reality, was its epitomisation. [3] It was a style equally suitable for sacred or profane buildings, in which the two elements could intermingle as they did in the minds of those who commissioned them. In baroque ceiling paintings while the central figure might be Christ in glory, the Virgin, a classical hero, a Virtue, or the Emperor according to the nature of the building which it adorned, the overall composition varied very little. Daniel Gran placed in the centre of his painting on the ceiling of the Imperial Library a large medallion of Charles VI supported by Hercules and Apollo the sons of Jove, surrounded by allegorical figures of Fame, the Virtues, Arts and Sciences, with symbolic figures of the Turks and French prostrate beneath his feet. In the iconography of the composition the Emperor occupies the position of the Pantocrator in a Byzantine mosiac sequence, the burning glass blending into one great harmony all the elements of earth and heaven. The Karlskirche, although ostensibly built for the glory of God and dedicated to a saint, also serves as a monument to Imperial grandeur. The two pillars in front of the main façade are symbolic of the Pillars of Hercules, the personal emblem of Charles VI, and the top of each bears, not the Cross of Christ, but a globe on which is poised the Imperial double eagle and crown. The Turkish Sultan might be named the Shadow of God on Earth but the Emperor, as portrayed by the baroque (few rulers have been endowed with a finer Public Relations medium), appears as the link between earth and heaven, and the Empire over which he ruled as the reflection in the world of the eternal harmony of the Divine Order.

The Spanish ceremonial of the Court of Vienna accorded with

this conception of the majesty of Charles VI. He and all his family were saluted with the 'Spanish reverence' performed by bowing low and dropping on to one knee. His name was never pronounced in public without a similar genuflexion. On gala days he appeared dressed in scarlet and gold brocade embroidered with diamonds. The Empress on these occasions was so loaded with jewels that she could hardly move. An elaborate ritual was observed when Their Majesties dined. The dishes (it can only be supposed to the detriment of the food), passed through twenty-four hands before they reached the Imperial tables. Wine was offered by a courtier, specially appointed for this purpose, kneeling on one knee. Nobody whosoever was permitted to sit at the Emperor's table. Electors or Princes might dine with the Empress, but no Minister unless he was a Cardinal.

Court life was governed by Charles's personal tastes and followed the same pattern year after year. Like other rulers of the day he had a passion for the chase amounting almost to a mania, and the various residences and movements of the Court were determined entirely by the hunting seasons. In April the Imperial family went to Laxenburg where they set their falcons at innumerable herons. At the end of June they moved on to the Favorita Palace on the outskirts of Vienna where the Emperor was wholly occupied with stag hunting till the beginning of October, after which he spent ten days at Schloss Halbthurn in the Burgenland shooting hares and pheasants. On his return to the Hofburg he went out nearly every day after wild boar, and at the end of January enormous drives of any game which remained were staged for the Imperial pleasure. Hunting in fact ceased only in Lent, for at the end of March woodcock shooting started and the round began again. Bags were large—Charles once killed 200 wild pigs in a single day—but he never tired of his favourite sport. When he accidentally shot and mortally wounded his Master of the Horse, Prince Adam Schwarzenberg, he was beside himself with distress, but a month later he was once again hunting stag at the place where the tragedy had occurred. Presumably the beat was too good to abandon.

A more attractive aspect of the Emperor's character was his

patronage of the arts. He appointed Fischer von Erlach, one of the greatest architects of the day, to a position at Court, and summoned the poet Metastasio from Italy, rewarding him handsomely for his compositions. Like many of the Habsburgs he had a real love of music, played the cembalo and would sometimes lead the orchestra in Court concerts. He imported Italian conductors, singers and instrumentalists and caused operas to be staged with an infinite variety of scenes and mechanical devices, quite regardless of cost. Since the beginning of the century all Austria had felt the stimulus of closer cultural contact with Italy. The Emperor took the lead in fostering it, and during his reign Italian became the second language of the Court.

A great deal of Charles's time was devoted to public appearances on Court festival days. These, the dates of which were unalterably fixed, occupied nearly a third of the calendar, recurred with monotonous regularity and were ceremonial rather than festive. On the innumerable birth and name days of members of the Imperial family courtiers and ambassadors were admitted to kiss hands and watch the Emperor dine; on '*Toison*' days all the Knights of the Golden Fleece in full regalia, wearing cloaks of crimson velvet embroidered with gold, marched in solemn procession to Mass and Vespers; on the frequent religious feast days the Emperor went on foot to Mass and his ministers and courtiers were compelled to do likewise. Ceremony was only somewhat relaxed during the week of carnival when there were balls which lasted until dawn, with fireworks and other entertainments. But carnival week was soon over. Lent was observed by Charles—and so perforce by all the Court—with the utmost strictness.

It was a very large Court indeed—there were about 2,000 courtiers on a permanently paid basis, and over 30,000 parasites, holders of titular posts, ever hopeful of a reward. Six different 'staffs' were fully occupied day in day out staging the minute detail of the Spanish ceremonial. The Imperial kitchen and cellar were run on a lavish scale. From the latter twelve cases of Hungarian wine a day were allocated for the nightcap of the late Emperor's widow and her entourage. Two casks of tokay were provided annually

Equestrian portrait of Prince Eugen of Savoy

The Battle of Belgrade 1717, from an engraving after a contemporary picture by van Huchtenburgh

for the ostensible purpose of soaking the bread of the Imperial parrots, and fifteen hogsheads of Austrian wine for bathing those luckless birds. So far as food and drink were concerned there must have been a great many pickings for the courtiers, who thereby possibly derived some consolation for the far from negligible discomforts of their existence. The main Imperial Palace, the Hofburg, lagged far behind Versailles or even the Escorial both in size and amenities. Into this confused mass of buildings with its unending corridors and dark staircases were crammed, not only the private and State apartments of the Emperor and his family, but also various government offices, a museum and a hospital. There were innumerable ante-chambers, but far too little accommodation for the multitude of courtiers which thronged them.

In the other palaces the situation was even worse. Laxenburg was far too small. As for the Favorita—'Never was any residence less princely or less commodious. Resembling rather a nunnery than the habitation of a sovereign, it stands in one of the streets of a dirty suburb.'4 In consequence, when Charles VI left the Hofburg to go hunting, most of his attendants were forced to migrate like members of a travelling theatrical company from lodging to indifferent lodging.

Courtiers of both sexes were required to conform to a number of rules with regard to dress. Jewellery could only be worn by the greatest aristocrats; nobody when in attendance in the Hofburg was permitted to dress in the French fashion. Ladies-in-waiting to the Empress were compelled to spend a great deal of money in order to equip themselves with the necessary clothes for a post in which they were on their feet from morning to night; nor did they ever have a hot meal. It was an exhausting existence, and to survive in it, it was necessary to be able to 'run like a postboy . . . wait like a dog, flatter like a cat, dissimulate like a fox, and to turn always in all directions like a weathercock'.5 There were, however, compensations. The Emperor conferred on certain Court officials the right of appointing their subordinates. The Lord Chamberlain for example could appoint new chamberlains, each of whom had to pay him 200 ducats for the honour. (There were in consequence a great many chamberlains.) Since the Golden Fleece was the only Order in existence at the time, Imperial approval was usually signified by gifts of land, lucrative appointments or money. On the whole it was worth putting up with the discomforts of attendance at Court in the hope of catching the Emperor's attention.

The aristocracy imitated the Court to the limit of their resources. Their palaces were furnished with Brussels tapestries, vast silver-framed mirrors, pictures, chandeliers and rich damask curtains covered with gold lace. They kept open house—at dinner as many as fifty dishes of meat would be served on silver platters, with a list of up to eighteen different kinds of wine laid beside each place. The splendour of their clothes matched their surroundings, but the result was not always aesthetically successful. When visiting Vienna in 1717 Lady Mary Wortley Montagu wrote that she had never in her life 'seen so many fine clothes ill fashioned. They embroider the richest gold stuffs: and provided they can make their clothes expensive enough, that is all the taste they show in them.'[6]

Lady Mary Wortley Montagu found that Vienna lacked the taste, elegance and sophistication to be found elsewhere in Europe, and most foreign visitors shared her opinion. Conversation was an art at which the Austrian aristocracy did not excel. The women had no education except in their prayer books and the externals of religion, 'this makes their conversation sometimes insipid; and unless now and then a love story falls in, rain and fair weather are their general topics'.[7] Most of the men were equally limited in outlook and, worse still, snobs to such a degree that 'the pedigree is much more considered by them than either the complexion or features of their mistresses'.[8] A contemporary observer advised any newcomer to Viennese society always to carry his pedigree in his pocket so that he might be in a position to produce that proof of his breeding which would undoubtedly be demanded of him.[9] Austrian 'pride and presumption' was a recurrent subject of adverse comment.

The foreign envoys, accredited to a Court no detail of the ceremonial of which was ever changed, found the Imperial capital

extremely dull. Their duties were tedious. They had to appear in
person to offer the congratulations of the rulers they represented
on the birthdays of the Imperial family, and whenever the
Emperor dined in public on gala days (there were a great many
of both). It was also necessary to attend at Court in gala clothes
on any day on which the Emperor or the Empress had taken a
purge, and to remain there without any kind of refreshment
until a happy result had been achieved, which was usually not
before the late afternoon. This occasion for felicitation again
occurred all too frequently.

One concession was made to the representatives of foreign
monarchs. When they were received in audience by the Emperor
they were not obliged to perform the Spanish genuflexion, and
several confined themselves to bowing. The lot of Protestants
was also somewhat easier than that of Catholics, for they were
not compelled to attend the Emperor to Mass every Sunday
and every feast day. As, quite apart from Sundays, there were a
great many feast days, and as whenever the Emperor walked to
church, the courtiers, Ministers, and foreign envoys had to do
likewise, this was a formidable chore. The envoys' sufferings were
summed up by the French Ambassador, the Duc de Richelieu,
who in 1726 wrote to the Cardinal de Polignac in Rome:

> I have led a pious life here in Lent which has not left me free
> for a quarter of an hour; and I avow that if I had known the
> life that an ambassador leads here, *nothing in this world* would
> have determined me to accept this embassy in which, under
> pretexts of invitations, and of representations at the chapels,
> the Emperor causes himself to be followed by the ambassadors
> as by valets. Only a Capuchin with the most robust health
> could endure this life during Lent. In order to give your
> Eminence some idea, I have spent altogether between Palm
> Sunday and Easter Wednesday, 100 hours at church with the
> the Emperor.[10]

To the foreign envoys Charles VI, the centre of so much
ceremony and apparent adulation, was not an impressive personality. The Spanish Court dress, black with point lace, a short

cloak, a hat turned up at one side, red stockings and shoes, which he habitually wore, did not conceal the fact that he was only of middling height, and that his legs were too short for his body. His face was swarthy with the protruding Habsburg lower lip, his manner stiff, haughty and unapproachable, and so cold that he seemed to be serious even on the rare occasions when he smiled. He appeared to have neither outstanding character nor ability. One of the more acute observers of the eighteenth century considered that he was 'endowed with the qualities which make a good citizen. . . . He had been brought up to obey, not to command.'[11] Bitter enemy though he was of the House of Habsburg Frederick the Great's verdict was apposite. Painfully conscientious, honest and anxious to be just, Charles had a number of virtues, but he was not a great man. He would have made an admirable ruler of a minor German principality, in which role he could happily have devoted his time to his real interests— hunting, music and the arts.

Unfortunately he was not the ruler of a minor German principality but the Holy Roman Emperor and imbued with the sense of his calling. He was also head of the House of Habsburg, and as such convinced that it was his duty to maintain the Habsburg hereditary lands undivided, to enlarge them if possible, and to ensure that his heirs succeeded to them. To Charles these two functions were perfectly reconcilable, for he genuinely believed that the well-being of the Holy Roman Empire was best furthered by maintaining the power and increasing the influence of the House of Habsburg.

The Princes of the Empire, however, took a different view of the matter. They saw not the slightest reason why they should assist the Emperor in his struggles with the French and the Turks.

In the perennial Habsburg wars with the Bourbons their principalities were fought over and devastated. Constantinople was far away, and once the Sultan's armies had been driven back from Vienna the Turkish threat seemed negligible. Those of them who were Protestants neither sympathised with the Emperor's particular brand of Habsburg Catholicism, nor felt themselves bound by the *mystique* of the Holy Roman Empire. Whether Protestant or Catholic they were all reluctant to support the Emperor in expensive wars from which, for the most part, he and not they derived the benefit. His position as their anointed overlord gave him no real authority over them. He could neither wage war, make alliances, nor conclude peace on behalf of the Empire without their consent. They were not bound to provide him with an army, nor with any significant amount of money. Charles's revenues from the Empire therefore amounted to no more than '14,000 florins (derived from a tax on the Jews of Frankfurt and Worms, and some small annual payments from the Imperial free cities)'.[12] The Princes, on the other hand, were free to contract alliances as they saw fit, provided that these were not contrary to the interests of the Empire as a whole, which in practice meant that they could do whatever they wished. If the Emperor needed their political support, he often had to buy it. If he needed their troops for his wars he had to hire them. If he wanted a subsidy he had to appeal to the central assembly of the Empire, the Reichstag. This was an outmoded, ineffectual and dilatory body, capable, regardless of the urgency of the situation, of spending an interminable time wrangling over such matters as whether the Prince Bishop of Passau should be called 'Cardinal of the Roman Church' or 'Cardinal of the Holy Roman Church'.[13] The relationship of the Emperor and the Princes was unsatisfactory to both sides and all too frequently only to be described as morose.

In the pursuit of his ambitions for the advancement of the House of Habsburg Charles VI was therefore compelled to rely mainly on the resources of his hereditary territories. These territories were extensive, communications within them were poor, and with the possible exception of the Netherlands, their economic development lagged behind the rest of Europe. They were a patchwork, and so was the machinery for administering them. There was an Austrian, a Bohemian and a Hungarian Chancellery, a 'Spanish Council' with different sections for Milan and Naples, and a Council for the Netherlands. All these Chancelleries and Councils had the right of expressing their views on questions of major policy, as had the Chancellery of the Empire, the Hofkammer or Treasury, and the Hofkriegsrat or Imperial War Council, which not only dealt with the army, but was also responsible for relations with Turkey. In theory they were all subordinate to the Imperial Privy Council—the Geheime Konferenz—the nominal head of which was the Chancellor, and which was responsible for advising the Emperor on all affairs of State. But in practice this Council lacked authority and there was continual friction between it and the other departments. It took a very long time indeed to reach any decision, and frequently so many conflicting interests were involved that there could only be a compromise which resulted in no action at all. As the British envoy in Vienna reported: 'The least business produces a referate, a referate produces a conference, and were the town on fire, there must be a conference to deliberate if the fire must be put out and how.'[14] If, after unending circulation of papers, quibbling, argument and counter argument, some sort of conclusion was reached, it had to be submitted to the Emperor for his approval, and this was frequently only given after much delay.

This 'unnecessary multiplicity of wheels and springs'[15] was of no assistance to an envoy abroad, such as the Imperial Ambassador in Constantinople, who required urgent instructions, or to a commander in the field asking for troops and supplies, and Prince Eugen himself complained bitterly about it throughout his career. Charles VI was temperamentally incapable of reforming it, or even of ensuring that the holders of high office were competent to carry out their duties. He was quite unable to take a broad or a detached view of a situation, slow to reach a decision (he had inherited the pathological immobility of his family) and, when he had done so would cling to it obstinately whether or not it proved to be correct in the light of subsequent events. A disastrous judge of character, he was obsessed by the fear of appearing to be over-influenced, and would frequently ignore good advice while on the other hand being only too susceptible to flattery.

With the exception of Prince Eugen, whose recommendations

in the decade following the capture of Belgrade Charles frequently rejected because they were unpalatable, the Emperor therefore had no ministers really capable of advising him as to how the machinery of government should be centralised and reformed. Nor had they any wish to do so. Many of the high officials were 'foreigners' from places outside the hereditary lands who, seeing no hope of advancement in their own countries, had come to Vienna to seek it in the service of the Emperor and were only too prone to put their careers before the good of his cause. A reform of the existing system with a reduction in the number of posts available would not have suited them at all. This opinion was shared by the majority of their colleagues who had no desire to advise the Emperor to streamline the machinery of government, for if this occurred they might lose powerful and well paid positions, the emoluments of which could be substantially augmented by accepting bribes.

Bribery of ministers and leading officials was common all over Europe in the eighteenth century, and in Vienna at the time of Charles VI where personalities were all-important and where there were so many conflicting interests, it was often the only means of achieving anything whatsoever. Count Sinzendorf, the Chancellor, was not in the least above indicating the sum which he was prepared to accept to reach a decision 'for', as he said on one occasion, 'at my age I must make provision for my family'.[16] Many of his subordinates followed his example, and would quibble over points of detail in order to raise their price. In 1726 the British envoy reached the conclusion that the only incorruptible people in the Imperial capital were Prince Eugen, Count Starhemberg, and the Emperor's confessor.[17] It was a system with which even the Emperor himself was to some degree forced to comply by the distribution of *pourboires* of various kinds in an endeavour to secure the loyalty of his officials. Sums expended 'for the maintaining of continued goodwill' were a recurrent item in the Imperial accounts.[18]

The size, magnificence and cost of the Court of Vienna bore no relation to the economic state of the Habsburg hereditary territories. When Charles VI succeeded to the throne the State was heavily in debt. Contrary to Prince Eugen's hopes the financial situation did not improve in the years of peace which followed the capture of Belgrade. But it never appears to have occurred to Charles to cut down the expenses of his Court, to curtail his personal munificence, or even to insist on exact accounting. The tradesmen working for the Court could (and did), charge what they liked—it was beneath the Imperial dignity to query their bills. State officials or the army might have to go short, but the Emperor always had money available for building, for the arts, for substantial gifts to those whose loyalty he wished to secure or who he considered had served him well. Court expenses, which in a normal year amounted to 2,000,000 gulden, were the first charge on the State finances. 4,500,000 gulden were allocated to meet the cost of the civil administration. The army, required to defend and garrison an area stretching from the Netherlands to Sicily, from Tortona to Wallachia, had to make do in time of peace with 8,000,000 gulden. [19]

The army indeed was one of the principal victims of the prevailing administrative and financial incompetence. The Hofkriegsrat was a cumbersome body which worked slowly and inefficiently, and had no control over supplies and finance since these were dealt with by the Hofkammer. Although the rates of pay were low they were still more than the military budget could stand, and cash was chronically and catastrophically short. The supply and provisioning of the troops was placed in the hands of Jewish contractors who frequently made 30 per cent on the transaction, and then failed to deliver the full quota of food and munitions. In spite of all Prince Eugen's efforts to suppress the practice, it was still possible to purchase a commission. In consequence many of the officers were decrepit old men, courtiers who spent little time with their regiments, or foreigners from the small nobility of the Empire who tended to quarrel amongst themselves and to think only of their own promotion. Only a commander of the calibre of Eugen could fight a successful campaign with such handicaps. In the time of peace which succeeded the capture of Belgrade even he failed to maintain the army in a state of efficiency.

Without a strong army and a full treasury there could be no question of exploiting the capture of Belgrade by a further attack on the Sultan. Charles in any case had no wish to do so, for he was wholly preoccupied by another and far more disastrous factor. He had no male heir. In 1713 he had promulgated the Pragmatic Sanction which laid down as a family law of the House of Habsburg that all his hereditary titles and lands should pass undivided to his son, or failing a son, to his eldest surviving daughter and, if he had no children at all, to the descendants of his brother the late Emperor Joseph I. The Pragmatic Sanction postulated the enduring unity and power of the Habsburg monarchy, and as such it inevitably aroused opposition abroad. Charles, however, was determined to get it legally recognised by as many foreign powers as possible, a determination which grew into an obsession dominating and distorting the whole of his foreign policy. Three years later his position greatly improved, for a son was born to him. But after a few weeks the infant Archduke died, and with him the Emperor's dearest hopes. Together with the Empress he made a pilgrimage to Mariazell, laid a silver statue of the Christ child weighing exactly the same as his dead son before Our Lady of Austria, and prayed for a male heir. His prayer was not answered. The succession devolved on the Archduchess Maria Theresia who was born in 1717.

All the forces of Imperial diplomacy were now brought to bear on the task of getting the Pragmatic Sanction recognised but, notwithstanding every effort, by 1725, three of the leading countries of Europe still held back. England (King George I was piqued at the Emperor's refusal to recognise the Hanoverian Succession), France and Prussia, neither of whom had any wish to contribute to the perpetuation of the power of the Habsburgs. Worse still, alarmed by the pact which the Emperor had concluded with Spain, all three countries joined together against him in the League of Herrenhausen. It was at this moment that the Russians renewed their approach to Vienna for an alliance.

The first Russian overture of this kind had been made by Peter the Great, searching for means to avenge the defeat inflicted on him by the Turks on the Pruth in 1711. It was rejected by Charles

VI who commented that the Czar was accustomed to demand far more than he contributed to an alliance. By 1725 the situation had changed. Peter the Great was dead and it could be hoped that his widow, Catherine I, who had succeeded him would be more amenable. The Spaniards were proving unco-operative, and it was clear that there was not a great deal of active support to be expected from Madrid. Charles needed an ally to strengthen his position against France and to threaten the Turks should they ever again become recalcitrant. Russia, a virile rising power, was implacably opposed to any extension of French influence in central Europe, she was the traditional enemy of Turkey and— a vital point to the Emperor—prepared to recognise the Pragmatic Sanction. There really seemed to be no alternative but to accede to the Russian proposal. In August 1726 a treaty was signed in Vienna whereby Austria and Russia mutually agreed to come to each other's help should any of their possessions be attacked from any quarter whatsoever.

On the whole it seemed not only that the Emperor had made a good bargain, but that so far as the safety and future expansion of his possessions in south-eastern Europe was concerned, he had made a very good bargain indeed. Austria and Russia had had both adopted as their emblem the double eagle of Byzantium. Together they could contain and in due course destroy the Turks, the conquerors of the Byzantine Empire. It was only later to become apparent that each had unrevealed but totally different ideas of the timing of the second part of this operation, and of the ultimate division of the loot.

CHAPTER II

ༀༀༀༀༀༀༀༀༀༀༀༀༀༀༀༀༀༀༀༀༀༀༀༀༀༀༀༀༀༀༀༀ

The Czarina and her Advisers

St. Petersburg, 1727–1730

When the Austro-Russian Treaty was signed, some of Charles VI's entourage feared that the Emperor had committed himself to a dangerous alliance. For a time their misgivings appeared to be unfounded. Catherine I died in the following year and was succeeded by Peter the Great's twelve-year-old grandson. A bitter struggle followed between competing factions of the Russian nobility, each of whom endeavoured to gain ascendancy over the young Czar Peter II. While it lasted the aggressive foreign policy of his grandfather was abandoned, and Russia, absorbed in her own internal problems, made no demands on her ally. Charles was left in peace to pursue his diplomatic manœuvres in support of his dynasty.

In 1730, Peter II died at the age of fifteen. Since he had been too young to follow the procedure laid down by his grandfather and to nominate a successor, the task devolved on the Supreme Privy Council, which had been set up by Catherine I in 1726 in an attempt to strengthen the executive by concentrating power in the hands of a few men. The attempt failed. During the reign of Peter II the Council had been unable to exert any real control and frequently did not meet for weeks on end. When the young Czar died, Prince Golitsuin, one of its most influential members, determined to reassert its position. At his suggestion, the Council offered the throne to Anne, Duchess of Courland, the daughter of Peter the Great's half-witted brother, on condition that she signed an agreement to govern solely through it, and relinquished all rights to confer titles or honours or to bestow gifts of money or land.

Severe though these conditions were, Golitsuin had every reason to hope that the attractions of a move from Courland to St. Petersburg would be such that Anne would accept them. Until 1730 her life had not been luxurious. Brought up in seclusion by her pious and narrowly superstitious widowed mother, she had been married off by Peter the Great in 1711 at the age of seventeen to Frederick William, Duke of Courland. Courland, a Polish fief, had been occupied by Russian troops in 1705 in the course of the Russo-Swedish war and the Czar was determined that they should remain there, for the Duchy lay on the Baltic and from it an enemy could threaten the approaches to St. Petersburg. To marry off his niece to Duke Frederick William appeared to be an admirable way of achieving this. The wedding was celebrated with the utmost splendour, and Peter himself presided at the nuptial banquet which was on a scale more appropriate to an orgy than a wedding feast. Unfortunately when the newly married pair set out for Courland, Frederick William died 'of a surfeit' before they had travelled thirty miles from St. Petersburg, and the succession to the Duchy was claimed by his uncle, Ferdinand, who was then in exile in Danzig. The Czar, however, refused to withdraw his troops unless Anne's dowry and the income of her late husband were made over to her. As Ferdinand was quite unable to raise the necessary money, the young widow was ordered to proceed alone to Mittau, the capital of Courland, whilst the new Duke remained as nominal ruler *in absentia* in Danzig.

Anne stayed in Mittau for nineteen years. Courland was a small, bleak Duchy. Her so-called palace lacked furniture. Her personal income was inadequate and irregularly paid, and her appeals for help were disregarded by her relations. When the Supreme Privy Council's invitation reached her in February 1730 she accepted it, signed the agreement curtailing her powers, and set out at once for St. Petersburg. It seemed to Golitsuin and his colleagues that they had achieved exactly what they intended, and had installed a docile figurehead on the throne of Russia.

They had miscalculated both the character of the new ruler and the extent of their own popularity. Anne showed her independence as soon as she arrived in St. Petersburg. When about to be solemnly invested with the Order of St. Andrew she exclaimed 'Why of course! I forgot to wear it', snatched the insignia from the senior Knight, and gave it to one of her ladies-in-waiting to put on for her.[1] She was received with great enthusiasm by the officers of the Preobrezensky Guards and appointed herself their Colonel, a direct contravention of the agreement which she had signed at Mittau. The Supreme Privy Council, seriously alarmed at the growing support for their new ruler, endeavoured to hold her incommunicado till she was crowned. They failed. On March 8th, 1730, within a few weeks of her arrival from Courland, a *coup d'état* took place. Anne repudiated the agreement, abolished the Supreme Privy Council, and replaced it by an Administrative Senate. She was reinvested with the powers of an autocratic ruler, and in May crowned with great splendour 'Czarina of all Russia, Lady of the lands of Siberia, Empress of all the Northern Coasts . . .'

In a special prayer at her coronation Anne thanked the 'Czar of Czars' for bestowing on her 'the grandest vocation on earth'.[2]

In appearance she was suited for the role. She was taller than any of her courtiers, and although not beautiful, had according to all contemporary observers great majesty of bearing:

She is a very large well made woman, well shaped for her size, and easy and graceful in her person. She has a brown complexion, black hair, dark and blue eyes . . . an awfulness in her countenance that strikes you at first sight, but when she speaks, she has a smile about her mouth that is inexpressibly sweet. She talks a good deal to everybody and has such an affability in her address, that you seem to be talking to an equal; yet she does not for one moment drop the dignity of a sovereign.[3]

Anne had never been expected to succeed to the throne of Russia; in consequence, she had received practically no education and, with the exception of a little German, spoke no foreign language. Although not brilliant, she had a certain basic common sense, never acted hastily, liked order and would listen to advice. Frederick the Great considered that, in contrast to Charles VI, she had the qualities appropriate to her rank, and noted that she was 'generous in her rewards, severe in her punishments, good natured, voluptuous but not debauched'.[4]

Voluptuous she certainly was, but also capable of lasting attachments, the outstanding example of which was her devotion to Biron, who became her lover about four years after she went to Mittau. Ernst Johann Biron, or Buhren as he was originally called, was the grandson of a groom to a former Duke of Courland. Having failed to get a position in St. Petersburg, he returned to Mittau and managed to obtain employment in Anne's household. He was extremely handsome, and soon supplanted her current lover. His influence over her remained paramount for the rest of her life. The liaison was in no way affected by Biron's marriage to a German of the minor nobility, for his wife, who shared his ambitions, took great care to remain on good terms with her husband's mistress. In 1721 he was appointed Court Chamberlain to Anne in Mittau and in 1730, together with his wife and family, he followed her to St. Petersburg. It has been alleged that it was he who advised Anne to accept the throne and then repudiate the conditions limiting her powers, assuring her that triumphs comparable to those of Peter the Great awaited her, and that her victorious armies would bear her standard far beyond the frontiers of Russia. The Czarina found this prospect wholly appropriate to her own conception of 'the grandest vocation on earth'. After the *coup d'état*, she showered honours on Biron, and seldom did anything without consulting him.

Biron—mean, treacherous, rapacious, and, while he could be agreeable if he wished, capable of great vindictiveness—was universally loathed, but his position with Anne was unassailable. As her Court Chamberlain, he was the 'gate' through which it was necessary to pass to obtain access to her. The bribes which he accepted in the course of this exercise of his office added substantially to his already not inconsiderable fortune. Foreign rulers, however reluctantly, had no alternative but to flatter this jumped-up, uneducated peasant who, according to one of his enemies, had only two accomplishments, cheating at cards, and horsebreeding. The King of Poland gave him the Order of the White Eagle, and Charles VI made him a Count of the Empire. He changed his name from Buhren to Biron, and took the arms of that French ducal house.

Anne was passionately fond of pomp and pageantry, a taste which she had lacked both the means and the setting to indulge during her nineteen years in Courland. When she succeeded to the throne of Russia, the Court of St. Petersburg though far larger than that of Mittau, was scarcely a Court in the eighteenth-century sense, and the reverse of luxurious. Arm-chairs, carpets and mirrors were lacking; during the long, cold Russian winter such light as there was was supplied by miserable tallow dips; on great occasions the nobles appeared in magnificent clothes, but these were so rarely worn that they were passed on from father to son. The Czarina was determined that her Court must become one of the most magnificent in Europe. As her Chamberlain it fell to Biron to organise this for her and with his love of splendour, it was an occupation no doubt entirely pleasing to him.

Western furniture (carpets, pictures, mirrors and chandeliers), was imported. Champagne and French wine replaced beer and vodka. Biron devised an endless succession of balls, masquerades, banquets, illuminations and firework displays. Courtiers were forbidden to appear twice in the same garments, a command which involved some of them in such expense that they were obliged to pawn part of their estates to pay for their clothes. The final effect was not always successful. The Czarina and Biron both adored bright colours and elderly courtiers were forced to attire themselves in unbecoming shades of pink or yellow. The richest dress was frequently ruined by a bad wig and coaches decorated with gold and upholstered in crimson velvet were drawn by miserable nags. The Court was thus a strange mixture of splendour and slovenliness. So were Anne's personal habits. She never used water for washing, preferring melted butter. Although she rose early to sign State papers and regulate the affairs of her household, she was still wearing a long Oriental *robe de chambre* when she dined with Biron at midday; no doubt it was convenient for the siesta which they took together after his family had discreetly retired.

The Czarina had the passion of all rulers of her day for the chase. An area of twenty miles round St. Petersburg was reserved as her personal hunting ground, and anyone caught poaching there was promptly imprisoned. Bears, wolves, stags, foxes, and hares were sent from all over Russia to stock it. The Russian Ambassadors in Paris and London were ordered to buy bassets and beagles. Once in the space of two and a half months Anne's personal bag included 374 hares, 68 wild ducks, 16 sea birds, a wolf and a large number of stags and deer. Loaded guns were stacked in odd corners of the palace, and in her spare moments she amused herself by shooting birds from the windows.

Like Charles VI, Anne spared no expense to ensure that her surroundings were appropriate to her exalted position, but there the resemblance ended. The Court of Vienna was 'a mixture of Olympian revelry, Spanish monastic severity, and barrack discipline'.5 There was no monastic severity at the Court of St. Petersburg. Although the revelry was on the largest scale that money could buy and Western ceremonial had been introduced, the effect was one of gorgeousness rather than taste, of a semi-barbaric Oriental splendour rather than of a grave, dignified protocol based on centuries of tradition. It reflected the preferences of the Czarina. While she commanded that Italian opera be performed at her Court in accordance with the prevailing fashion of the day, she really enjoyed gross knockabout farces. Like her uncle, Peter the Great, she had the old Russian traditional love of dwarfs, fools and mountebanks; also like him while frequently kind and generous, she was capable of outbursts of ferocity. When, during some public celebrations, her soldiers deliberately discharged their muskets into the crowd she laughed as heartily as any of her suite. One of her courtiers had the misfortune to incur her displeasure by contracting an unsuitable marriage. When his wife died Anne promptly forced him to marry one of her hideous Kalmuck dwarfs, organised at great

Emperor Charles VI, from a portrait in Schönbrunn by an unknown
artist

Czarina Anne I, from an engraving by Joseph Wagner after a painting
by Jacopo Amigoni

expense a wedding ceremony of barbaric splendour, and then had
the couple conducted to a house built of ice in which all the
furniture was also made of ice. There they were compelled to
pass their wedding night. She had a feline sense of humour.

The Czarina's moods and the entertainments devised to gratify
them inflicted some startling experiences on the diplomatic corps.
The wife of the British Ambassador described one of the winter
diversions at Court as being:

> A machine made of boards, that goes from the upper storey
> down into the yard. . . . This had water flung on it, which soon
> froze, till it was covered with ice of a comfortable thickness.
> The ladies and gentlemen of the Court sit on sledges, and they
> are set going at the top, and fly down to the bottom. . . .
> Sometimes, if these sledges meet with any resistance, the
> person in them tumbles head over heels; that, I suppose is the
> joke. Every mortal that goes to Court has been down this
> slide. . . .[6]

Unavoidable routine appearances to pay court to the Czarina
when she removed to her summer palace outside St. Petersburg,
involved a journey of three and a half hours each way with no
possibility of getting a meal en route. The entire diplomatic corps
had to do this twice a week. Any exceptional festivity was a
major physical ordeal. When the Czarina's niece married the Prince
of Brunswick the day began with a lengthy church ceremony
and ended with a State banquet at which regardless of the heat
(it was July), the guests were obliged to wear their most
splendid (and therefore their thickest) clothes, and from which
they got home 'half dead with fatigue' at half-past three in the
morning.[7]

One event which occurred with sickening inevitability year
after year, and must have been dreaded by all foreign envoys, was
the celebration of the anniversary of the Czarina's accession to the
throne. This took the form of a very large drunk on a very large
scale. That it should have been so is one of the curious, and
possibly revealing, facets of Anne's character. When she came
to the throne, Russian drunkenness was proverbial throughout

Europe. After the inaugural banquet of the Supreme Privy Council in 1726, according to the Prussian envoy, their Excellencies were unable to sit round the Council table, for the simple reason that they were all lying beneath it.[8] Peter the Great had been renowned for his hard drinking, so amongst Russians this occasioned little surprise. Drunkenness was, however, a trait which Anne had not inherited from her uncle. But, on occasion, it amused her to see others drunk.

> Last Monday being the anniversary of Czarish Majesty's accession to the Crown the same was observed here with all greatest solemnity. In the morning all the foreign Ministers and Russ Nobility appeared at Court in the most magnificent clothes that could be got. After dinner Her Majesty presented every one of us with her own hand with a large glass which contained above a bottle of wine and we were obliged to drink the same as well as several lesser glasses. In the evening there was a Ball at the Court, but as most of the company was very drunk, it did not last long. . . .[9]

Although in the opinion of most foreign envoys the banquets and festivities at Anne's Court were not worth the enormous amount of money spent on them, they were as the Czarina wished. She was in need of distractions, not only to make up for her nineteen years in Courland, but also to take her mind off her anxieties. She had been solemnly crowned ruler of Russia, but this was no guarantee that she would remain on the throne. A number of her predecessors had been disposed of when they became unpopular or were considered to be unsatisfactory. Any sign of opposition must be ruthlessly exterminated, and for this the instruments of repression were already to hand. Russia was a country of savage punishments where women who murdered their husbands were buried up to their necks in the ground and left to die. The penalties for real or suspected political crimes included breaking on the wheel, flogging, cutting out the tongue, and frequently, in addition, exile to Siberia. It was a ferocious age. A Russian Princess of the day calmly announced to her guests when they arrived at her country house: 'I am delighted you have come,

I was so bored that I was going to have my negroes beaten to pass the time.'[10] Even if Anne wished to reform the system of justice she dared not relax it. She made Biron the head of the Chancellery of Secret Investigation with full powers to stamp out any sign of treason. During the ten years of her reign he arrested 37,000 people, of whom 5,000 were put to death, and the rest sent to Siberia.

It was, however, not enough to stamp out opposition. To maintain her position Anne had to assemble around her a band of followers on whom she could rely. She never forgot the circumstances of her accession and the attempt of the Russian nobility in the Privy Council to curb her powers. She was never prepared to trust them again, an attitude in which she was encouraged by Biron who did not hesitate to voice his dislike of the entire Russian aristocracy. The only course was to attach to herself foreigners—German, Livonians or Courlanders, and buy their loyalty with substantial rewards. Fortunately the preferences of the ruler and the interests of the State coincided, for there were virtually no Russians capable of holding high office. Nevertheless, if all the foreigners had been of the limited intellectual attainments and self-seeking character of Biron the experiment would have been disastrous. Happily there were two notable exceptions, both originally recruited by Peter the Great, and both of whom were prepared to devote all their talents to the service of Russia. One of them became Foreign Minister and executive head of the Government in all but name. The other rose to be a Field-Marshal and Commander-in-Chief of the Russian army. Ostermann and Münnich were two of the most valuable legacies which Peter the Great bequeathed to his country.

Ostermann, a German of middle class origin from Westphalia, entered the service of Peter the Great while he was still a young man. In 1711 he took part in the peace negotiations which followed the crushing defeat inflicted by the Turks on the Russians at the Pruth. It was his first experience of dealing with the Porte and one which he never forgot. Ten years later, as the Czar's principal plenipotentiary, he succeeded at Nystedt in negotiating a peace with Sweden on terms exceptionally favourable to Russia.

Peter the Great appointed him Vice-President of the Ministry of Foreign Affairs in 1723 and thereafter constantly sought his advice.

By this time Ostermann had identified himself with Russia. He married a Russian, changed his Christian name to Andrej Ivanovič, and was baptised into the Orthodox Church. This was a necessary step for the advancement of his career in Russia and, since he was no more than a coldly rational Deist, probably caused him little heart-searching. His progress continued to be spectacular. During the reign of Peter's three successors the conduct of foreign affairs remained for all practical purposes in his hands. A year after Anne came to the throne, he induced her to set up an Inner Council of Three through which all communications from the Senate, the Synod and the Government departments had to pass before being presented to her. The Council consisted of himself and two leading members of the Russian nobility of which the latter were ciphers. Ostermann, working day and night, was aptly described as the 'peg' which held Russia together.

'Ostermann', Peter the Great is reputed to have said when he was dying, 'is indispensable to Russia. He best knows her needs, and he is the only one of us who has never made a diplomatic blunder.'[11] Of those needs few seemed to the Count to require more urgent attention than the backward economic state of his adopted country. He was convinced that this could only be improved if new outlets for trade were developed. Peter the Great's 'window on the Baltic' was not enough. Russia must have access to the Black Sea. To gain this the alliance with Austria was indispensable, and he lost no opportunity of impressing the importance of preserving it on the Czarina.

Of medium height and corpulent, Ostermann did not resemble the conventional portrait of a magnificent eighteenth-century statesman. His clothes were 'positively disgusting from their dirty condition', his house 'abominably furnished', his servants 'dressed like beggars' and the plate he used every day 'so dull that it looked like lead'.[12] He was apparently uninterested in using his position to further his material advancement and unconcerned about honours and distinctions. All observers agreed (sorrowfully in the case of foreign diplomats), that in a notoriously venal government he was the one Minister who could not be bribed.

In St. Petersburg the Count was known as 'the Oracle'. Nobody was ever certain what he thought or might do, or indeed how to interpret what he thought and did. If he wished he could, when in society, be an entertaining companion. He was reputed to have had a number of love affairs, but to have regarded them merely as light relaxation, carefully avoiding any form of serious entanglement with his mistresses. This was characteristic of his whole method of working, for he always left himself room for manœuvre. A consumate judge of what was possible, he was prepared to wait and procrastinate or, if need be, to withdraw until the situation was more favourable. A quiet, seemingly inoffensive man, he was in fact a formidable opponent. He did not break his enemies, he simply edged them off the stage. Ostermann excelled at dissimulation. According to a contemporary observer he never looked anyone in the face and 'lest his eyes betray him he had acquired the art of rendering them immovable'.[13] He could weep at will. If pushed into a corner during a diplomatic discussion he would be afflicted with an uncontrollable fit of coughing or, although an accomplished linguist, suddenly and unaccountably be quite unable to express himself in anything but Russian. If the situation became too difficult he would be smitten with a bad attack of gout and retire to bed. 'When Ostermann is not pleased he pretends to be sick, and during his absence, all the members of the Council are at a stand; sit a little, drink a dram, and then are obliged to go and court the Count.'[14] Foreign ambassadors frequently discovered that after a discussion with him they were none the wiser, for everything which he said could be interpreted in a variety of ways. But, infuriating though they found him, they all acknowledged his ability and his unrivalled knowledge of his adopted country.

By contrast to Ostermann who spent all his working life in Russia, Burchard Christoph Münnich, the other great servant bequeathed by Peter the Great to his successors, had considerable experience of other countries before he entered the service of the Czar at the age of thirty-eight. He came from Oldenburg where for three generations his family had been employed in canal construction and marsh drainage. In 1701 he was commissioned into the forces of Hesse-Darmstadt, with whom he fought under the command of Prince Eugen, first in Italy, and then in Flanders where, at the battle of Denain, he was captured by the French. They treated him well, and the experience left him with a lasting regard for France. After his release he obtained employment in Warsaw and rapidly rose to be Inspector-General of the armies of Saxony and Poland. His career there was cut short by a quarrel with one of the King's favourites, and it was clear that if he wished for advancement he would have to look elsewhere. In all Europe no country offered greater scope for his boundless ambition than Russia, where foreigners were welcomed and richly rewarded. Münnich had inherited his family's engineering talent. He drew up a plan for the fortification of the Baltic provinces which interested Peter the Great, and the Czar offered him the post of Engineer-General of the Russian army. In 1721 Münnich hastened to St. Petersburg confident that a brilliant future lay in front of him.

At first he was disappointed. Peter, unimpressed by the fact that in addition to his engineering ability he could write equally well in English, French and Latin, disliked what he considered to be his affected manners, and found his appearance juvenile. But the German was a good engineer and there were all too few of them in Russia. One of the Czar's most cherished projects was the construction of a canal to by-pass Lake Ladoga and give St. Petersburg a commercial shipping route down the Volga to the Caspian. This project was not going well, and eventually it was entrusted to Münnich. He laboured at it for twelve years and finally, long after Peter's death, completed it successfully. Catherine I conferred on him the Order of Alexander Nevsky, and Peter II made him a Count but, gratifying though these honours were, they did not carry with them the promotion which Münnich considered to be his due. For this he had to wait until

Anne came to the throne when, in accordance with her policy of placing foreigners in leading positions, she promoted him Field-Marshal and appointed him Minister of War and Governor of St. Petersburg.

Münnich was tall, handsome, witty, a good dancer and a great success with women. His elegant appearance was, however, deceptive. The army knew him a strict disciplinarian with a violent temper apt to strike out with a cane if his orders were not obeyed. He was a tremendous worker, drove his subordinates unmercifully, and had little regard for human life. It was said that to kill one of the enemy he would sacrifice the lives of three of his own men. Yet his troops, who called him Sokol—the Falcon—were devoted to him. Frederick the Great considered that he had 'the virtues and the vices of great generals' and was 'capable, bold and fortunate, but also proud, self-confident, ambitious and sometimes too tyrannical, sacrificing the lives of his soldiers to enhance his reputation'.[15] Münnich had come to Russia determined to establish himself as one of the greatest commanders in Europe. To do this he must achieve a brilliant victory. No victory he considered, could more redound to his fame than to succeed where the great Czar himself had failed, to annihilate the Turks and avenge the defeat of the Pruth. He was confident that he, and he only, could do this. In one respect he was right. He possessed the essential qualification for the exacting role of commanding the Russian army. In a ruthless country he too was capable of being utterly ruthless.

Ostermann, Münnich, Biron—these three foreigners held the real power in Russia during Anne's reign. Each had his own method of maintaining his position in the extremely difficult circumstances of the Court of St. Petersburg. Ostermann, subtle and evasive, side-stepped his way round opposition; Münnich bulldozed ahead without regard for circumstances or personalities; Biron, far the least intelligent of the three, survived, partly because when he wished he could be all things to all men, but above all because with the Czarina as his mistress he held a trump card. They were all aware that if Anne fell they would almost certainly fall with her, that if she was to remain on the throne her reign must be a reign glorious for Russia in the tradition of Peter the Great and that the beginning of its achievements must not be long delayed. Apart from this they had nothing in common, nor was any love lost between them. Ostermann and Münnich both hated Biron and resented his influence over Anne. Biron mistrusted Ostermann, found Münnich's manner offensive, and feared that the Field-Marshal would supplant him in the Czarina's favour. Ostermann resented Münnich's attempts to interfere in matters outside the military sphere. They were an ill-assorted triumvirate, but confronted by the bitter jealousy of the Russian nobility they had no alternative but to stick together.

The Russian nobility disliked not only the presence of foreigners in influential positions, but any sort of reform or progress. Russia, for all the innovations of Peter the Great, still remained a backward country. There were vast stretches of uninhabited territory. The provincial towns consisted of mean houses and unpaved streets, and Western travellers found even St. Petersburg not particularly impressive. 'There reigns in the capital a bastard kind of architecture', wrote one of them, and added that the palaces of the nobles there were so badly built that their walls were already cracked and out of the perpendicular.[16] The poor lived in conditions wretched even by eighteenth-century standards, 'one really sees human creatures so debased, and the poor wretches are so low and poor, that they seem to have only the figures of human creatures'.[17]

As an illustration of the general filth one diplomat described a tavern in St. Petersburg. The beer stood in open vats. Each customer dipped in his drinking vessel and drank leaning over the vat, letting quite a lot of beer run back into it through his dirty beard. If he was unable to pay immediately he left as a pledge that he would do so one of his garments, such as an old sock, which was hung over the vat and often fell into it.[18] Outside the Court the only real magnificence and colour was to be found in the Church, but splendid though its vestments and ornaments might be, it hardly provided a means of enlightenment and the priests, who were often very drunk, were incapable of checking the superstition which was rife amongst all classes of society.

This backwardness had one advantage. The country was cheap to run. Little was spent on communications, for there were so few roads; the Ministry of Health had only two doctors and one physician on its payroll; the standing army (which in 1730 amounted to 174,000 men) cost comparatively little for rations were meagre, the soldiers' pay infinitesimal, and those units stationed in the provinces lived off the country as best they could. In consequence, the total state income of 8,500,000 roubles when Anne came to the throne in 1730, although small in view of the size of Russia, and even though a substantial proportion of it was earmarked for the Court, was fairly adequate. Unlike the Emperor, the Czarina was not burdened by interest on loans raised abroad.

Here was a reasonably solvent ally for Austria with a large standing army. To all appearances Charles VI had not made a bad bargain. He was further reassured when Anne on her accession declared that she would honour the Austro-Russian Treaty. Ostermann, now all powerful in the conduct of Russian foreign affairs, was known to be a firm protagonist of the alliance. The Emperor had no hesitation in warmly reciprocating the Czarina's declaration.

But the new reign in Russia had only just begun, and the factors which would influence it were still masked. Biron's attempt to flatter his mistress by holding before her the vision of herself as the ruler of a great and expanding empire, Münnich's ambition to lead the Russian army to victory on the battlefield, and Ostermann's cold calculation that the defeat of the Pruth must be reversed in order to give Russia that access to the Black Sea, were all unknown to the Emperor. Neither, and this was particularly unfortunate, was he aware that these aims all coincided in one objective, the early dismemberment of the Ottoman Empire for which, under the terms of the Treaty, his assistance would undoubtedly be invoked.

CHAPTER III

The Cardinal and his Ambassador

Paris–Constantinople, 1726–1728

'Probably the first great revolution in Europe will be the conquest of Turkey . . . every day a feather is plucked from her wing.'[1] This prophecy was made by a Frenchman. His country more than any other had reason to be concerned by the threat to Turkey implied by the Austro-Russian alliance.

France enjoyed a special relationship with the Porte from which she had derived considerable political and commercial advantages. It originated in 1526 when King Francis I, defeated by the Emperor Charles V and a prisoner in Madrid, sought the help of that other sworn enemy of the Habsburgs, the Sultan Suleiman the Magnificent. The interests of the King and the Sultan coincided for, acting together, they could attack Charles's possessions on two fronts. Suleiman was quick to respond to Francis's overture. 'Your appeal has been heard at the steps of our throne', he replied, 'Night and day our horse is saddled and our sabre girt.' A few months later his forces routed the Imperial army at the battle of Mohács. But, wholly agreeable though this victory was to Francis, it was impossible for His Most Christian Majesty of France to enter into a formal alliance with the infidel Turks against the Holy Roman Emperor without outraging Christendom and risking excommunication. The agreement which he concluded with Suleiman in 1536 was therefore restricted to a statement of friendship and mutual interest, with which were coupled advantageous concessions to French merchants trading with the Ottoman Empire. These concessions (subsequently known as the Capitulations) were renewed five times before the end of the seventeenth century. In 1581 the Sultan awarded the French Ambassador in Constantinople precedence over the ambassadors of all other nations.

During the reign of Louis XIV France, while taking every care never to appear as the declared ally of the Turks, manipulated them to the utmost in her struggle with the Habsburgs. As Louis himself noted in 1676, the Turks must not be incited to war against Christendom as a whole; but it was permissible to insinuate to them that, for example, instead of attacking Poland, a Christian country friendly to France, they should embark on a further campaign against the Emperor.[2] Vienna was under no illusions about this. A directive to Imperial ambassadors in the following year said of the King of France, 'In order to weaken us so that he may bring us under his yoke, he is inciting the Turks, the enemies of Christendom, to attack us.'[3] In March 1683 an Imperial communiqué put the position even more bluntly— 'The Turkish war is essential to the King of France for the accomplishment of his designs.'[4] Four months later the Turks reached the gates of Vienna. There was no French contingent in the Christian army which eventually defeated them. By the end of the century the advantages to France of her special relationship with the Porte were so great that the preservation of the Ottoman Empire had become a cardinal principle of French policy.

These advantages were not confined to assistance against the Habsburgs. The concessions granted by Suleiman the Magnificent to French merchants led to a spectacular increase in trade with Turkey. A century later Colbert, Louis XIV's Minister of Finance, convinced that this was vital to the economy of France, declared Marseilles a free port, and set up a Chamber of Commerce there charged with the responsibility of exercising on behalf of the State strict control over every aspect of it. No young man could go to Turkey to trade without the approval of the Chamber of Commerce: once this had been obtained he was sent out for ten years, and forbidden either to take his wife with him or to contract a local marriage. French merchants in Turkish cities lived in self-contained communities with their own doctors, bakers and artisans, their existence governed by regulations laid down by the authorities in France for every conceivable contingency, down to and including the number of Masses to be said. The manner in which trade was conducted was no less strictly regulated, and exports to the Sultan's dominions (by far the most important of which were textiles), were subjected to rigid Government inspection to ensure that their quality was maintained. By the end of the seventeenth century trade with Turkey was organised as part of the public service, and an important section of French industry was wholly dependent on it. It offered to France all the commercial advantages of a colonial empire without imposing on her any comparable administrative burden.[5]

There was one other sphere in which France exploited her special relationship with Turkey to her own advantage. The Capitulations of 1604 awarded to His Most Christian Majesty the guardianship of pilgrims going to the Holy Land, and by implication he became the protector of the Latin Christian minorities in the Ottoman Empire. Throughout the seventeenth century there was a steady infiltration of French priests and monks into Turkey. Ardent for the faith, regardless of hardships, able to move about more freely than the merchants, they travelled to places which few Europeans had previously visited. Since they were strictly forbidden to try to convert Muslims, they concentrated on ensuring that the Latin Christians did not lapse or fall into heresy, and on the conversion of the Armenians and the Orthodox. By 1700 the Jesuits and the Franciscans, working directly under the protection of France, had so extended their activities that they had virtually created a French enclave in the midst of the Sultan's dominions, and in 1710 the Jesuits even succeeded in reaching the Crimea, a feat which paved the way for the establishment of a French consular agent there. As a source of information both they and their fellow monks were most useful to the French Ambassador.

In 1719 the British Ambassador in Constantinople considered that the Turks trusted the French more than any other Christian nation. During the next few years, however, it became more and more apparent that the French position was not as strong as this statement implied. After their resounding defeat by Prince Eugen at Belgrade in 1717, the Turks, determined to avoid a further trial of strength with the Emperor, made far-reaching concessions to appease him. The Imperial Resident rather than the French Ambassador began to call the tune at the Porte. Commercial competition was increasing. The British who had also managed to extract favourable trading terms from the Sultan were becoming formidable rivals, and the Dutch too were extremely active. When the Treaty of Passarowitz was concluded in 1718, the Emperor obtained special trading privileges and founded the Imperial Ostend Company to exploit them. By 1726 it seemed probable that Austria would become yet another competitor for the Levant trade. Finally the conversionary zeal of French priests and monks gave rise to an increasing number of bitter quarrels with the schismatic clergy and, since the latter were the Sultan's subjects, this inevitably led to friction between France and the Porte. The Latin Christians, losing faith in the power of the King of France to protect them, began to turn towards the Emperor.

The weakness of the Turks after their defeat at Belgrade, and the emerging threats to the position of France in the Ottoman Empire, were therefore among the more serious of the many problems confronting the elderly prelate to whom in 1726 Louis XV entrusted the direction of the affairs of his kingdom.

André Hercule Fleury was seventy-three when he was made First Minister of France. He came from Languedoc, and after entering the Church, had the good fortune to attract the notice of Bossuet, through whose influence he became Almoner successively to the Queen and then to King Louis XIV. He was popular at Court. Although neither tall nor strikingly handsome his wit made him a sought after guest, and his affable manner gained him many friends. Temperamentally well suited to Court life, he had every reason to suppose that a pleasant if not particularly distinguished career lay ahead of him. This agreeable prospect was apparently wrecked when in 1701 he was appointed Bishop of Fréjus, a poor and unimportant diocese over 300 leagues from Paris. In France at that time everything centred on Paris and to be dispatched to the provinces was the equivalent of being sent into exile. Fleury, bored and detesting every moment of it, remained at Fréjus for fifteen years. But, dreary though his sojourn there was, it was to prove the turning point in his career. Occupying a position coveted by nobody he had no enemies, and in consequence when, on the death of Louis XIV, the problem arose of appointing a tutor for his grandson and successor, all factions at Versailles agreed that the non-controversial Bishop of Fréjus was the ideal choice.

In 1715, determined never again to leave Paris, Fleury returned to the capital to take up his new post. He made a great success of the task entrusted to him, and succeeded in winning his pupil's affection and confidence. In 1726 his patience and perseverance were rewarded. The young King dismissed the Duke of Burgundy who had been a disastrous failure as First Minister and appointed Fleury to succeed him. The appointment suited everyone admirably. It left Louis free to pursue his pleasures, confident that the affairs of his kingdom were being directed by a wise old man who was personally devoted to him. It aroused little jealousy amongst the courtiers who saw in the new head of the government merely a septuagenarian who in the natural course of events would not hold office for very long and who, in the meantime, was unlikely to disturb their intrigues. In consequence Fleury, awarded a cardinal's hat by the Pope, was left with the minimum of interference to carry the whole burden of the affairs of the State.

According to a contemporary song Richelieu bled France and Mazarin purged her, but Fleury adopted the far less drastic course of simply putting her on a diet.[6] The Cardinal's policy was dominated by his conviction that the supreme need of the country was to recover economically from the wars of Louis XIV. Understanding little of finance he did not attempt to introduce any new system of taxation or commerce, but confined himself to insisting that his subordinates cut down expenditure and, having done this, simply left the rest to the basic health of the economy. A diet takes time to effect a cure and most men of his age, anxious to see results before the end of what might only be a short term of office, would have tried a speedier remedy. Fleury, however, was well prepared to wait. He took absolutely no account of his age, correctly as events were to prove, for he remained in power for seventeen years until his death at the age of ninety-three. The epithet of '*Votre Éternité*' said to have been applied to him by the Archbishop of Paris was singularly appropriate.

If France was to gain the time she needed for her recovery at home she must have peace abroad. The Cardinal set himself to obtain this for her by diplomacy, an art at which he excelled. He had an unrivalled capacity for concealing his real intentions, and for disarming suspicion by conveying the impression that he was a timid simple old man, buffeted by fate and uncertain how to proceed. No impression could be more misleading; the whole act was part of a subtle calculated technique. St. Simon considered that Fleury with his outwardly gentle and unassuming manner was inwardly the most self possessed and determined man he had ever met.[7] According to d'Argenson he had 'the wiles of an old monkey'.[8] Both were right. The mild modest exterior concealed a character of extreme determination and obstinacy. Once he had decided what he wanted, the Cardinal was prepared to exploit every asset which he possessed—his age, his health, his experience of the court and its intrigues—and to use every means, however small, to obtain it. Tenacity of purpose is formidable when combined with flexibility of method. Fleury was a very formidable old man. Like Ostermann he was quite unbribeable and cared nothing for splendour or riches; like Ostermann too he was an adept at the art of evasion. He had a small house at Issy outside Paris and if he was displeased, or wished to appear so, would simply retire there and wait for the situation to clear. Foreign envoys found him impossible to pin down. Lord Waldegrave, the British Ambassador, reported that it was useless to question him: 'He himself has told me many times that he cannot bear "*des Questions*". He says they either put him upon equivocating, or make him break off the conversation.'[9]

The Cardinal was an exacting taskmaster and his subordinates did not find him easy to work with. He demanded absolute submissiveness and encroached constantly on their authority.

He kept all the strings of policy in his own hands, and French ambassadors abroad were left in the dark as to the interconnections of his negotiations with foreign governments. Nevertheless they served him well. Their reports were clear, concise, and to the point and they prided themselves on their descriptions of the personalities at the Courts to which they were accredited. On the whole these diplomats were far superior in calibre to most of their colleagues from other countries, and they worked for a Ministry of Foreign Affairs at home which was better organised and a great deal more competent than any other in Europe.

In 1727 one of the most important posts in the French diplomatic service fell vacant when M. d'Andrezel the ambassador at the Sublime Porte died in Constantinople.

Of all the representatives of His Most Christian Majesty of France none had a more difficult task than the ambassador in Constantinople. The distance of his post from Versailles meant that a great deal had to be left to his own initiative; and the diversity of his country's interests in the Ottoman Empire required him to be not only a diplomat but also an administrator. In addition to trying to persuade the Porte to conduct its foreign policy in a manner beneficial to France, he was required to promote French trade and to enforce the innumerable regulations governing it. He was responsible for the protection of the French mercantile communities in the Ottoman Empire from the rapacity of the local Turkish pashas, for protesting (all too often) on their behalf against infringements of their trading rights; and for adjudicating (only too frequently) in internecine squabbles between his countrymen. Finally he had to defend the interests of the Latin Christians, and to restrain the religious zeal of the French priests and monks, whose missionary ardour often caused more trouble than all the vagaries of the merchants put together. The duties attached to the post were in many ways those of a viceroy rather than of an ambassador. It demanded a man of exceptional ability, and never more than in 1727 when French prestige and influence in Constantinople were suffering a progressive erosion, French trade was declining, and the existence of the Ottoman Empire, one of the vital pivots of French policy, was menaced by the Austro-Russian alliance.

The situation appeared to call for the appointment of a highly experienced diplomat, or at least, given the importance which the Porte attached to outward display, for an ambassador who was 'rich, well born and handsome'.[10] The Cardinal took a different view of the matter. He chose a competent fifty-three-year-old civil servant with no previous experience of diplomacy who was neither outstandingly aristocratic nor rich, and most certainly not handsome.

The Marquis de Villeneuve, Lieutenant-General of Marseilles, came from a family of minor provincial nobility. His career had been honourable rather than brilliant, and he might have remained a provincial official in Marseilles for the rest of his life had not official business caused him to visit Paris. There he came to the notice of the Chancellor d'Augesseau who recommended him to the Cardinal. To Fleury, searching for a successor to d'Andrezel in Constantinople, Villeneuve had one obvious asset. He came from Marseilles, the port through which the whole of the French trade with Turkey passed, and therefore had a first-hand knowledge of those commercial interests, the protection and furtherance of which was one of the main functions of the French Ambassador at the Porte. Fleury also found Villeneuve's personality congenial. The Marquis was an ugly tough little man who expressed himself vividly in a broad Provençal accent. He was agreeable, had an easy manner, and gave the impression of possessing energy tempered with good judgement. The latter quality, however, the Cardinal felt certain, would not in Villeneuve's case be vitiated by any considerations of forbearance towards an opponent, a quality the exercise of which would be most detrimental to the interests of France in the Ottoman Empire. Confident that he had found a man who would conform to the classic definition of an ambassador and 'say, advise, and think whatever may best serve the preservation and aggrandisement of his own state',[11] the Cardinal laid the name of his chosen candidate before his sovereign. In 1728 Louis-Sauveur, Marquis de Villeneuve was appointed Ambassador of His Most Christian

Majesty King Louis XV of France at the Sublime Porte.

Before leaving for Constantinople Villeneuve received the thorough briefing given to every French ambassador before proceeding to a new post. The directive for the mission he was to undertake, although signed by Chauvelin, the Keeper of the Seals and Fleury's deputy for Foreign Affairs, reflected the Cardinal's appreciation of the situation. It opened by stating that, in view of the weakness of Turkey and the determination of the Sultan Ahmed III and his Grand Vizier, Ibrahim, to do nothing to offend the Emperor, it was, for the time being, useless to attempt to persuade the Porte to adopt a more active policy in favour of France. So far as politics were concerned Villeneuve was therefore to confine himself to establishing good personal relations with the Sultan's Ministers and to wait for the situation to improve, for past experience had shown that Sultans and Grand Viziers came and went with disconcerting rapidity. The Marquis was, however, in the meantime to try to negotiate a truce under French auspices between the various Christian sects, to do everything in his power to further trade, and generally to neglect no opportunity of defending and strengthening the French position in the Ottoman Empire.

In September 1728, Villeneuve together with his wife and family set sail for Constantinople. They were accompanied by a suite of over a hundred persons which included scholars charged with the purchase of antiquities for the King's private collection; gentlemen who, curious to see the city of the Grand Seignor (as the Sultan was then generally called in Europe), were making the journey for their own pleasure, and two abbés who optimistically hoped to study certain manuscripts reputed to be lodged in the Sultan's private library. Two months later the *Léopard* and the *Alcyon*, the French ships of the line carrying the party, flags flying and bristling with guns, entered the Bosphorus, doubled the Serail point and dropped anchor. The Ambassador had arrived at his post.

Constantinople, protected by walls fourteen miles long, situated on the join of two continents, looked back on a turbulent history since its foundation as the Second Rome by the Emperor

Constantine. It had witnessed the rise and glory of the Byzantine Empire, and its final destruction on that day in 1453 when Mehmet II, the Conqueror, rode up to the Cathedral of Santa Sophia and from the altar proclaimed Constantinople to be the capital of the victorious Ottoman Turks. From it the forces of Suleiman the Magnificent had marched to bear the standard of the Sultan far into Asia and to the gates of Vienna. Rulers changed. Constantinople took part in their vicissitudes and survived them all, imbued with the cynical wisdom of a courtesan who has charmed many men—and found them all much the same—still capable of flashes of passion, incapable of sustained enthusiasm. Approached from the sea the beauty of the city, its domes and minarets set in the midst of gardens and cypresses, arranged, as Lady Mary Wortley Montagu wrote, like 'tiers of jars, canisters, and candlesticks in a cabinet',[12] must have impressed Villeneuve as it did all travellers. Like them too he was no doubt disillusioned when, escorted by his countrymen, the monks among them chanting the Te Deum, he rode in procession to the '*palais de France*', the French Embassy in Pera. All the houses were built of wood. The streets were dark, filthy, infested with stray dogs, and so narrow that in many of them two loaded horses could scarcely pass each other. He must have been relieved when the procession emerged into the comparative cleanliness and light of Pera, the diplomatic quarter of Constantinople.

The French Embassy was built on a hill. Of all the views from it the finest was to the west, where on one of the most beautiful sites in the world formed by the junction of the Golden Horn and the Bosphorus rose a high wall, broken here and there by rectangular towers and more than a league in circumference. This wall enclosed the Serail Palace, a series of pavilions linked by courtyards, surrounded by colonnades, and set in gardens in which there were fountains, avenues of cypresses, and beds of tulips. It was a view of exceptional interest to Villeneuve. In the Serail Palace, withdrawn from the gaze of his subjects except on ceremonial occasions, lived Sultan Ahmed III the ruler of the Ottoman Empire, to whom he would shortly be summoned to present his credentials.

CHAPTER IV

ﾡﾡﾡﾡﾡﾡﾡﾡﾡﾡﾡﾡﾡﾡﾡﾡﾡﾡﾡﾡﾡﾡﾡﾡﾡﾡﾡﾡﾡﾡﾡ

The Sultan, the Porte and the Foreign Envoys

Constantinople, 1728-1729

The Serail was a self-contained community. According to a contemporary chronicler the provinces of the Ottoman Empire were required to supply it annually with very large quantities of 'rice, sugar, peas, lentils, pepper, coffee, sena, macaroons, dates, saffron, honey, salt, plums in lemon juice, vinegar, water melons, 199,000 hens, 780 cartloads of snow, and tin for the cooking pots and fodder and forage for the horses.'[1] Thus sustained and provided for, a very large number of officials attended day and night to the needs and personal affairs of the Shadow of God on Earth. The preparation of the Sultan's food was presided over by the Chief Attendant of the Napkin, assisted by the Senior of the Tray Carriers, who had on his staff the Sherbert-maker, the Fruit-server and the Pickle-server. There was a Chief Turban-Folder, and Chiefs of the Laundrymen, Barbers, Bathmen and Bandsmen, each with an appropriate number of assistants. The Baş Çokadar or Head Valet, had the special privilege of walking on the Sultan's right in processions, holding the Privy waterproof and scattering silver coins to the crowd; the Rikabdar Aga held his ruler's stirrup when he mounted; the Silihdar Aga or Sword Bearer was in constant attendance carrying his sword, and the Mir Alem was in charge of his personal standard, as well as commanding a corps of special messengers called the Chief Doorkeepers. Great attention was paid to the supervision of the Sultan's private treasury which contained gold, money, jewels, furs, guns, and articles in general household use. To look after this glorified store cupboard there was a Purse-Keeper, Keepers of the Guns, of the Aigrettes, and of the Gala Robes, the Senior of the Dishes, who was responsible for the porcelain dinner services, and the Chief Guardian of the Gifts to whom was entrusted the task of listing and maintaining registers of the innumerable presents offered to the Sultan.

One of the senior officials had a title which in no way corresponded to his functions. This was the Bostançi Başi or Chief Gardener. The two thousand Bostançis under his command were so named because their corps was first formed to undertake the conversion of the rough ground about the palace into gardens and vegetable plots, but by the eighteenth century most of them had been diverted to other tasks and were watchmen, guards, porters and refuse removers. Their commander, the Bostançi Başi, was therefore responsible for a variety of odd jobs in the Serail, but since his duties also included the execution of sentences passed on delinquent members of the Sultan's household, he occupied a position of considerable importance. Even he, however, was overshadowed by the Chief Black Eunuch, the Kizlar Aga, or, as he was sometimes called, the Aga of the House of Felicity. As controller of the harem he was the principal ministrant to his master's personal pleasures and, as the channel through which all communications passed between the Sultan and his ministers, in a unique position to influence affairs of State. His power was such that not even the Grand Vizier could afford to neglect him.

On his appointment the Grand Vizier was entrusted with the Sultan's seal, and so, in the words of the official Turkish historians, 'attained the signet of the Sovereign of the world'.[2] From the vast building near the Serail, known to Europeans as the Sublime Porte, he controlled the administration and armed forces of the Ottoman Empire, and represented the Sultan as chief dispenser of justice. He was assisted by the great Officers of State, such as the Captain Pasha who commanded the Ottoman Navy and the Janissary Aga, and by three principal lieutenants. These were the Kahya Bey who acted as his general deputy, particularly in home and military affairs; the Reis Effendi who was head of his Chancery with a special responsibility for foreign affairs (in which he in turn was assisted by the Porte Dragoman or Interpreter); and the Çavuş Başi who combined the function of Vice-President of the Law Courts with that of Chief Pursuivant or Herald and Master of Ceremonies to the Sultan.

The Ottoman civil service was organised in a rigid bureaucratic hierarchy of the utmost complexity and the Grand Vizier, as the head of it, occupied a position of great power. But, although he was designated the Sultan's 'absolute representative', two spheres lay outside his jurisdiction. One of these was the Sultan's Household in the Serail dominated by the Kizlar Aga. The other was the 'Learned Profession' presided over by the Sheikh ul Islam. The administration of the Ottoman Empire was governed by the principles incorporated in the Şeri'a, the Sacred Law of Islam. In theory these principles were all embracing, the 'Gate of Interpretation' was shut, and no further definitions were either admissible or necessary. [3] But the Şeri'a had been drawn up to legislate for conditions in a primitive and long since outmoded society, and by the eighteenth century there were many situations for which it could provide no ruling. To deal with these the Sultan issued Kanuns or supplementary regulations which were supposed in no way to conflict with the Şeri'a. The final decision as to whether or not they were in order rested with the Sheikh ul Islam, who was a consultative jurist chosen from amongst the Muftis and assisted in his work by a staff headed by the Chief Judges of Rumelia and Anatolia. He had (in theory) the right to depose the Sultan if the latter transgressed the Sacred Law; war could not be waged without his consent; he acted as a check on the Grand Vizier.

Exalted though the position of the Grand Vizier might be, it was surrounded by restrictions and hazards. Any holder of the office had to be contend not only with the Sheikh ul Islam, (who was inevitably opposed to innovation), and with the Kizlar Aga (who was always liable to undermine his position with the Sultan), but also with the Janissaries. This was a formidable body of men, the *corps d'élite* of the army, paid and fed by the Government, and enjoying a number of privileges designed to bind it more closely to the Sultan. The importance attached to the problem of feeding the Janissaries adequately in order to keep them contented was reflected in the designations of some of their junior officers—Corbaçi (soup man), Asçi (cook), and Baş Kara Kullukou (head scullion). The most treasured possession of any section of the corps, and revered far more than its standard, was the huge copper cauldron in which its food was cooked. But this aura of domesticity was misleading. The Janissary head cook, in addition to his culinary duties, was responsible for arresting, putting in irons, and, if so commanded, garotting prisoners. On the battlefield the Janissaries were dreaded by every Christian commander; at home the efforts of the Government to satisfy and control them were by no means always successful, and they were prone to assume the role of a Praetorian Guard. When discontented they hammered on their cooking cauldrons. All too often that sound was the death knell for the Grand Vizier of the day.

The Ottoman hierarchy had altered very little during the two centuries which had elapsed since the reign of Suleiman the Magnificent. Villeneuve had his first sight of it when, shortly after his arrival in Constantinople, he presented his credentials to Ahmed III. This ceremony, the details of which never varied, was conducted with the utmost formality. It was far from agreeable.

On the appointed day the Ambassador and his suite rose at three in the morning, put on their finest clothes, and were ferried across the Golden Horn. On landing in Stamboul they were conducted to a miserable house 'the stairs of which' as one ambassadorial sufferer complained, 'are no better than a ladder and the room fit rather for the reception of a Polish Jew'.⁴ There they waited for the Çavuş Başi, who was alleged to be detained at prayer in the mosque. When he finally condescended to arrive there was a protocol quarrel, the Çavuş Başi demanding to ride in the place of honour on the Ambassador's right and the Ambassador insisting that the Çavuş Başi should precede him. The wrangle, to which every Ambassador was subjected, was always prolonged and frequently acrimonious, but the point was considered to be of such importance that foreign envoys were accustomed to estimate their colleague's standing at the Porte by the extent to which he managed to get his own way. When some sort of agreement had been reached, the Ambassador and his suite (in no very good temper), rode slowly up the hill until they came to the Sublime Porte. Here, whatever the weather, they were obliged to halt until the Grand Vizier, magnificently attired and attended, had preceded them into the Serail.

The first courtyard of the Serail was an irregular rectangle the size of a city square, adorned with clumps of trees and thronged with officials. At the far end of it the foreigners were compelled to dismount and hand over their swords. A procession was then formed. The Çavuş Başi and the Chief Intendant of the Door-keepers wearing blue ceremonial robes led the way. They carried long staffs of office covered with gold leaf which they struck on the ground to give notice of their approach and to clear a way through the spectators. The Ambassador and his suite followed them into a second smaller courtyard. Here they were confronted by a remarkable sight. A number of cauldrons filled with *pilau* stood in the centre of it and to the right of them several thousand Janissaries were drawn up. At a given signal they fell upon the cauldrons, scooping up the *pilau* with their hands, each man pushing and kicking in an endeavour to get the largest possible share for himself. In a few minutes all the food had disappeared. Having witnessed this edifying spectacle the ambassadorial procession resumed its progress and entered the Diwan or Grand Vizier's audience chamber. This was a large domed hall, the walls adorned with mosaics, arabesques, and gold and blue hangings, round three sides of which ran a low stone bench. On this bench the great officers of the Porte reclined, the colours of their fur-trimmed widesleeved ceremonial robes—green, violet, silver, blue or yellow—denoting their rank. The Ambassador was motioned to seat himself on a small stool placed by the door, but his staff were obliged to stand.

After a short pause the Grand Vizier, wearing a robe of white satin and a turban bound with gold, entered and seated himself in the place of honour on the Diwan bench from which he spent the next two hours dealing with petitions. The proceedings were conducted in Turkish of which most of the ambassadors understood not a word. The Janissaries were then paid from a massive stack of bags of coin deposited in a corner of the Diwan. This ceremony took some time. When it was over the Ambassador, who had been sitting in a draught for several hours on his backless stool, was exhausted, but found little to restore him in the banquet which followed. He was compelled to remain on his stool while fifty dishes or more 'came in like a torrent'.[5] The plates were not changed, but as one diplomat put it 'occasionally wiped', and the food was most unpalatable. The best that could be said about the meal was that it did not last very long.

After the dishes had been cleared away the Ambassador put on the robe of honour or caftan presented to him by the Sultan. This was made of fur embroidered with gold and silver, reached to the ground, and was so heavy that it was difficult for the wearer to stand upright. He was then conducted to the courtyard leading to the Sultan's audience chamber where, pending the arrival of the Grand Vizier, he sat on a bench which was no more than 'a single old board, on which, at other times, grooms, ostlers and scullions lie to sun themselves though it sometimes serves for less decent purposes'.[6]

After another interminable wait the Grand Vizier, surrounded by high dignitaries, appeared and swept into the Sultan's audience chamber on the far side of the courtyard. Two officials seized the Ambassador under the arms and half carried, half propelled him forwards. The weight of his robe was such that it was nearly impossible for him to move without their assistance, so it was an undignified form of progress. Jerked to his knees at intervals by his two escorts in order that he might make the suitable form of reverence, struggling to keep on his feet, he eventually arrived breathless, and with his wig awry, before the Shadow of God on Earth. The Sultan was enthroned on a marble altar covered with cloth of gold, under a canopy which, together with its supporting pillars, was ornamented with silver and precious stones. He wore cloth of gold trimmed with sable, a white turban in which was affixed a black and white aigrette, and sat turned sideways so that no infidel might gaze upon his face. The blue ceiling of the audience chamber was decorated with yellow and red plaster work, the walls covered with blue, white and yellow tiles, and there were great crimson carpets on the floor. No effort had been spared to achieve an impression of splendour and mystery.

From this point the proceedings were brief. The Ambassador made a short speech which was translated into Turkish by the Porte Dragoman, and handed over a richly embroidered case containing his credentials. This was passed from hand to hand until it reached the Grand Vizier who, bowing very low, laid it beside the Sultan's throne. The Grand Vizier replied briefly to the Ambassador. The Porte Dragoman translated again. The Sultan inclined his head. The Ambassador and his suite were half carried half frogmarched backwards out of the Sultan's presence, hoisted on to their horses, and then compelled to wait until the Grand Vizier had left the Serail. A dawn rising, and considerably more than six hours hanging about, had culminated in an audience which had lasted for ten minutes and during which absolutely nothing of significance had been said. All the foreign envoys agreed that it was a mortifying experience. Villeneuve in his report to Versailles commented that there had been a good many thorns among the roses.

A few days after presenting his credentials to the Sultan the new French Ambassador was received in audience by the Grand Vizier Ibrahim Pasha. After an exchange of compliments which lasted over an hour the Grand Vizier invited Villeneuve to smoke a pipe with him. This was an honour which, as a non-smoker, the Frenchman did not relish, but which he was forced to accept in the interests of diplomacy. He then attempted to raise the question of the Porte's failure to implement the Capitulations. Ibrahim replied by interrogating him about the gardens of Versailles. Villeneuve departed having obtained nothing more than an assurance that he would be given a further audience 'after the festivities', but when these would end was quite unspecified.

The Marquis consoled himself with the thought that in his first audiences with the Sultan and the Grand Vizier he had avoided the errors committed by some of his predecessors. M. de Ferriol had tried to enter the Sultan's presence wearing his sword and, when attempts were made to remove it from him, had cast his robe of honour on the floor and stalked out without presenting his credentials. M. de Vantelac, having lost his temper with the Grand Vizier, had flung the papers which he had come to discuss on the Diwan bench from where they had rebounded hitting the Grand Vizier on the stomach, an involuntary insult for which M. de Vantelac had been punished with three days' close arrest. M. de Nointel had so enraged the Grand Vizier of his day by advancing the stool on which he sat too close to that dignitary that he had never again been received in audience. But, as Villeneuve fully realised, although there had been no disagreeable incident at either of his audiences, the Porte regarded him with no more favour than any other Christian envoy.

The Porte disliked all the Christian envoys very much indeed. Ottoman historians, when describing their audiences with the Sultan, referred to them as 'the accursed' whose presence polluted the audience chamber. This was more than a figure of speech. The Turks held the Christians in contempt, regarding their envoys as potential spies and hostages for the good behaviour of their rulers. A Russian ambassador was twice incarcerated in the Seven Towers, an unpleasant prison on the Bosphorus, but this after all was normal Turkish practice when war seemed to be imminent. A French ambassador spent three months in the Seven Towers merely because a shipload of merchandise from France for the Serail had inadvertently been sold *en route* in Italy.

By 1728 when Villeneuve arrived in Constantinople the situation was rather easier. After the defeat inflicted on the Sultan's armies by Prince Eugen, the Turks could no longer afford to be quite so high handed with the representatives of foreign monarchs. But, and as the French Ambassador soon began to discover, they were still extremely difficult to deal with. Although the Sultan, concerned only with his pleasures, left the administration of his Empire to the Grand Vizier, he retained the right to veto the actions of his First Minister and to dismiss him and, when exercising this prerogative, he was frequently influenced by the officials of his household, or even by favoured members of his harem. In consequence the Grand Vizier lived in constant dread of dismissal, as did his subordinates who, having bought their positions, were concerned only to retain and exploit them for their own profit. The Janissaries, although still spasmodically capable of formidable action in battle, were undisciplined and susceptible to any disaffection which might be stirring in the bazaars of Constantinople. The façade of magnificence mingled with contempt presented by the Ruling Institution of the Ottoman Empire to the foreigner was therefore no more than a hollow shell and, in the vacuum behind it, ministers and officials gyrated in an apparently endless series of permutations and combinations, intriguing against each other, intent solely on maintaining their own positions. In this confusion there was, it seemed, only one unassailable man. The Kizlar Aga Beshir aged seventy-six was a former Abyssinian slave who had been bought for thirty piastres in Cairo for the Sultan's household and, having spent over sixty years in the Serail, was a pastmaster at manipulating its intrigues. It was generally agreed that he was the *Éminence Noire* behind the Sultan's throne, but no foreign envoy had direct access to him and, as Villeneuve soon realised, attempts to approach or bribe him through intermediaries were unproductive.

The French Ambassador therefore could only hope that the festivities would soon be over and that he might once again be summoned to the Grand Vizier. Time passed; festivities of some kind or another appeared to be unending. They were essential to the remarkable balancing feat by which Ibrahim Pasha remained in office. Ahmed III was interested only in riches and diversion. He loved the sight and possession of gold, and nothing pleased him more than some new kind of entertainment. Ibrahim cut down the expenses of the administration and extorted money by every means at his disposal, thereby both enriching the Sultan's personal treasury and acquiring the means to finance an unending variety of these essential diversions. Ahmed had a passion for building. Ibrahim embellished mosques, commissioned fountains, summoned architects from abroad and, at the Sweet Waters of Europe outside Constantinople, built a series of pavilions and cascades in imitation of Marly. By his orders religious feasts were celebrated with greater splendour then ever before, and lasted for several days during which time the whole city was illuminated. On special occasions, such as a royal marriage, more than two thousand musicians and fifteen hundred cooks were employed.

These festivities, on a scale exceeding those of the greatest courts of Christendom, were staged with a grave measured formality. There were no orgies of drinking and gambling as was all too often the case elsewhere. The Sacred Law forbade the Turks to do either, nor did they wish to. In the intervals between entertainments the Sultan passed his time in his harem, sat in the shade listening to poetry, inspected his buildings, and gave orders for the cultivation of new and exotic kinds of tulips. Superficially it appeared that his court had achieved a refinement by no means always to be found at the other courts of the day, and that the imitation of Marly was a sign that he and his Ministers were prepared to copy the best which Christendom could provide. In fact this was not so. A pleasing style of architecture might be imitated, a printing press set up, or improved types of cannon imported from Europe, but this was all. There was no interest in the new ideas which were beginning to stir elsewhere and education made no progress. The same Sultan who delighted in the cultivation of tulips did not hesitate to inflict ferocious punishments on any of his subjects who displeased him—beheading, strangling and the strappado were amongst the mildest of them. The Grand Vizier Ibrahim was reported on one occasion as being in an exceptionally good humour because he had just received the heads of two rebels who had been executed in Cairo. Altogether the veneer of refinement and civilisation in Constantinople was very thin.

To Villeneuve and his colleagues the veneer seemed to be non-existent. They were not invited to the great court festivities, but from their residences in Pera looking out across the Golden Horn to Stamboul, they could see the splendid cavalcades which accompanied the Sultan and the Grand Vizier as they rode through the streets of the capital. The foreign envoys were not impressed by the colours of the robes of the high officials of the Porte, the ostrich plumes of the Janissaries, or the splendour of the horses' trappings studded with gold and precious stones. They found the garments bizarre and the colours crude. The architecture of the city did not appeal to them, and Turkish food they considered disgusting. On the rare occasions when they were invited to a ceremonial banquet they were bored by the interminable juggling, wrestling and other entertainments which accompanied it. They had a genuine horror of Islam, little comprehension of its practices and ceremonies, and no desire to acquire more. Constantinople in their opinion was totally lacking in either fascination or glamour.

The Sultan's capital was also, as Villeneuve discovered within a very few weeks of his arrival, a most uncomfortable place to live in. It was said of its inhabitants that 'if anyone is asked his age, the answer will always refer the enquirer to the year of some great plague or famine, some rebellion or conflagration.'[7] Of these recurrent disasters plague occurred annually, fires almost daily, and the diplomatic corps were no more exempt from such hazards than the rest of the population. Their official residences, constructed like most other buildings in the city of wood and plaster, were vulnerable to fire and cold in winter. When the summer outbreak of plague occurred, the only safe course was to leave the capital for one of the villages outside it, and to remain there until the epidemic had subsided, or, if this was not possible, to remain indoors and see nobody. In addition to the plague there were smallpox epidemics, fever and dysentery to contend with. Eighteenth-century dispatches from Constantinople contained frequent references to the writer being 'out of order'. Servants, a great many of whom were required to maintain the pomp and ceremony appropriate to an ambassador's status, were a perpetual problem. If they were Europeans they either did not survive long, 'the heat of the country and the wine ruin them, they are either drunk or sick in bed',[8] or caused embarrassment to their masters by brawls with the local inhabitants. Most envoys were reduced to engaging Arabs as grooms and Greeks and Armenians for housework, and putting up with their incompetence and squabbles.

Life was very dull. Foreign envoys rarely travelled outside Constantinople and, when in the capital, seldom left Pera. Their wives could only cross the Golden Horn to Stamboul if, like the Turkish women, they wore a veil. Amongst the Sultan's subjects social relations were possible only with the Phanariot Greeks, and this left much to be desired. These Greeks, so called because they lived in the quarter of the Phanar in Constantinople, constituted a closed caste from the ranks of which were drawn the Hospodars or Governors of Moldavia and Wallachia, the Patriarch and other high dignitaries of the Orthodox Church, and the Porte and Embassy Dragomen. They controlled much of the trade of the Ottoman Empire, and, unlike the Sultan's Muslim officials and citizens, had some knowledge of Europe and its ideas. But for the sophisticated European diplomat a visit to a Phanariot Greek household had little to offer. Food was served 'with more profusion than elegance or cleanliness'.[9] The women were of limited charm, appearing in the height of the summer in robes of crimson or black velvet, loaded with gold embroidery, 'the weight of such a dress, added to the heat of the weather, had almost rendered these ladies immovable and nearly dumb.'[10] Altogether there was not much enjoyment or profit to be derived from social contact with the Phanariot Greeks. Although they were Christians, they were not in the least interested in furthering the cause of the Christian powers, for their existence depended on the goodwill of the Porte, and their unreliability and rapacity were notorious.

It was not surprising that, after a few months in Constantinople, Villeneuve confessed in a letter to a friend that there was nothing in the Ottoman capital which could replace for him the delights of Paris. The discomfort and boredom of Constantinople would have been tolerable had he been able to make some progress with the mission with which he had been entrusted. He made no progress at all. Month succeeded month without a further summons to the Grand Vizier, and the latter's deputy for foreign affairs, the Reis Effendi, consistently fobbed the Marquis off, as he did all the Christian envoys, on to the Porte Dragoman.

The Porte Dragoman, as the official with whom they were most in contact, was of paramount importance to Villeneuve and his colleagues. He was always chosen from one of the leading Phanariot Greek families. Unlike other countries the Porte maintained no permanent ambassadors abroad, and its sources of information about other countries were therefore extremely limited. During the era of military conquest and expansion this was no great handicap, but by the beginning of the eighteenth century the position had changed. Ottoman military strength was declining, but contact with Europe was increasing, and a great deal more accordingly devolved on the Porte Dragoman. His duties were arduous. In addition to conducting day to day business with the foreign envoys, he had to interpret when they were received in audience by the Sultan, and at all discussions between them and the Reis Effendi or Grand Vizier. He was also required to translate all written communications between the Porte and foreign countries, to read foreign newsheets, and to extract and translate any items of interest which they might contain. Although in a position to influence the conduct of affairs, and so to derive considerable profit for himself, he never knew how long he would remain in office. If anything went wrong it was on him that the wrath of the Porte descended: the Grand Vizier could one day make him his confidant, and on the next cut off his head.

The post of Porte Dragoman was aptly described as that of 'the principal slave of the Porte'.[11] His attire, a long robe *à la Turque*, and a bonnet trimmed with ermine, was a constant reminder that he was one of the Sultan's subjects and as a Phanariot Greek he belonged to a community considered by many foreigners to be exceptionally unreliable, and prepared for money to sell 'their God, their faith, their soul, and their sovereign.'[12] Villeneuve found the Porte Dragoman courteous and apparently easy to deal with, but had a number of reservations about his integrity and professional competence, and a poor opinion of his linguistic ability. This left much to be desired, a factor which could, and did, lead to serious misunderstandings.

The language problem bedevilled the existence of every foreign envoy in Constantinople, for their ignorance of Turkish compelled them to employ their own dragomen interpreters. Since it

Field-Marshal Münnich, from an engraving by Bornigoroth after
a painting by an unknown artist

Cardinal Fleury, from an engraving by François Chereau
after a painting by Rigaud

was beneath an envoy's dignity to have contact with any other than the senior officials of the Porte, and since he only demanded audience of them on ceremonial occasions or when there was business of great importance to discuss, a great deal was left to the dragomen, who were in addition expected to serve as general intelligence agents. Most of them were Levantines of Italian extraction or Phanariot Greeks. This was unavoidable for they were the only people who possessed the necessary linguistic qualifications, but it was also all too frequently disastrous. According to a contemporary rhyme, 'In Pera sono tre malanni: Peste, fuoco, dragomanni.'[13] The general concensus of opinion in the diplomatic corps was that the dragomen were the worst of the lot, and that it was 'hell on earth to have to deal with them.'[14]

The dragomen inevitably became privy to the secrets of the mission of the envoy whom they served, and so were well placed to influence negotiations by transmitting, withholding or providing information as they saw fit. They endeavoured to carry out their duties without endangering themselves for, while nominally under their employer's protection, and so enjoying a form of diplomatic immunity, this did not exempt them from punishment by any official of the Porte whom they might offend.

If required to deliver a communication likely to arouse the wrath of the Porte, they would either water it down or not deliver it at all. One ambassador having sent his dragoman with an urgent message to the Reis Effendi had him followed, and found that he had simply gone to a house which was a rendezvous for other dragomen 'where they passed the day very agreeably at cards and other diversions.'[15] Over their cards they no doubt exchanged information about the secrets of their respective employers, and concocted the stories which they would tell them. In the cut-throat existence of eighteenth-century Constantinople the dragomen had a freemasonry of mutual interest. Apart from some very rare exceptions they were all concerned to exploit their positions to their own advantage.

One of these exceptions was Delaria, the First Dragoman of the French Embassy, who was both intelligent and loyal. From him, during his first six months in Constantinople, Villeneuve learnt a great deal about the intrigues within the Porte, and about the all important subject of bribery.

Bribery was another factor which bedevilled and rendered most expensive the existence of every foreign envoy in Constantinople. In the Turkish capital the transaction of any business whatsoever involved a continual outlay of 'presents' either in kind or in cash. It was essential to give 'presents' when summoned to an audience with the Sultan, at the Muslim feast of Bairam, to any newly appointed senior official, before an important conference, and on all too many other occasions. The minimum stock of presents in kind for a newly appointed envoy to bring with him was once defined as: 'Vests of cloth of the most fanciful colours, gay silks with gold flowers more showy than costly. . . . a few of the smallest gold repeating watches, fine spying glasses, large looking-glasses.'[16] Grander—and more expensive—presents were of course even more acceptable. Villeneuve arrived in Constantinople with a cargo of inlaid furniture encrusted with ormolu, crystal chandeliers, firearms inlaid with silver, Chinese and Japanese porcelain, watches, jewellery, damask, brocade and silk. The greater part of the cargo was soon distributed, and it seemed to bring in remarkably little in return.

An audience of the Sultan cost a great deal in presents, for they had to be distributed, not only to the Sultan and the Grand Vizier, but also to a great many of the senior officials of the Porte and the Serail. After having been carefully listed by the Chief Guardian of the Gifts, the offerings to the Sultan were stored in his private treasury. In return an ambassador might, with luck, be given a horse, the splendour of the gold and silver trappings of which often far exceeded the quality of the animal, and for which the slaves who delivered it had to be given a tip at least double its value. But it was exceptional to be given a horse. The Sultan's standard presents to ambassadors and senior members of their suites were caftans or Turkish ceremonial robes. Their cut did not appeal to European taste, 'they conceal the finest garment like a sack';[17] they were made of indifferent cloth, and the gold and silver embroidery on them was skimped. It was customary for the recipient of one of these garments to sell it for what he could get to a Jew, who resold it at a profit to the Porte. It was then presented to the next envoy to be received in audience by the Sultan, and the whole cycle repeated until the caftan was worn out. Scarves of 'not much value' were considered adequate for junior members of the ambassadorial suite.[18] The Sultan had brought present giving to a fine art, and what he received was a great deal more valuable than what he gave.

Present giving was not confined to ceremonial occasions. As Villeneuve learnt from his First Dragoman, it was constantly necessary to produce those 'little presents and gratifications which here make an essential part of all intercourse and are expected as Tokens of Respect . . . when an acquaintance is once made, there is a constant train of little wants'.[19] These 'little wants' were sometimes for novelties. A group of English merchants had a great success with a gift of clipped box trees for the Serail garden.[20] But novelties could be inconvenient to provide. The donor of a parcel of chocolate and sugar subsequently had great difficulty in keeping his own pot and mill for grinding them. The Sultan once took a fancy to the only violin and piano in the Imperial Ambassador's orchestra. A desperate struggle to retain them only succeeded when it was suggested that there was an organ in the Dominican monastery which would suit the Serail far better. The Dominicans lost their organ.[21] It was essential to have a store of presents handy for unexpected contingencies, and every Venetian Bailo was dispatched to Constantinople with a present chest or *ragionateria* as part of his standard equipment. In addition to the usual lengths of cloth, mirrors and, no doubt, watches, it contained a remarkable assortment of items which ranged from cheese to canaries. It was in constant need of replenishment.[22]

Cardinal Fleury had given orders that Villeneuve was to be well supplied with money. This was essential if the French Ambassador was to succeed in his mission for there were also many occasions for which a present in kind was inadequate and only cash would do. According to one of the Venetian Bailos 'there is no door which the key of gold will not open when it is guarded by a vile and venal people'.[23] The *'passion enragée de l'argent'* of the Turks shocked even the eighteenth-century diplomat. Bribery could conclude a treaty; induce a Grand Vizier to declare war, or make him refrain from doing so, appease a Pasha, or procure a copy of a State paper from the Reis Effendi's office. Every Turk had his price and, in the distribution of largesse, it was necessary to pay attention not only to powerful dignitaries such as the Grand Vizier and the Reis Effendi, but also to intermediaries wielding influence behind the scenes and liable in the near future to emerge from obscurity to high office. The question of where bribes could most profitably be distributed was foremost amongst the many problems which perplexed representatives of foreign monarchs at the Sublime Porte.

During his first six months in Constantinople Villeneuve paid out a great deal of money in order to induce influential Turkish officials to adopt a more favourable attitude to France. By June 1729 he came to the conclusion that this expenditure had been wasted. He was still ignored by the Grand Vizier; his chances of stiffening the Porte to play an active part in support of French interests appeared to be very poor indeed. As he confided to the Venetian Bailo in a moment of depression, the Turks 'revealed a weakness which he would never have conceived at a distance; desolate provinces, a discontented people, an inefficient undisciplined militia which lacked leaders'.[24] Unable to make any progress in matters of high policy, the Marquis spent most of his time dealing with tiresome minor chores such as the settlement of petty squabbles over precedence in the French trading communities, and the purchase of antiques for the King, coffee for the Court, and horses for the royal stables.

PART TWO

Prelude to the Struggle

CHAPTER V

ﺸﻜﺸﻜﺸﻜﺸﻜﺸﻜﺸﻜﺸﻜﺸﻜﺸﻜﺸﻜﺸﻜﺸﻜﺸﻜﺸﻜﺸﻜﺸﻜﺸﻜﺸﻜ

Diplomatic Stalemate

Constantinople, 1730–1732

When Villeneuve arrived in Constantinople at the end of 1728 one of the only subjects on which he and his colleagues agreed was the expense, the fatigue and the frustration of their assignments. Apart from this they had little in common. They devoted a great deal of time, energy and money to spying on one another, in order to learn the contents of a recently arrived dispatch, what had been discussed at an audience with the Grand Vizier, or indeed to obtain any sort of information whatsoever in a country where the acquisition of intelligence was extremely difficult. Dragomen often sold not only the secrets of one envoy to another but the secrets of both to the Porte. Ambassador's secretaries, inadequately paid, were by no means invulnerable to financial inducements, and their loyalty was a constant source of anxiety to their masters. Constantinople, a city in which there was at least one potential bidder, if not more, for any intelligence which could remotely be described as secret, offered unlimited scope for the paid informer, and the foreign envoys made full use of their services.

The result was that it was extremely difficult for any member of the diplomatic corps to prevent information about his activities leaking to his colleagues. In addition no envoy could be certain that his reports to his home government would not be intercepted and read *en route*. Dispatches were normally forwarded either by sea to Marseilles, or by land northwards via Nish, Belgrade and Vienna. The disadvantage of the sea route was that it was slow;

sailings from the Bosphorus to Christendom were infrequent, ships were often delayed by contrary winds and storms in the Mediterranean, and liable to be attacked by the Barbary pirates. The land route was faster but, except on occasions of great emergency, most governments grudged the expense of employing a special courier. The envoys were therefore forced to entrust their dispatches to whatever courier might be available, and he was more often than not the courier of the Imperial Resident. This suited the Austrians admirably.

Most governments at that time had a *cabinet noir* or 'Secret Office' which was engaged in the interception and copying of dispatches between other governments and their representatives abroad. One of the most active and competent of these was sited in Vienna, ably seconded by similar offices established on the Emperor's behalf in Liége, Brussels, Frankfurt and Ratisbon. A dispatch entrusted by an envoy in Constantinople to the Imperial courier was therefore almost certain to be copied for the benefit of the Emperor's ministers at some point in its journey across Europe. Dispatches addressed to Constantinople and sent via Vienna were exposed to the same hazard, and to add insult to injury the Austrians took no great pains to close the envelopes in such a manner as to conceal what had occurred. The encipher-ing of important dispatches did not effectively safeguard the information which they contained. The ciphers used in the eighteenth century could be broken without much difficulty, and all the principal European governments employed special officials for this task who were quite capable of holding up an enciphered dispatch for weeks while they worked on it, and then destroying it if they were unsuccessful. In England one of them was eventually rewarded for his labours with the Bishopric of Bath and Wells. [1] Altogether ciphers were an unsatisfactory means of transmitting secret information and their operation frequently caused great confusion.

The time-lags in communications were even more serious. A courier was unlikely to ride from Vienna to Constantinople in much less than eighteen days, a letter from St. Petersburg took about six weeks, and mail from Paris, London and The Hague anything from six weeks to three months to reach the shores of the Bosphorus. Months therefore could and did elapse before an envoy at the Porte received a reply to an urgent request for a directive.

The foreign diplomats in Constantinople, isolated from their home governments and suspicious of each other, were quick to take offence about questions of precedence and protocol. In an age when ceremonial was all important, no ambassador could ever permit himself to forget that an insult to him was a direct infringement of the dignity of the monarch whom he represented. There were consequently continual squabbles over matters such as who should give 'the hand', which was the place of honour on the right, to whom. These squabbles, which involved not only the envoys but also their wives, occupied a great deal of time and energy, and often resulted in a situation where, as one harassed participant wrote 'envy is sometimes as troublesome . . . as the plague'.[2] They did not ease existence in a post from which, since no home leave was granted, there was no escape until recall, resignation or death. The diplomatic corps, boxed up together in what one of them described as 'no country of delight and joy',[3] frequently got on one another's nerves. Its members were in any case by no means mutually congenial, the Venetian envoy or Bailo being the least controversial figure amongst them. Venice was declining, and therefore no longer to be regarded as a dangerous competitor for the favours of the Porte. The Bailo was urbane, civilised, and a highly intelligent observer of the local situation. He was no doubt a sought after guest.

The British Ambassador was in the unhappy position of having to serve two masters—His Majesty's Government and the Levant Company. Turkey was at that time of minor political interest to England, and King George II and his Prime Minister, Walpole, saw no reason to make any substantial contribution out of public funds to the cost of the Constantinople Embassy. It was considered that the Ambassador's main function was to protect and further the commercial interests of the Levant Company, and the Company therefore paid the greater part of his salary. Such letters as were addressed to him by the Foreign Office, might

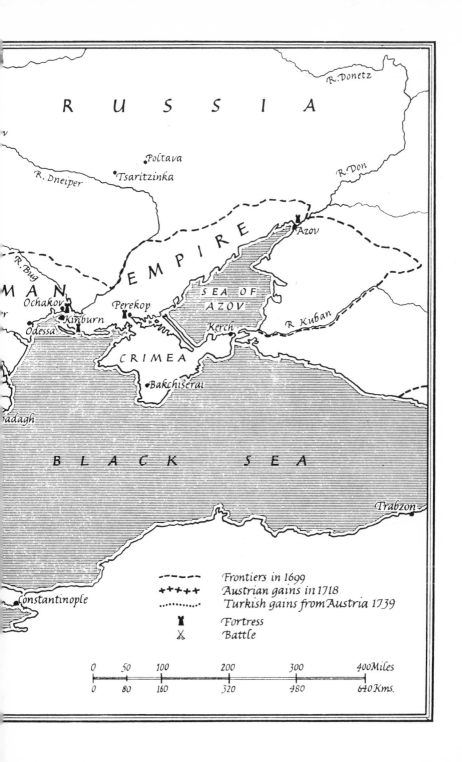

R. Donetz

R U S S I A

•Poltava

R. Dneiper   •Tsaritzinka   R. Don

                    E M P I R E   🛡Azov

R. Bug   🛡Azov

M A N   Ochakov🛡   Perekop🛡   SEA OF
      •Kinburn🛡   AZOV
Odessa•   Kerch   R. Kuban

              C R I M E A

adagh   •Bakchiserai

B L A C K   S E A

                                                      Trabzon⹀

onstantinople

        - - - - -   Frontiers in 1699
        + + + +   Austrian gains in 1718
        ··········· Turkish gains from Austria 1739
           🛡   Fortress
           ⚔   Battle

0   50   100   200   300   400 Miles
0   80   160   320   480   640 Kms.

deal with nothing more important than the procuring of sherbert for Queen Caroline or seeds for His Majesty's kitchen garden. In 1728 the post was held by Abraham Stanyan who, after ten years of struggling with the Porte, had settled down to take the line of least resistance and live as agreeably as possible. He was succeeded in 1730 by Lord Kinnoull, who was preoccupied with his debts and his women, habitually drunk and a bore.

The British Ambassador was required by his government to work closely with his Dutch colleague. This was a trial, for Cornelius Calkoen was disliked by the entire diplomatic corps. A lawyer by training with no previous experience of diplomacy, he was self-important, an intriguer, bad tempered and rude. Villeneuve eventually refused either to speak to him or to have anything to do with him, and it was generally agreed that it was necessary to have great patience to endure him at all.

The French Ambassador's chief rivals in Constantinople, the envoys of the Emperor and the Czarina, both held the rank of Resident. The Imperial Resident, Leopold von Talman, arrived a few weeks after Villeneuve. His father had also represented the Emperor at the Porte, and Talman had no doubt learnt much from him about ways and means of handling the Turks. Known as 'the Dwarf', he was married to the daughter of an English merchant and led an irreproachable private life. As the representative of a country which had inflicted a crushing defeat on the Sultan; taking his orders from Prince Eugen, the architect of that defeat; well supplied with funds, and in closer touch with his home government than any of his colleagues, he was admirably placed to further the interests of his ruler. He was to prove himself determined and persistent.

Ivan Ivanovich Neplyuev, the Russian Resident, held one of the most exacting positions in his ruler's service. Until 1700 Russian diplomatic contacts with the Porte had been confined to the dispatch from time to time of envoys on special missions: they were liable to be beaten up *en route* by the Tartars or thrown into prison when they reached Constantinople, and were invariably insulted by the Turks. In 1700 the Porte grudgingly agreed to accept a permanent Russian Resident, and nominally accorded him the same recognition as the ambassadors of other Christian nations. But, since relations between the two countries were always strained, the activities of any occupant of the post were regarded by the Turks with the greatest suspicion.

Neplyuev was one of Peter the Great's 'fledglings'—those young men whom the Czar had trained and inspired—and only twenty-eight years old when in 1721 he was appointed Russian Resident at the Porte. But although he had had no previous diplomatic experience, he became in the course of the next few years a distinguished member of 'that advance guard of diplomats which Russia posted on the Bosphorus to precede and inform her armies'.[4] A devout member of the Orthodox Church and totally devoted to his ruler's cause, he furthered his country's interests with great skill and won the personal respect of his colleagues. By the end of 1728, however, his health was beginning to fail and in 1729 Alexsej Veshniakov, rumoured to be equipped with 80,000 ducats for intelligence and bribes, arrived to assist him.[5] The Ottoman Empire was a major sphere of Russian interest, and Count Ostermann was determined that the Czarina should be adequately represented there. By the end of 1729 the Count was well satisfied with the position. All reports reaching him confirmed that the Porte was prepared to go to any lengths to avoid offending the Russian and Imperial Residents.

In view of the internal weakness of the Ottoman Empire, the determination of the Porte to remain on good terms with Austria and Russia was not surprising. In the case of Austria this was comparatively easy. Since the Peace of Passarowitz the 1,200 mile long frontier between the Emperor's and the Sultan's territories had been more or less stabilised. There was, admittedly, continual frontier raiding, but this was only to be expected in an area so wild that it was known in Vienna as '*desertum primum*' and '*desertum secundum*',[6] and there was tacit agreement between the two governments that these raids constituted no reason for going to war. The Porte's relations with Russia were far less happy. The question of whether certain tribes in the Caucasus should pay tribute to the Czar or to the Sultan had long been the subject of acrimonious correspondence between Constantinople and St. Petersburg, and the problem of the Cossacks and the Tartars remained quite unresolved.

The Cossacks were freebooters and outlaws, mainly of Polish or Russian origin, who had taken refuge in the marshes and wilderness of the southern Ukraine around the lower reaches of the Don, Volga and Dnieper. They made their living by hunting, fishing and robbery, elected their own chiefs and enforced their own laws. At the beginning of the eighteenth century they were nominally under the suzerainty of the Czar to whom, for all their unreliability, they were useful both as a source of auxiliary troops and as a buffer against the Tartars. St. Petersburg needed all the help that could be mustered to hold the Tartars in check. These were descended from a splinter group of the Golden Horde of Genghis Khan which had settled in the Crimea and along the northern shore of the Black Sea. Like the Cossacks their principal occupation was raiding, their most spectacular exploit being in 1571 when they burnt Moscow and thereafter compelled the rulers of Russia to pay them an annual tribute. Subsequently they confined themselves to objectives nearer at hand, killing, burning and carrying off thousands of prisoners and vast herds of livestock. When the Turks went to war the Tartars furnished the advance and rearguard of the main army. Mounted on small hardy ponies, each man carrying his supplies, they were ideally suited both for this role, and for guerrilla operations in the wastes of the southern Ukraine.

Although their Khan was the Sultan's vassal, Constantinople had as little control over the Tartars as St. Petersburg had over the Cossacks, and unending complaints were exchanged between the two governments about the behaviour of each other's turbulent frontier subjects. These complaints were generally drafted in the most undiplomatic language, but by 1727 the Grand Vizier could no longer permit himself the luxury of returning invective for invective, for the Ottoman Empire was then threatened not only from Europe but also from Asia. As the Reis Effendi explained to the French Dragoman, 'We have our hands and heads so full of the affairs of Persia that we have not the leisure to attend to any others.'7

The 'affairs of Persia' had been a subject of concern to the Porte ever since Ibrahim became Grand Vizier in 1718. At that time the Safavid dynasty was collapsing and Persia seemed ripe for dismemberment. Russia was the first to move in, and Peter the Great invaded Daghestan. The Turks, anxious to get their share of the loot and to prevent Russia from gaining control of the Caspian area, riposted by invading Georgia, starting off a chain reaction by no means to their advantage. It led to further friction with Russia, for the demarcation lines of the Russian- and Turkish-occupied areas of Persia were ill defined. It also involved the Porte in an intermittent and expensive war with Persia. In these circumstances the Grand Vizier had really no choice but to soothe Neplyuev, flatter Talman, and avoid seeing the French Ambassador.

It was an extremely trying situation for Villeneuve who after a year in Constantinople was still unable to make progress with the tasks with which he had been entrusted by Fleury. French trade continued to languish; it was impossible to obtain any improvement in the position of the Latin priests and monks; when one of the French consuls was imprisoned in the Seven Towers, the Grand Vizier, the Kahya, and the Reis Effendi successively refused to grant the Marquis an audience to discuss the matter. His personal relations with the Turkish officials were not improved by a punitive expedition launched by Versailles against the Sultan's piratical vassals in North Africa, an incident which left the Porte with a smouldering resentment against France.

But in Constantinople 'the military and political wheel', as the Venetian Bailo once described it,8 was perpetually turning. In 1730 'the affairs of Persia' finally upset the Grand Vizier's balancing act.

The Persians had been rallied by Nadir Shah, 'one of those extraordinary personages which appear seldom'.9 By origin a shepherd-boy, he had worked his way up to the position of an outstanding general, and in the spring of 1730 started to expel the Turks from those parts of Persia which they had appropriated.

Popular opinion in Constantinople clamoured for revenge, and the Grand Vizier was forced to give at least the appearance of taking up Nadir Shah's challenge.

On August 3rd, accompanied by the Sultan and the ministers of the Porte, Ibrahim crossed to Scutari on the Asiatic side of the Bosphorus to join the army which had been assembled there. The procession took four hours to pass the applauding crowds. The standards and relics of Islam were borne before the Sultan, and the spectacle was calculated to convey the impression that a major campaign was about to begin. In fact nothing happened at all. The Sultan and his Ministers sat at Scutari and procrastinated, heavy taxation was imposed to maintain the army and the Court, and popular discontent mounted. At the end of September a dissident Janissary organised and led a successful revolution. The Sultan was deposed and replaced by his nephew Mahmoud who had been imprisoned in the Serail for twenty-three years. The Reis Effendi, the Sheikh ul Islam, and the Grand Vizier were beheaded.

The Persian Nadir Shah was instrumental in bringing about a change wholly favourable to France. In October 1730, a fortnight after the revolution, Villeneuve reported to Versailles that, the Grand Vizier Ibrahim having fallen, it would soon once again be possible to enlist the active co-operation of the Porte in support of French policy.[10] Within a few months it seemed that his optimism was justified. Djanum Khoda, the newly appointed Captain Pasha, removed a number of excessive duties on French merchandise, and early in 1731 Topal Osman Pasha was appointed Grand Vizier. Twenty-three years earlier Topal Osman had been ransomed from captivity in Malta by a French officer. Thereafter he remained a staunch friend of France. 'You may write to the King', he declared to Villeneuve, 'and tell him that if the Sultan had chosen a Frenchman as Grand Vizier, he could not be more French than me.'[11]

In the game of diplomatic poker between the French Ambassador and the Austrian and Russian Residents the first hand had been won outright by Talman and Neplyuev, but now it seemed that the cards had turned against them. The new Grand Vizier made peace with Persia. Villeneuve was in constant conference with him and all reports reaching the two Residents suggested that Topal Osman, at the behest of the French Ambassador, was preparing for action against Austria and Russia.

These reports appeared to Talman to be confirmed when, towards the end of 1731, he learnt that Count Bonneval, the Emperor's sworn enemy, had been summoned to Constantinople.

Bonneval, a French aristocrat and the son-in-law of a Marshal of France, was one of the most extraordinary figures of the eighteenth century. A general at the age of twenty-nine in Vendôme's army in Italy, three years later he was condemned to death and hanged in effigy in Paris. By the time he was forty-one he was a member of the Emperor's Imperial War Council, a close friend of Prince Eugen and regarded as one of his most brilliant subordinates. His exploits at Eugen's victory over the Turks at Peterwardein in 1716 were celebrated in an ode by Jean Baptiste Rousseau; the Prince himself referred to the Count as '*grand capitaine*'; the Emperor promoted him to the second highest rank in the Imperial army.

Bonneval had courage allied with a capacity for making rapid decisions, and for leadership on the battlefield. He was known to princes and statesmen throughout Europe and could have excelled in any one of a number of professions—as a soldier, statesman, courtier, geographer or engineer—for he was a versatile and talented man. Unfortunately he lacked the less spectacular qualities which give staying power. Indiscreet, impatient, tending to act on impulse rather than judgement, and pathologically proud, he was quite impossible to fit into any established system. Pride caused him to leave the service of Louis XIV, when his handling of certain funds in Italy was questioned, and offer his sword to the Emperor; pride caused his downfall in Vienna where Prince Eugen, he considered, had failed to procure for him the position to which he felt himself to be entitled. He therefore attacked and ridiculed the Prince, quarrelled with the latter's deputy in the Netherlands, and exacerbated the situation to a point where Eugen used all his influence to procure Bonneval's ignominious dismissal from the Emperor's service.

After the death of Louis XIV Bonneval made his peace with the Bourbons and the sentence against him was annulled. There was no peace to be made with the House of Habsburg, which had dismissed him in such circumstances as to render it impossible for him to obtain suitable employment elsewhere. He was determined to devote the rest of his life to pursuing a vendetta against the Emperor, but to do this he needed an ally. The Sultan was the traditional enemy of the Habsburgs, so to the Sultan's court he determined to go. In 1729, after an arduous journey and accompanied by only six followers, he arrived in Sarajevo the capital of Bosnia.

Bonneval was by then fifty-four, plagued by gout, and compelled to wear a silver plate over the wound in his stomach which he had received at Peterwardein, and which had never healed. His total worldly wealth amounted to no more than 1,500 ducats. He had no letters of introduction and spoke not a word of Turkish, but his self-confidence was unshaken. The Bonneval family motto was after all *Victorieux à tous les hazards.*[12]

At first, however, it looked as though that motto might be misleading. The Pasha of Bosnia received the Count hospitably, but detained him in Sarajevo, explaining that he could not be allowed to continue his journey to Constantinople until permission had been obtained from the Porte. Bonneval had no alternative but to comply with the Pasha's orders.

When the alarming news of Bonneval's arrival in the Sultan's dominions reached Vienna, Prince Eugen at once dispatched a special courier to Constantinople instructing the Imperial Resident to make every effort to frustrate the Count's plans. Talman immediately demanded an audience with the Grand Vizier. Employing a mixture of requests and threats, and elevating the whole affair into a major incident between Austria and Turkey, he pointed out that if Bonneval was permitted to come to the Sultan's court relations between the two countries would be seriously endangered. His *démarche* was successful. The Pasha of Bosnia was instructed to continue to detain Bonneval in Sarajevo.

Talman then received further urgent instructions from Vienna. He was to 'discredit' Bonneval (what precisely this meant was

The Sultan and two court officials, from a contemporary painting by
J. B. Vanmour

View of Constantinople and the Serail, *c.* 1730, from a painting by J. B. Vanmour

tactfully not defined), and if possible to have him expelled from the Sultan's dominions. Since the Count was a French citizen this was more than the Imperial Resident could formally demand. He was compelled to resort to bribery, and this took time. By September 1730, after much effort and expenditure, he induced the Porte to dispatch a secret order to the Pasha of Bosnia instructing him to get rid of his detainee by any means which he could devise. It was too late. Bonneval had become a Muslim and thereby both secured his continued residence in the Turkish Empire and rendered himself eligible to enter the Sultan's service. Although he was still unable to obtain permission to come to Constantinople, he was now far better treated in Sarajevo than he had been before. The ground had been cut from under Talman's feet. Bonneval, far from having been eliminated, remained on the scene and, as the attitude of the Porte towards Austria and Russia stiffened, there was every prospect that he would one day advance to the centre of the stage. While far from pleased by this addition to his list of problems, the Imperial Resident was not altogether surprised when he was informed by his spies in January 1732 that the Grand Vizier Topal Osman had summoned the Count to Constantinople.

Vienna had reacted immediately to the news of Bonneval's arrival in the Sultan's dominions. Versailles by contrast had not reacted at all, and no instructions had been sent to the French Ambassador at the Porte as to the attitude which he should adopt towards this renegade and controversial Frenchman. When therefore Villeneuve received a letter from the Count asking for help to get to the Ottoman capital, he found himself in a dilemma. He was well aware of Bonneval's military abilities and of the threat posed to the Emperor if they were placed at the disposal of the Sultan. But Bonneval also had a long record of untrustworthiness, and his proclaimed intention to enter the service of the heathen Turk was something which His Most Christian Majesty of France could not support without incurring the execration of every Christian ruler. The Marquis was by training a civil servant, and he adopted a civil servant's compromise. He advised the Grand Vizier to keep Bonneval at Sarajevo for the time being, did not reply to the Count's letter, and wrote urgently to Versailles asking for further instructions. When these arrived they were unequivocal. Bonneval, Fleury's deputy Chauvelin replied, was someone with whom His Most Christian Majesty did not wish to be associated, and Villeneuve was therefore to have no personal contact of any kind with him. If by his own efforts the Count managed to get to Constantinople, and if his presence there embarrassed the Emperor, so much the better, but this was something in which the French Government could take no active part. The Ambassador should confine himself to observing the renegade and reporting on his activities.[13] Thus instructed the Marquis made no reply to a second appeal from the Count. When, towards the end of 1731 he learnt from the Grand Vizier that Bonneval had been summoned to the capital, he received this news without comment.

Late on the evening of January 17th, 1732, after two and a half years of exile and obscurity, Count Bonneval rode into Constantinople, was honourably received by the Grand Vizier, and given the task of training a Bombardier Corps for the Turkish army. He was now well placed to pursue his designs against the Emperor and, since his interests coincided with those of France, it seemed that Villeneuve's hand must be still further strengthened. But two months later the wheel of the Porte turned again. The Grand Vizier Topal Osman, having quarrelled with the all powerful Kizlar Aga, was dismissed and sent into exile. His fall was preceded by that of the Captain Pasha, and Villeneuve lost his two principal allies at the Porte.

Topal Osman was succeeded by Hakimouglou Ali Pasha 'the Doctor's son'. The new Grand Vizier, a small man with a neat, well-trimmed beard, was courteous, intelligent and well versed in all the subtleties of diplomacy. He was determined to remain uncommitted and, although he sought the French Ambassador's advice, did not act on it.

A few months after he took office, war with Persia flared up again. Nadir Shah who had made himself Regent of that country, secured his flank by an agreement with Russia, and in the autumn of 1732 attacked the Turks.

It seemed that Villeneuve had lost all the ground which he had gained during the past two years. Ali Pasha reverted to the old policy of conciliating Austria and Russia. Bonneval, who had been preparing memoranda for the Porte on the strategy of a further war with the Emperor, was ostensibly restricted to his task of training the Bombardiers.

At this moment, when the attention of the Turks was once more fixed on Asia, Europe was thrown into a turmoil by the death of King Augustus II of Poland and the beginning of the struggle for the succession to the Polish throne. The envoys at the Porte were dealt a new hand for their next round of diplomatic poker.

꙰꙰꙰꙰꙰꙰꙰꙰꙰꙰꙰꙰꙰꙰꙰꙰꙰꙰꙰꙰꙰꙰꙰꙰꙰꙰꙰꙰

CHAPTER VI

The Discomfiture of the French Ambassador

Constantinople, 1733–summer 1735

The King of Poland was elected by the Polish nobility but, owing to the geographical situation of the country, the outcome of the election was of interest not only to the Poles, but also to a number of other states. Poland served both Austria and Russia as an east–west bridge or buffer as the situation demanded, each country having a frontier which marched with hers, and neither the Emperor nor the Czarina could lightly acquiesce to the installation of an unfriendly ruler in Warsaw. For France, on the other hand, a King of Poland subservient to her interests was both a useful thorn in the side of the Habsburgs and an additional safeguard on one of the most vulnerable frontiers of the Ottoman Empire, for the southern boundary of his kingdom adjoined the Sultan's province of Moldavia. In 1733, Austria and Russia jointly backed the candidature for the Polish throne of Frederick Augustus, Prince of Saxony, son of the late King, whilst France supported Stanislas Leszczynski, the father-in-law of King Louis XV and the choice of the majority of the Poles.

The personal wishes of the rulers of all three countries were bound up with this alignment. Frederick Augustus promised that if he was elected King he would recognise the Pragmatic Sanction, than which no cause was dearer to Charles VI. The Czarina hoped that if Russian influence secured Frederick's election, he would not oppose the investiture of her lover, Biron, with the Polish fief of Courland. Louis XV wished to place Stanislas Leszczynski on the throne of Poland because it was wounding to his self-esteem to have a commoner as a father-in-law. Therefore in August 1733 Stanislas was bundled by a devious route to Warsaw, and duly elected King of Poland. His stay in Warsaw was brief. The Russian armies advanced, Russian money was liberally distributed, the election reversed and Frederick proclaimed King Augustus III. Stanislas fled to Danzig, and France declared war on the Emperor. It was a lopsided triangle of a war. Although Russia was Austria's ally she never formally declared war on France, and St. Petersburg and Vienna had no joint plan of campaign. The Emperor was left alone to bear the whole brunt of the French attack, which was launched across the Rhine and in northern Italy. The Russians contented themselves with fanning out over Poland and eventually settled down to besiege Stanislas in Danzig.

In the spring of 1733 Count Ostermann in St. Petersburg, Prince Eugen and his colleagues in Vienna, and Cardinal Fleury at Versailles drafted instructions to their envoys in Constantinople as to the attitude which they should influence the Porte to take towards the struggle for the Polish throne. To Ostermann the installation of Frederick Augustus in Warsaw, who was amenable to Russian policy, was essential to the plan for the expansion of his adopted country on which he had been working for several years. Turkish intervention in support of Stanislas would upset the whole of his carefully phased programme. The Count accordingly directed the Czarina's representatives at the Porte to ensure at all costs that the Sultan remained neutral in the War of the Polish Succession.

The Austrians, with characteristic lack of thought for their Russian ally, were far more concerned about the forthcoming French attack on their positions on the Rhine and in Italy than about the possibility of a Turkish advance into Poland. Vienna's sole fear was that Bonneval, the implacable enemy of the Emperor, might persuade the Grand Vizier to take advantage of their preoccupations with the French to launch an attack north-west towards Belgrade. Prince Eugen therefore instructed Talman to keep a close watch on Bonneval.

Cardinal Fleury took quite a different view of the situation. He did not care in the least whether Louis XV had a King or a commoner as a father-in-law, and whatever the advantages to France of having a friendly ruler in Poland, they were not in his view worth a war. However, confronted with the unavoidable, he set himself to extract from it the greatest possible gain for France at the least possible cost. He was reasonably confident about the outcome of the campaigns on the Rhine (where Prince Eugen, worn out and ill, was no longer to be feared), and in Italy (where the Imperial army was to all intents and purposes leaderless). The Russian advance into Poland was another matter. When the Russians moved into a country they tended to stay there. Once established in Poland they would occupy a position similar to that of the Emperor in Belgrade from which they could threaten the Sultan's European provinces. But to march an army from France across Europe to dislodge them was far too hazardous and expensive. There was, Fleury considered, only one alternative, and that was to induce the Sultan to take the necessary measures for his own defence, and to attack the Russians in the flank as they moved through Poland.

Towards the end of May 1733 the Cardinal ordered Chauvelin to forward his instructions to the French Ambassador in Constantinople. Villeneuve was directed to obtain a declaration from the Porte that, if Stanislas Leszczynski was not permitted to occupy the Polish throne, the Ottoman army would advance into Poland. Even Chauvelin appears to have felt that this was a formidable task. 'These,' he ended his letter to Villeneuve, 'are all the instructions which I can give you about this most important affair. In view of the distance which separates us, the manner in which you approach the Porte must be left to your own judgement.'[1]

It was a tacit admission that Versailles was unable to offer the Ambassador either advice or comfort.

The War of the Polish Succession did not affect life in the capitals of the contending countries. In St. Petersburg, Vienna and Paris the rulers hunted as usual, and the round of Court festivities and receptions remained unaltered. Ostermann, the Emperor's ministers, and Fleury, having issued their instructions to the envoys of their respective monarchs in Constantinople, turned their attention to other matters. Those envoys, working under arduous conditions in a remote and unhealthy city, and hampered by the perennial difficulty of assessing the shifts of influence within the Porte, were left to play out their next hand of diplomatic poker as best they could.

The Russian Resident and his assistant, instructed by Ostermann to ensure that the Turks did nothing at all, had the easiest task. Still at war with Persia, inactivity in other directions was all that the Porte asked, and the Grand Vizier found no difficulty (in return for a bribe of 850 purses), in assuring Neplyuev that he would take no action to intervene in Poland before the end of the year. Ostermann considered the money well expended and saw to it that the Russian Resident was well provided for any similar contingency which might arise in the future.

Vienna's instructions to Talman to keep a close watch on Bonneval were occasioned by the alarming reports which the Imperial Resident had submitted on the renegade since his arrival in Constantinople. Bonneval, it appeared, was in touch both with Delaria, the senior dragoman of the French Embassy, and with Prince Rákóczi, another sworn enemy of the Habsburgs who, some years previously, having failed to raise Hungary against the Emperor, had fled to Turkey with a price on his head. Prince Eugen and the Emperor were apprehensive that Rákóczi might be used by the Turks to stir up disaffection in Hungary. Bonneval, whose influence at the Porte was steadily growing, clearly had some most undesirable associates, but happily, and to the great consolation of Vienna, Talman was well informed about his activities. Rákóczi's secretary Bohn acted as the exiled Prince's intermediary with the Porte, Bonneval and Villeneuve, and was regarded by them all as being entirely trustworthy. This was an opinion to which the Imperial Resident, for quite different reasons, heartily subscribed. Bohn was his principal agent, and provided him with information of inestimable value not only about the contact between Rákóczi and Bonneval, but also about the activities of the French Ambassador.

Villeneuve, directed by Versailles to prod the amorphous mass of the Porte into action of a kind which neither the Grand Vizier nor his colleagues had the slightest desire to take, was faced with a far more difficult task than either the Russian or the Imperial Resident. There were only two personalities in the Ottoman Empire from whom he might hope for assistance. One was the Tartar Khan who was known to support Leszczynski and to be in touch with the latter's adherents in Poland; the other (or so it seemed reasonable to assume) was Bonneval. As soon as Villeneuve received Chauvelin's instructions he dispatched Baron Tott, one of his attachés, to the Crimea on a special mission to the Tartar Khan. Tott, who had a natural gift for handling Oriental rulers and was well supplied with 'presents', succeeded in persuading the Khan to mobilise his forces to harass the Russians. By the end of August 1733, Villeneuve was able to report to Versailles that, provided the Porte gave its consent, the Tartars were ready to march.

Meanwhile, in Constantinople, the French Ambassador worked unremittingly to incite the Grand Vizier against the Emperor and the Czarina, and to extract a letter from the Sultan supporting the election of Stanislas to the Polish throne. He was not unhopeful of success. Sultan Mahmoud I was reported to be favourably inclined towards France; the Porte Dragoman who had great influence with the Reis Effendi was in French pay; finally there was Bonneval. Villeneuve, convinced that they were working for the same ends, did not hesitate to recommend him warmly to the Grand Vizier, in the hope that Ali Pasha would seek his advice. The Grand Vizier did so, but with results which were the reverse of those which the Marquis had anticipated. A few months later he presented Villeneuve with the most disagreeable ultimatum. Unless a formal alliance was concluded between the Sultan and His Most Christian Majesty the King of France, the Porte could not contemplate any offensive action against the Russians in Poland.

The French Ambassador had no power to conclude such an alliance. There was nothing for it but to inform Versailles that if Louis XV wished the Turks to support the cause of his father-in-law in Poland, he must reverse the policy of his predecessors

and conclude a formal and public treaty with the infidel. Villeneuve employed all his powers of persuasion when drafting this
difficult dispatch. He stressed that he fully appreciated that
such a course must be repugnant to a Prince so pious as His
Most Christian Majesty but, he reasoned, surely it was justified
by the needs of the situation.[2] Then, having arranged a special
system of couriers to bring him the reply from Versailles by the
fastest route via Rome, Ancona and Durazzo, he addressed
himself once more to the task of maintaining the *status quo* in
Constantinople by any means which he could devise.

As soon as Villeneuve's dispatch reached Versailles, Fleury
called a meeting of the French Council of Ministers and addressed
it with unusual vehemence. As a priest and a Prince of the
Church, he could not, he declared, possibly advise King Louis
XV to conclude a treaty with the infidel; neither as a statesman
could he countenance such a risky alliance. The Cardinal could,
when he chose, be a most obstinate old man. On this occasion he
did so choose, and there was no moving him. The Council then
proceeded to consider whether some counter-proposal could not
be made. After prolonged debate and hesitation, Chauvelin was
instructed to write to Villeneuve authorising him to declare to
the Porte that, when a peace was concluded, the King of France
would not forget the interests of the Sultan.

This directive was useless. The Grand Vizier required a treaty,
not a vague oral assurance. The situation was by now acute. The
Russians, confident of the neutrality of the Porte, had moved all
their available troops up to the north to besiege Danzig, and the
frontiers of the Polish Ukraine were left practically undefended.
Now, if ever, was the time for action. It was impossible to tell
how long Danzig could hold out, and its fall would release over
70,000 Russians to repel any Turkish attempt to advance into
Poland. Villeneuve eventually managed to induce the Grand
Vizier to agree that a formal treaty would take too long to
negotiate, and that in the circumstances the Sultan would be
content with a written declaration of French support. He wrote
repeatedly to Versailles stressing the need for the immediate
dispatch of this declaration. But Versailles continued to dither.

Chauvelin, try as he might, could not persuade Fleury to take action until he had examined every other possibility of sending help to Danzig. Finally the Cardinal agreed with the utmost reluctance that there was nothing for it but to do as Villeneuve urged, and a declaration was drafted. It bristled with reservations, promised only that the King of France would not make any peace detrimental to the Porte and was dispatched, not by Villeneuve's special system of couriers, but by sea from Marseilles. The ship bearing it was delayed by contrary winds in the Mediterranean and did not reach Constantinople until July 10th, 1734. Eight days earlier Danzig had fallen.

The most favourable moment for intervention had been missed, but all was not yet lost. Stanislas had managed to escape from Danzig to Prussia, and the armies of France were inflicting defeat after defeat on the Emperor in Italy and on the Rhine. So far as the Polish Succession was concerned France still had her pawn in the game, and her victories increased her attractions as a potential ally. Villeneuve bribed, intrigued, cajoled and redoubled his efforts. At the end of July he had a secret meeting with the Grand Vizier in a garden outside Constantinople, handed over the declaration to him, and for three hours tried to extract some kind of counter-assurance. All his arguments were met with evasions. Later in the evening the Porte Dragoman appeared, explained that Ali Pasha would be content with nothing less than a letter to the Sultan signed by Louis XV himself, and handed the French Ambassador yet another project for a treaty.

The continued evasions and obstinacy of the Porte could not be accounted for solely by Austrian intrigues and Russian gold. Villeneuve began to suspect that Bonneval, far from collaborating with him, was working against him. He decided to risk his career and position, disobey orders, meet Bonneval face to face, and endeavour to enlist his support. In due course he had several meetings with him in a secluded villa outside the capital. They were fruitless; the clash of personalities was too great.

Bonneval by then exercised considerable influence at the Porte. He had been made a Pasha, and was in daily conference with the Grand Vizier and his colleagues, who took few decisions with

regard to the Christian powers without first seeking his advice.
The Count had gained the position which he had marked out for
himself when he first arrived in Constantinople and, even more
important to a man of his temperament, re-established himself
as a factor to be reckoned with by the rulers of Europe. But one
mark of recognition was still denied him. The French Ambassador
still refused to meet him in public or to have anything to do with
him officially. Bonneval had never forgiven Villeneuve for the
latter's failure to answer his appeals for help when he first
arrived at Sarajevo, and the Marquis' continued shunning of
him increased his bitterness. Therefore when they met in 1734,
he was in no mood to be either pleasant or co-operative. Villeneuve left no record of his personal impressions of Bonneval.
Bonneval was less reticent. He described the Ambassador as
being the great grandson of a Jew, a common jumped up little
man with all the pettiness of a minor civil servant and referred to
him as an upstart and *'ce petit ambassadeur'*.

The Count turned Pasha not only disliked and despised the
Marquis; personal feelings apart, he had no intention of collaborating with him. Villeneuve summed up the situation when he
wrote to Chauvelin: 'M. de Bonneval should no longer be
regarded as a Frenchman who has changed his religion in Turkey;
but rather as a Muslim who has been raised to the rank of Pasha,
and is playing a leading part in the conduct of affairs.'[3] Villeneuve
was prepared to manipulate the Turks to serve the interests of
France, but Bonneval (as the Ambassador finally realised in the
summer of 1734) was not. He considered that it was not in the
interests of the Porte to attack Russia without a treaty of alliance
with France, and the Grand Vizier's insistence on this was the
result of his advice.

Villeneuve next discovered that not only had he been mistaken
in hoping for Bonneval's support, but also that the Pasha was
dangerously indiscreet. His house was the rendezvous of all the
doubtful adventurers and exiles who aspired to make a career
in the Sultan's service and were prepared to sell any information
to the highest bidder. Bonneval talked freely to them of his plans
and negotiations, and in consequence the Imperial and Russian

Residents were well informed of the approach which the French Ambassador had made on Chauvelin's instructions to the Porte. Before the end of the summer of 1734 Vienna and St. Petersburg openly accused King Louis XV of making common cause with the infidel, and the British and Dutch Governments instructed their Ambassadors to do everything in their power to frustrate their French colleague.

Villeneuve's task now became even more difficult, and for this he blamed Bonneval's indiscretion 'the effects of which', he described as being 'even more damaging than those of his obstinacy'.[4] But in spite of all this he persevered, convinced that if only Versailles would send the letter signed by the King which the Grand Vizier demanded, the Turks would march. He succeeded in conveying the impression that he was by no means to be discounted as an adversary. In October 1734 both London and The Hague were convinced that he was on the verge of bringing the Turks into the war, and in St. Petersburg Ostermann informed the British envoy that he had every reason to believe 'that the French Ambassador at Constantinople was actually far advanced in his negotiations with the Porte to engage the Turks to attack this Court or that of Vienna'.[5] But in the middle of 1735, when Villeneuve had great hopes of final success, he received an order from Versailles to take no further action. It had been decided that Stanislas Leszczynski's cause should be abandoned. Cardinal Fleury was secretly negotiating peace with the Emperor.

In Versailles in July 1735 the Cardinal permitted himself some unflattering comments on the Court of Vienna. 'The Austrian pride', he told the British Ambassador, 'would not condescend to acts of common civility.' It was impossible, he asserted, 'to gain anything from the Emperor by complaisance'.[6] In return he was neither civil nor complaisant to Charles VI, compelled him to agree to a peace which deprived him of Naples and Sicily, and wrecked his hopes of adding Lorraine to the Habsburg possessions by insisting that this rich Duchy must be given to Stanislas Leszczynski to compensate him for the abandonment of his claim to the Polish throne. (It involved the Emperor in the embarrassment of persuading his prospective son-in-law, the Duke of Lorraine, to divest himself of his birthright, but that was of no concern to the Cardinal.)

By October 1735, Fleury was well pleased with himself. He had extricated France from a situation in Poland about which he had never been enthusiastic, and in the process had added a valuable province to the possessions of Louis XV, for Lorraine was to revert to the French Crown when Stanislas died. The Emperor was cut down to size and left with a depleted treasury and a demoralised army. It was regrettable of course that no similar humiliation could be inflicted on Russia, but unfortunately France had never been formally at war with her. However, His Most Christian Majesty could signify his disapproval of the Czarina, and this the Cardinal duly did by breaking off all diplomatic relations between Versailles and St. Petersburg.

There remained the somewhat awkward problem of Turkey. The Cardinal knew that his *volte-face* over the question of inducing the Sultan to intervene in Poland, must have revealed all too clearly to the Porte that King Louis XV was concerned, not for the welfare and security of the Ottoman Empire, but for the furtherance of his own interests. However, Fleury reasoned, for two centuries Turkey had been used by France as a piece on the European chessboard, to be advanced or withdrawn as the occasion demanded, and similar occurrences in the past had caused no lasting damage to the relations between the two countries. He felt confident that in time any resentment engendered in Constantinople against France by this episode would die down, and was prepared to wait for it to do so. He had after all reduced the Emperor, the only European ruler to defeat the Turks for over a century, to a state where he was in no position to undertake any kind of offensive action. The safety of the Ottoman Empire was therefore assured, and in due course France would resume her position of most favoured nation at the Porte. Admittedly relations between Constantinople and St. Petersburg were strained. There was the question of the march of the Tartar Khan through the Caucasus to attack the Persians in the rear. The Khan's route lay through an area the overlordship of which had long been in dispute between the Turks and the Russians, and at the beginning of July Ostermann had sent a threatening note to the Grand Vizier accusing the Khan of violating Russian territory. But the Cardinal paid no particular attention to this. The Tartars after all, for decades had been a subject of controversy between the two governments. Like many old gentlemen, Fleury preferred to disregard anything disagreeable which did not appear immediately to concern him.

꙳꙳꙳꙳꙳꙳꙳꙳꙳꙳꙳꙳꙳꙳꙳꙳꙳꙳꙳꙳꙳꙳꙳꙳꙳꙳꙳꙳꙳꙳꙳

CHAPTER VII

Russia Attacks

St. Petersburg–Azov and Crimea–Constantinople
Autumn 1735–1736

The Cardinal for once was mistaken. The Russian Note to the Porte protesting about the march of the Tartar Khan, far from being merely the latest of a long series of threats and complaints about the behaviour of the Sultan's vassals, had been carefully drafted by Ostermann with the object of establishing Russia as the victim of an entirely unprovoked infringement of her territorial rights. He concluded it with an adjuration to the Grand Vizier to co-operate in preserving the 'perpetual peace' between their respective nations, observing that injustice was most displeasing to the Almighty. This was pious duplicity, for as he dictated those sentences nothing was further from Ostermann's thoughts than the preservation of peace of any kind with the Porte. A fortnight earlier it had been secretly decided in St. Petersburg to attack and dismember Turkey.

All parties to this decision were convinced that Russia would be victorious in the forthcoming war, and each had a vision of the advantages which would be derived from it. Ostermann saw it as a means of opening up the Black Sea to Russian trade, which he was certain was essential to the economic development of his adopted country. Münnich, who for six years had worked unceasingly to prepare the army for this war, was convinced that it would be the culmination of his career. Biron knew that anything which enhanced the Czarina's riches and glory could not fail to benefit him. To Anne nothing was more desirable than the abasement of the Sultan. The only defeat which her illustrious predecessor Peter the Great had ever suffered had been inflicted on him twenty-four years earlier by the Turks on the Pruth, and it still rankled. To avenge it and to open a window on the Black Sea, as Peter the Great had opened a window on the Baltic, would establish her as the mightiest ruler in Europe.

In the summer of 1735 it seemed to Anne and her advisers that everything favoured the realisation of their aims. The Russian candidate, Augustus III, was established as King in Warsaw, so the Polish flank was secured, and over 150,000 Russian soldiers were now available to carry the Czarina's standards in triumph to the Bosphorus. From Constantinople the Russian Resident reported that the military resources of the Porte were strained to the limit in Persia, and that the Sultan's Orthodox subjects were only waiting for the arrival of the conquering Russian army to rise against their hated overlord. There was, it was true, still some difficulty over the Emperor. While the performance of his army in the War of the Polish Succession had been most unimpressive, and the state of his finances was known to be deplorable, he possessed Belgrade, an impregnable base from which he could threaten the Sultan's European territories, engage part at least of the Ottoman army and greatly facilitate the Russian advance. He was the Czarina's ally, and it was generally agreed in St. Petersburg that it was only right and proper (as well as being most desirable), that he should enter the war on her side. Admittedly there was this awkward clause in the 1726 treaty which stated that he was only bound to do so if Russia was the victim of a Turkish attack, but happily the march of the Tartar Khan presented the perfect opportunity of maintaining that such an attack had occurred.

Ostermann had no doubt that he could lever the Emperor into the war, but it was by then July, and only a short campaigning season remained. Even if Charles was as amenable as the Count hoped, he would not be able to put an army into the field before the winter set in. In a few months the Tartar Khan would return from the Caucasus and the chance of overrunning the Crimea in his absence would be lost. Cautious though he was,

Ostermann fully agreed with his colleagues that the Crimea should be grabbed without waiting for the Emperor to declare himself, and that in the meantime preparations should be made for a full scale attack, in which it was confidently expected Austria would participate, on the Turks in the following spring.

There was much to be gained by concealing the Czarina's real intentions from the Porte for as long as possible and Veshniakov, who by this time had succeeded Neplyuev as Russian Resident in Constantinople, was therefore instructed to represent to the Grand Vizier that the forthcoming attack on the Crimea was no more than a punitive expedition against the Tatars. Veshniakov played his part admirably when, towards the end of October, he was summoned by the Porte and asked to explain the presence of 40,000 Russian troops 120 hours march within Turkish territory. He professed astonishment at the news and assured the alarmed Turkish ministers that since he personally knew nothing about the Russian advance, it was certainly nothing more than one of the usual attempts to hold the Tartars in check. He was so convincing that the Porte took no action other than sending orders to the Tartar Khan to return home immediately. This was fortunate for the Russians, for the campaign was a failure. Winter set in far earlier than had been expected, supplies were inadequate, the Russians lost 9,000 men through cold and sickness, and were forced to retreat without even having reached the Crimea.

It was perhaps as well for the Czarina's prestige and *amour propre* that the expedition had not been proclaimed to all Europe as the opening phase of a drive to dismember the Ottoman Empire, and in St. Petersburg Ostermann, thoroughly alarmed, was now all for abandoning the whole enterprise. Münnich flatly disagreed with him. Owing to illness he had not been in command of the expedition to the Crimea, and he was confident that in the following spring he would lead the Russian army to victory. He was wholeheartedly seconded by Veshniakov who was certain that it could only be a matter of time before the Russian flag flew over Constantinople. He assured his ruler that in Turkey there were neither politicians, nor military leaders, nor able financiers. 'As formerly they were aggressive and intent on glory, so now they are craven and fearful. They appear to sense that the end of their tyranny is at hand. May God permit your Majesty to destroy them for ever.'[1]

At the beginning of 1736 Münnich submitted his operational plan to Anne, Czarina of all Russia. It outlined a victorious progress during which the northern coast of the Black Sea would be overrun, the Crimea captured, and the Sultan's vassal Principalities of Moldavia and Wallachia occupied. The stage would then be set for the grand finale and the ultimate triumph. The Field-Marshal described this in a fine flight of rhetoric:

> The banners and standards of the Czarina will be erected, where? . . . In Constantinople! The Czarina will be crowned Empress of the Greeks in the oldest Greek church, in the renowned cathedral of Santa Sophia, and will bring peace— to whom? . . . to the whole world. . . . Who will then question whether the Imperial title belongs to him who is crowned in Frankfurt, or to her who is crowned and anointed in Stamboul?[2]

It was a dazzling prospect. Peter the Great himself had never hoped for more than to be buried in Santa Sophia.

But, in order to realise this vision, it was necessary to get to Constantinople. The obvious route lay through southern Poland, Moldavia and Wallachia. The army would advance through easy country and, according to Veshniakov, be welcomed and assisted by the Orthodox in the two Principalities. From there they would link up with the Austrians to launch a devastating combined attack southwards towards the Ottoman capital. Ostermann, Münnich and the Czarina each, however, saw reasons for objecting to this plan. It could only be interpreted as a direct attack on the Sultan and must lead to a full-scale war with the Porte. Ostermann was doubtful about the wisdom of Russia undertaking this alone and preferred to confine the conflict, until such time as the Emperor had been dragged into it, to operating against the Tartars. Münnich was reluctant to advance through southern Poland with his left flank opposed to attack from an undefeated Tartar Khan. The Czarina took a personal view of the problem. She was determined that Biron should succeed to the Duchy of Courland, and feared that if the neutrality of Poland was violated by the Russian army, King Augustus III might refuse to invest her lover with this Polish fief. It was finally agreed that the 1736 campaign should be devoted to the capture of Azov; the invasion of the Crimea, and the final defeat of the Tartar Khan.

Azov was the most easterly of the chain of fortresses built by the Turks in the seventeenth century to guard the estuaries of the Don, Dnieper and Bug, and so deny Russia access to the Black Sea. It stood sentinel at the mouth of the Don, a complex of bastions, redoubts and palisades, dominating the vast estuary which formed an ideal natural harbour. During the past hundred years the Russians had twice captured Azov, only to lose it again to the Turks. So long as it remained in Turkish hands one of Russia's most important trade routes was blocked, but to regain it was a major operation. Supplies for the besieging army must be shipped down the Don, and to reach the fortress that army must cross a long stretch of barren territory infested by roving bands of Tartars. But it was 600 miles from Constantinople, and Münnich calculated that, if a surprise attack were launched, it would be possible to capture it before reinforcements arrived.

In March 1736, and without declaring war or waiting for the arrival of his siege guns, the Field-Marshal appeared with a large force in front of Azov, and took the Pasha commanding it by surprise. The Russians overran two outposts higher up the Don and broke the chain across the river, Russian warships appeared, and Azov was surrounded. A few days later Münnich handed over the conduct of the siege to General Lacy. In his opinion it was no more than a routine operation which would soon be brought to a successful conclusion. He now proposed to assume command of the main Russian army and to lead them to the supreme victory of the campaign, the capture of the Crimea. To achieve this he must march across 300 miles of desolate and largely unknown territory into which no Russian army had ever ventured. It was a feat which Peter the Great himself had never attempted, but Münnich was confident of success. He had interrogated the Cossacks, who alone amongst the Czarina's subjects knew the area; he had studied such few maps as existed; he was sure it could be done.

As the Field-Marshal galloped back over the dusty tracks across the steppe to his base at Tsaritzinka, he reflected that during the past winter he had spared no effort to prepare for the greatest triumph of his career. He had paid great attention to supplies and ensured that the army was provided with 8,000 wagons and enough flour to give each man a daily ration of two and a half pounds. The Cossacks had told him that he would at times find no water for twenty miles or more, and would be confronted with ravines sixty miles long, forty feet deep and a quarter of a mile wide. Therefore he had assembled casks for transporting water and adequate bridging equipment. He commanded the hardiest soldiers in Europe, self-sufficient, accustomed to bivouac on the bare ground, patient, courageous, and—although their appearance was rough—capable of accomplishing great feats if they were well led. Under his personal leadership he did not doubt that they would destroy the forces of the Tartar Khan.

Münnich permitted himself no rest at Tsaritzinka. He reviewed his troops, rechecked stores, and appointed Prince Trubetskoy to organise the supply lines—an unpleasant assignment as the Field-Marshal threatened to have the Prince hanged if he failed in this task, remarking 'Seemingly impossible things can be brought about in a very short time in this country by such threats.'[3]

On the 20th of April the army, 50,000 strong, their Commander-in-Chief at their head, moved out of the camp and disappeared slowly over the horizon into the southern steppes on the first stage of their long march to the Crimea. As day succeeded day they laboured on through a wilderness, a vast expanse of nothing except grass and sky, in which, with the exception of hares and birds, the only living creatures were bands of Tartars, who could be seen several miles away across the unending flat plain, circling round and waiting for an opportunity to attack. Münnich, aware of the havoc which a sudden Tartar onslaught could cause to his baggage train, had ordered the army to advance in a formation of five large hollow squares, in the centre of each of which the supply waggons were grouped. This, while effectively protecting the supplies from the Tartars, slowed up the advance, and over four weeks elapsed before, on May 26th, the Russians, by now near the limit of their endurance, reached the isthmus of Perekop, the gateway to the Crimean peninsula.

Although he knew that the Tartars had constructed defence lines across the isthmus, Münnich, possibly inaccurately informed of their strength, had brought no siege equipment with him. He reconnoitred the lines and found them formidable. They consisted of a dry ditch about seventy feet deep and seventy feet wide along the far side of which ran a high wall; behind this lay a fort garrisoned by 4,000 Janissaries, and a few miles away from this the Tartar Khan was reported to be encamped with a force of 100,000 men. Only two courses were open to the Field-Marshal, to retreat, or to attack and risk losing the entire army. To a man of his temperament retreat was unthinkable, and three days later he gave the order to advance. His soldiers had marched 300 miles on a staple diet of biscuit, and for the past week had only been able to find brackish water to drink, but they obeyed him without hesitation, stormed the lines and routed the Tartar Khan. It was a considerable feat of arms, and as a result of it the Crimea for the first time lay at the mercy of the Russians.

Constantinople was far away from Azov, the Crimea and the main Russian base. During the first three months of 1736 the French Ambassador and his British, Dutch and Venetian colleagues were quite unable to gauge the intentions of Russia, or to determine whether the spring would bring peace or war. The Porte kept its own counsel; the exact whereabouts of the Tartar Khan were unknown; the Russian Resident would divulge nothing and the Imperial Resident professed to know nothing. It was possible to conjecture from the demeanour of the Turks, which the British Ambassador found 'dejected, reserved and silent',[4] that the Porte, still entangled in the Persian war, was anxious to avoid another military adventure, but no firm information even on this subject was available.

At the beginning of April Villeneuve and his colleagues received some unpleasant enlightenment on the situation when, during the celebration of the Muslim feast of Bairam, the first news of the Russian attack on Azov reached Constantinople. The outraged Grand Vizier described it as 'an assassination'.[5] The capital was in a state of panic, troops marched through the streets, high officials of the Porte were in continual conference in the Serail, but no army was assembled, and war was not declared.

A month later a courier arrived from St. Petersburg with a letter from Count Ostermann for the Grand Vizier. Veshniakov remained as inscrutable as ever, but his colleagues deduced from the agitation which it caused at the Porte that this letter must be most disagreeable. They were right; it was. In order to demonstrate the extent to which the Porte had broken the 'eternal peace' Ostermann began by enumerating in detail all the Tartar raids between 1700 and 1732, and there were a great many of them. He then roundly accused the Porte of double dealing in Persia and the Tartars of violating Russian territory during their march through the Caucasus. Finally he pointed out that the Czarina had put up with a great deal and now, unless the Sultan immediately sent plenipotentiaries to the frontier with full powers to negotiate a peace, had no alternative but to take up arms in defence of her rights. The reference to peace negotiations was rhetorical for the letter was dated April 12th, and Ostermann was perfectly aware when he drafted it that, by the time it reached the Grand Vizier, the siege of Azov would be well advanced and Münnich would have launched his attack on the Crimea. Shortly after the arrival of this ultimatum, as every foreign envoy was able to inform his government, the situation was no longer in doubt. A courier arrived from the Pasha of one of the frontier provinces to announce that a Russian captain had entered Turkish territory and 'formally announced war by sound of trumpet and beat of drum'.[6]

It was now clear to the Porte that the Russians would not stop at Azov and that, unless they were checked, warships with the Russian flag flying at the masthead would appear on the Black Sea, that 'pure and immaculate virgin'[7] on which the Turks had vowed no foreign ship should ever sail. As was customary the Grand Vizier summoned the leading dignitaries of the Ottoman

Empire, and in solemn council asked the Sheikh ul Islam whether to declare war on Russia would be in accordance with the law of the Prophet. The answer was given in the traditional form: 'Peace with the infidels is but legal, if advantageous to all Muslims, but if not, it is not legal at all: as soon as it is useful, it is allowed to break the peace, be it concluded for a fixed time, or for ever.'[8]

At sunrise on the 28th of May the Sultan's standard was unfurled in front of the Serail, the three horse-tails surmounting it pointing north-east towards Russia. After sheep had been sacrificed and prayers recited, it was borne in solemn procession through the gates of the city to Daoud Pasha, the place of assembly of the army.

With the obvious exception of the Russian Resident all the foreign envoys gathered to watch the Alay, or traditional procession, when the army left Constantinople for the war. It had the appearance of a fête, rather than the prelude to a struggle on the outcome of which depended the future of the Ottoman Empire. It included contingents from all the guilds of the city, wearing their finest clothes and bearing the tools of their trade. There were bakers, pastry-cooks, butchers, sherbert sellers, sweetmeat makers, fishmongers, poulterers, fruit merchants, gardeners and cattledrovers, armourers and shipwrights, goldsmiths resplendent in red and green turbans. The slave dealers were accompanied by their most beautiful slaves, the surgeons carried saws, lancets and other surgical instruments. There were bands, tumblers, and mimers. The lion and bear keepers led their animals on golden chains. The executioners carried drawn swords, and were hung about with nails, gimlets, matches and all 'the seventy-seven implements of torture . . . they pass with great vehemence but no light shines from their faces for they are a sombre set of fellows'.[9] The Janissaries, bombardiers, cavalry and artillery followed the guilds. Last of all came the Grand Vizier and the great officers of State, riding on magnificent horses. Nothing could have exceeded the splendour of their attire, but the Venetian Bailo noticed that they looked pale and grave.[10]

The Russian Resident had meanwhile shut himself up in his

house and, after burning his papers, was composing a final dispatch to the Czarina. He assumed that he would be treated as a hostage and imprisoned in the Seven Towers, and even doubted if he would leave Constantinople alive. However, for years he had dedicated himself to the task of preparing the way for the triumphal entry of the Russian army into the Sultan's capital, and now that this task was completed he was prepared, if need be, to die. He reiterated to his ruler that the Turks were now at her mercy and added 'I am but an insignificant and unworthy victim, but I am ready to shed my blood in confirmation of the truth of my reports if only Your Majesty will set this enterprise in motion. Nothing stands in its way; all are paralysed with fear.'[11] In fact this ultimate sacrifice was not demanded of him. He was neither arrested nor maltreated, but a few months later conducted honourably to the frontier and allowed to return to St. Petersburg. It must have been a sad anticlimax.

Russia's declaration of war removed Veshniakov, one of Villeneuve's principal opponents, from the stage. But, as he watched the great Alay, the French Ambassador was most uneasy. He knew too much about the weakness of the Turks to have any confidence that they would be successful in a war against Russia and reports from Vienna indicated that the Emperor, while he had not yet committed himself, would probably succumb to pressure from St. Petersburg to enter the war on the Czarina's side. If he did so the chances of the Ottoman Empire surviving in any form likely to be of use to France were small, the Levant trade would be lost, the Austrians and the Russians would dominate the eastern Mediterranean, and the prestige of King Louis XV would suffer irreparable damage.

Villeneuve was not prone to depression, but he was bound to concede that the future looked very dark indeed, for it seemed that the ultimate disaster was at hand, and he was powerless to avert it. Since the end of the War of the Polish Succession Cardinal Fleury appeared to have lost interest in Turkey, and the Marquis lacked both support and instructions from Versailles. The Grand Vizier Ali had been dismissed; since then he had been excluded from the inner councils of the Turks, and obliged to endure the recurrent mortification of watching Bonneval with the escort allotted to a great officer of State ride by on his way to the Porte where, Villeneuve reflected sourly, the advice which he tendered was unlikely to take account of the interests of France. There was no alternative but to put the best face he could on an extremely difficult situation in the hope of deluding his colleagues into thinking that he was still an opponent to be reckoned with; to hope for a directive; and to wait with what patience he could muster for some indication that France was not entirely excluded from the calculations of the Turks.

The French Ambassador's patience was rewarded sooner than he had dared to expect. When in June he made his farewell call on the Grand Vizier at Daoud Pasha before the latter set out with the army for the Danube, he was astounded to be asked by that dignitary whether he would be prepared to join him in his camp if invited to do so. The Marquis, still without instructions from Versailles, could only reply with a smile that, since the Grand Vizier could turn to the Imperial Resident, and to the British and Dutch Ambassadors, all of whom were certainly only too anxious to help and advise him, and in all of whom he appeared to have entire confidence, he doubted whether an envoy such as himself, so little informed of the policies of the Porte, could have anything useful to contribute. This reply provoked from the Grand Vizier a fervent expression of friendship for France, which was subsequently echoed by the Kahya who lamented that the Sultan's real friends were silent.[12] Villeneuve, sweating in the summer heat of Constantinople, immediately dictated a report of these conversations to Versailles, devoutly hoping as he did so that it might stimulate Cardinal Fleury into some sort of action. His need for a directive was now acute, for the Porte had let it be generally known that mediation to settle the dispute between the Sultan and the Czarina might be favourably considered by the Grand Vizier.

In Europe at that time mediation was often employed in the settlement of differences between nations. It eliminated the quarrels over protocol and precedence which were inseparable from large conferences and which frequently delayed the start of proceedings for weeks. The ruler who agreed to undertake the mediation had an excellent opportunity of ensuring that the final settlement was favourable to his own interests. His representative in the actual negotiations, usually his ambassador in one of the contending countries, was handsomely rewarded by all sides when an agreement was reached, and it was therefore a role to which every ambassador aspired. But certain conditions had to be fulfilled before mediation could begin. The ruler undertaking it had to be accepted by all the contending parties, his representative on the spot briefed as to terms on which each side would make peace, and invested with special powers for his task. It was the diplomatic equivalent of the lover's age old problem of assembling together the time, the place and the loved one—and often as difficult to solve.

By the end of June 1736 every foreign envoy in Constantinople except the Venetian Bailo, who continued to observe the situation with sardonic amusement, had reported to his home government that the Porte might be prepared to accept his ruler's mediation. All of them were anxiously awaiting instructions, and each of them wished to assume the role of mediator; Villeneuve and the Imperial Resident, Talman, because they hoped to manipulate the mediation to their ruler's advantage; the Dutch Ambassador, Calkoen, for reasons of personal ambition, and the newly arrived British Ambassador, Sir Everard Fawkener, because his pay and allowances were quite inadequate and he was sorely in need of money. In the meantime the Grand Vizier, the army, and all the senior officials of the Porte were lumbering north-eastwards up the coast towards the estuary of the Danube. Such officials as were left in Constantinople had no power to take any important decision, and appeared to be quite uninformed as to the Grand Vizier's intentions. For all practical purposes the foreign envoys were no longer in contact with the government to which they were accredited, and each of them was uncomfortably aware that, if he was empowered to act as mediator, it would be necessary to obtain the Grand Vizier's consent to go to his camp for discussions before negotiations could begin.

Talman, to the envy of the rest of the envoys, was the first to receive powers to act as mediator. Villeneuve, however, could console himself with the thought that this indicated that the Emperor was apparently still disinclined to enter the war. As the weeks went by he observed with satisfaction that, try as he might, the Imperial Resident was quite unable to extract an invitation from the Grand Vizier to come to his camp and, as one member of the diplomatic corps maliciously put it, remained in the uncomfortable position of a man with one foot in the stirrup quite unable to mount.

The Grand Vizier had meanwhile settled down at Babadagh near the mouth of the Danube over 250 miles from Constantinople. His camp with its streets, squares, bazaars and fountains, resembled a town rather than a military base. In addition to the regular troops it was thronged with Arabs, Circassians and nomads, all of whom had attached themselves to the army in the hope of loot; and by a strange medley of hangers on, Greeks, Armenians, Jews, merchants, contractors and spies who had come there in search of profit. In the centre of the camp stood a group of magnificent tents, shaded by artificial trees and surrounded by stacks of brightly coloured tin boxes which contained the money for paying the troops. Five red horse-tails on poles surmounted by golden balls, symbolising the Grand Vizier's authority, were erected before them. Beside them, a grim reminder of that authority, criminals were executed. Here, closely guarded, the Grand Vizier sat in council; here the major decisions were taken and forwarded to Constantinople for the Sultan's approval. It was not a streamlined method of dealing with affairs of State.

But the Grand Vizier was disinclined for immediate action, and as summer merged into autumn he remained uncertain as to what course to pursue. The situation admittedly had improved, for peace had been concluded with Persia and, although Azov had fallen, the Russians had been forced to retreat from the Crimea.

But in spite of this, and although public opinion was clamouring for war to recover Azov, he was still reluctant to take the field against Russia. He decided to hedge and see what turned up. An order to the frontier Pashas to raise troops and prepare to defend their Pashaliks, and the dismissal of the Tartar Khan for his failure to keep the Russians out of the Crimea, pacified public opinion. Meanwhile all the would-be mediators were kept dangling in the hope that by playing off one against the other more favourable terms for a settlement might be secured.

Reports of Münnich's enforced retreat had also reached Constantinople, and recounted a disaster rather than a failure. After routing the Tartars at Perekop the Field-Marshal had detached a force to take Kinburn, a fortress on the mouth of the Dnieper and then, disregarding the protests of his generals, had advanced into the Crimea. For the next three weeks he ravaged the peninsula and burnt and sacked the capital of the Tartar Khan at Bakchiserai. The supply position then deteriorated. No attempt was made to conserve and ration captured stores of food and, since the Tartars had burnt the grass and destroyed the wells, there was neither fodder nor drinking water. The sick rate rose sharply, for the Field-Marshal forced his men to march throughout the heat of the day. Finally he retreated to Perekop, but the supplies which he had hoped to receive there failed to arrive. He was forced to blow up the defence lines on the isthmus and withdraw to his winter quarters in the Ukraine, having lost 30,000 men of whom only 2,000 were killed by the enemy. He had been defeated by two of the principal allies of the Porte, climate and geography, and by the defects of his own supply system. The campaign had been brilliant but murderous. Altogether the Russian balance sheet by November 1736 was not impressive. All that had been achieved at great cost was the capture of Azov and Kinburn and 'the burning of a few towns in Tartary'.[13] To Villeneuve, still waiting impatiently for his instructions, it was encouraging, for it showed that the Russians were by no means all victorious.

At last the instructions arrived. Early in December a French frigate dropped anchor off Pera. On board her was Baron Tott who had already distinguished himself on his mission in 1734 to the Tartar Khan. Before leaving Versailles he had been ordered to place himself at Villeneuve's disposal for all tasks which the Ambassador could not personally undertake without compromising his position, and he carried with him a long memorandum addressed to the Marquis. This was signed by Chauvelin but undoubtedly had Fleury's full approval, for it was drafted as the result of a thorough reappraisal of the importance of the preservation of the Ottoman Empire to the French conception of the balance of power. As a result of this reappraisal it had been agreed in Versailles that it would be disastrous if the Czarina and the Emperor succeeded in dismembering Turkey, and it had also been agreed that they could only be frustrated by a diplomatic offensive launched with the dual aim of splitting the Austro-Russian alliance, and of stiffening the Turks so that they would under no circumstances accept a damaging peace settlement. This conclusion was acceptable to the Cardinal, for it advocated the kind of action which he understood, and he had taken immediate steps to implement it.

A courier was dispatched to Vienna, with instructions to the French agents there to lose no opportunity of insinuating to the Austrians that the Russians were not to be trusted. The memorandum brought by Tott to Villeneuve ordered the French Ambassador to emphasise to the Porte that, while France did not seek the role of mediator, in His Most Christian Majesty the Sultan had a powerful friend and supporter. He must, Chauvelin wrote, win the confidence of the Grand Vizier and his ministers, have them seek his advice, and ensure that they concluded no settlement which was prejudicial to the interests of France.[14] This was all very well, but the Grand Vizier was over 250 miles away at Babadagh, and Villeneuve had no direct access to him. It was a very difficult assignment and one which could not be carried out speedily. But the Marquis reflected that something might be achieved, for the Russians were back in winter quarters, the Emperor had not yet entered the war, and recent reports from Vienna suggested that his relationship with his Russian ally had for some months been far from happy.

PART THREE

Trial of Strength

CHAPTER VIII

Austria goes to War

Vienna–Hungary–Serbia, January–July 1737

Villeneuve was correctly informed. Relations between Vienna and St. Petersburg were very strained indeed, and for some time communications between the two governments had been conducted in language more appropriate to relatives squabbling over an inheritance than to allies considering joint action against a mutual enemy. Ostermann's recurrent attacks of gout and their effect on his temper did not assist matters; neither did the Emperor's unfortunate choice of Count Ostein as his representative in St. Petersburg. According to a contemporary Ostein always tended to be 'high in business, satirical in conversation, and perhaps too refined in both'.[1] Tact was not one of the Count's outstanding virtues. He was unwise enough to lecture Ostermann on the disadvantage of attacking the Crimea and Azov and consistently managed to infuriate Biron. The Czarina's lover in any case had no love for the Court of Vienna 'who', he said, 'by her haughtiness had found the secret to disoblige all her old friends'.[2]

This 'haughtiness' masked the state of confusion which had prevailed in the Imperial capital ever since Eugen of Savoy had become too ill to exercise any real influence over affairs.

The Prince, who had been failing for some time, died in April 1736. The Jesuit father who officiated at his funeral said in the course of his sermon '. . . here in a coffin lies everything which we human beings call great'.[3] The Emperor by contrast noted in his diary on the day of Eugen's death:

Heard at 8.30 that Prince Eugen of Savoy, who has served my
House since '83, commanded and accomplished much on the
battle-field since '97, became President of the Hofkriegsrat in
1703, served me in everything since 1711, has, after a long
illness been found dead in bed. God have mercy on his soul.
He was 73.[4]

It was a bare record of service, such as might have been noted
for an old and faithful valet. Charles VI apparently failed to
realise that a glorious era in the House of Habsburg was lowered
with the Prince's small coffin into the vault beneath St. Stephen's
cathedral in Vienna.

Eugen had directed both the political and the military affairs
of the State. After his death these responsibilities were split
between several ministers, none of whom were possessed of
outstanding ability, and all of whom were elderly.

Count Königsegg who succeeded the Prince as President of the
Hofkriegsrat, and therefore directed relations with Turkey, was
sixty-three, a lover of pomp and good living, and afflicted with
gout. Königsegg's senior colleague, the Chancellor Count Philipp
Ludwig von Sinzendorf, had only two qualifications for high
office, a knowledge of foreign affairs gained through some forty
years experience, and a capacity for flattering the Emperor and
telling him what he wished to hear. All his contemporaries agreed
that he was not an admirable character. One of them summed
him up as 'Naturally timorous and when things go ill with him,
he abandons himself to sighs and groanings . . . when they go
well he is too elated.'[5] He must have been anathema to his colleague, Count Gundaker Starhemberg, who was highly intelligent
and totally incorruptible. Had Starhemberg been younger he
might have exercised a considerable influence for good on the
conduct of affairs, but he was seventy-three, tired, and unsup-
ported by his fellow ministers, the third of whom, Count Harrach,
was only a few years younger, and not a strong personality.

After Prince Eugen's death these four, Königsegg, Sinzendorf,
Starhemberg, and Harrach formed the Inner Cabinet of the
Imperial Privy Council. Charles VI preferred to deal with his

ministers in writing, and communications between him and them were channelled through the Protokollführer or Permanent Secretary of the Council, Hofrat Johann Christoph von Bartenstein. All the aristocratic members of the Inner Cabinet disliked the commoner Bartenstein and his habit, contrary to all precedent, of taking part in their discussions but, because he was a first-class draftsman, was energetic, and stood high in the Emperor's favour, they had no alternative but to put up with him.

Bartenstein was an exceptionally able civil servant, but lacked the breadth of vision and detachment of a statesman. Sinzendorf and his immediate colleagues lacked in varying degrees energy, competence and singleness of purpose. Collectively they were far from being the ideal team to advise a ruler in whom ultimate power was vested, but who was deficient in the necessary qualities to exercise it. After Prince Eugen's death Charles VI was more determined than ever to rule as an absolute monarch, and insisted that no measure was to be executed without his prior approval, but he devoted more and more time to music, hunting and court ceremonies, and less and less to affairs of state. Documents accumulated on his desk which he had neither the leisure nor the inclination to examine. He shrank from taking decisions, but paid little attention to the advice of his ministers, blaming each of them in turn and setting them against each other, 'Following', as the British envoy reported, 'the family political principle of governing over them by keeping them in divisions.'[6]

This ill-assorted collection of ministers was quite incapable of dealing with Ostermann's repeated demand that the Emperor should honour his treaty obligations and enter the war on the Czarina's side. They procrastinated, and finally replied with an offer of the Emperor's good offices to mediate. Ostermann retorted curtly that, while in any event the good offices of the Emperor would have been useless, unless they were accompanied by a specific declaration to the Porte that Austria was mediating as Russia's ally, now nothing less than an immediate declaration of war by Charles VI would satisfy the Czarina.

A great deal of dithering and heartsearching then took place in Vienna. Every commonsense reason dictated against embarking on another Turkish war. It could not be presented to Europe as a crusade against the infidel, and Charles could therefore expect from the Princes of the Empire neither voluntary contributions to finance it, nor troops to help him fight it—unless he paid for them. In addition he was required to take the field in support of an ally who refused either to reveal her ultimate war aims or to discuss a joint plan of campaign. But to Charles common sense was subordinate to one fact. He was head of the House of Habsburg, and so bound, not only to ensure that his hereditary possessions descended complete and undivided to his successor, but also to increase and multiply them if possible. All observers at the Porte agreed that the Ottoman Empire was decaying. As the Emperor saw it if he did not enter the war he would lose the chance of acquiring part of the Sultan's European provinces, and might expect to see the Russians established on the eastern frontier of Hungary. He needed the Czarina as an ally, but as an ally whose possessions were separated from his own by a series of buffer territories. He was in a dilemma, neatly summarised by the British envoy in Vienna, who wrote to Walpole: 'If the Turks beat the Muscovites, the Emperor cannot abandon the latter, and if the Muscovites beat the Turks, he cannot be too much on his guard against the former.'[7]

Had Prince Eugen been alive a solution might have been found. But the Prince was dead, and his successors, anxious as they were to curry favour, had no desire to advise any course displeasing to their ruler. Money, they assured him, could be raised, troops recruited and no doubt, once the Czarina knew that he was prepared to do as she wished, she would be more amenable. Moreover the announcement that he was preparing to take the field might frighten the Turks into accepting the Imperial offer of mediation which Talman was endeavouring to force on them. The risk that Bonneval or the French Ambassador would meanwhile succeed in inducing the Porte to forestall the Emperor and invade Hungary could, Sinzendorf and his colleagues were comfortably certain, be discounted.

No Court in Europe was more given to wishful thinking than the Court of Vienna, and no ruler more prone to succumb to this failing than Charles VI. He readily accepted his minister's assurances. Count Ostein in St. Petersburg was instructed to inform Ostermann that the Emperor would enter the war if the Porte refused to accept his offer of mediation; Talman in Constantinople was urged to redouble his efforts with the Grand Vizier (there was after all no harm in trying to extract the greatest possible gain with the least possible risk); steps were taken to put the Imperial forces on a war footing.

Six million gulden were reckoned to be necessary for equipping the army, and the cost of keeping it in the field for a six months campaign was estimated to be a further 4,811,667 florins and 39 kreutzer precisely. Charles imposed a tax on property throughout the Habsburg hereditary lands and made an eloquent appeal to the Reichstag, which reluctantly agreed to advance him 3,000,000 gulden. Emissaries were dispatched to scour Europe for funds, in return for which they were empowered to pledge (for several years to come) the revenues of Bohemia, Silesia and the Imperial copper mines. They succeeded in raising loans of 1,000,000 gulden from Genoa and 3,500,000 gulden from Holland. The Pope agreed to continue the tax which he had imposed on the clergy throughout the Empire and in Naples, Sicily and Milan to pay for maintaining and strengthening the fortifications of Belgrade and Temesvár. One other means of raising money remained. Drastic economies could be effected in the expenses of the Court, which was still costing more than 2,000,000 gulden a year, but even Starhemberg dared not suggest this, and it certainly did not occur to Charles VI.

Money, by some means or other, was coming in. It was not so easy to find the necessary recruits to bring the army up to strength. Recruits must be between the age of eighteen and forty-six, obedient and always ready to face the enemy, but most of the men provided by the hereditary territories failed to reach this standard. Bohemia sent either habitual deserters or boys unfit to bear arms; Carinthia flatly refused to furnish any recruits at all. Negotiations for the hire of contingents from Saxony, Hesse and Brunswick hung fire and there was, in any case, little hope that these states would be able to furnish large numbers of men.

The transit of reinforcements from the Imperial garrisons in Italy was held up by the reluctance of the provinces through which they must march to make any provision for them. Units already stationed in Hungary had been severely affected by sickness following the flooding of the Danube. The air there was so damp that it was impossible for the soldiers to keep their shirts dry and, according to reports reaching Vienna, the supply situation was so bad that the men were 'in total want of shoes and stockings'.[8] The whole state of the army in Hungary was clearly in urgent need of review, and the Emperor ordered that a full inspection of it should be made, and a report submitted for his personal consideration.

The report reached him in February 1737. It was devastating. Inadequate barracks, shortages of munitions and provisions; the frontier fortresses and the warships of the Danube flotilla in urgent need of repair; full hospitals and far too little medical attention; slack and incompetent generals. The list of deficiencies to be made good was unending. Charles cannot have found it agreeable reading, particularly as a few weeks earlier he had formally committed himself, by a solemn agreement with the Czarina which had been signed in Vienna, to mobilise an army of 80,000 men, and if peace was not concluded during the winter, to open hostilities against the Turks in the following spring. There was now nothing for it but to attempt to remedy the supply situation as rapidly as possible, hope that Talman might yet be successful in persuading the Porte to start peace negotiations, and endeavour to tie the Russians down to some plan of campaign which would ensure that if the Imperial forces had to take the field they were not left alone to confront the main Ottoman army. The Hofkriegsrat and the Hofkammer creaked into action. Orders were placed for stores. Eighty thousand tons of flour and a large number of iron baking ovens, 5,630 carts and 12,565 oxen to draw them, 300,000 bundles of straw, and 60 iron bridging pontoons were some of the items in a very large assortment of requirements. Königsegg inundated Talman with directives. Ostein was urged to lose no opportunity of impressing on the Russians that they should march through southern Poland to link up in Moldavia and Wallachia with the Imperial forces. Another month passed. It became clear that even if the Jewish contractors, with whom orders for supplies had been placed, for once fulfilled their contracts, it would be impossible to assemble on the Danube the necessary transport fleet of 700 ships. There was still no satisfactory news from Talman. A courier then arrived from St. Petersburg with an exceedingly unpleasant letter from Ostermann. The Emperor, the Count wrote, might conduct his campaign as he wished. The Czarina was sending a force under Lacy to invade the Crimea while Münnich, with the main army, proceeded to besiege Ochakov. It was anticipated that this fortress (which commanded the estuary of the Dnieper), would fall before the end of May and Münnich would then advance through the southern steppes in the direction of Bender, the Turkish stronghold on the next great river, the Dniester. Ostermann concluded with a demand that the Imperial forces should invade Turkish territory as soon as they heard that the siege of Ochakov had begun. This was his sole reference to any form of combined operations.

It was now painfully clear to Charles and his ministers that the Russians had not the least intention of being either co-operative or amenable, but it was too late to make a further protest, for the Czarina's armies had already begun to advance. It could only be hoped that Talman could succeed in deluding the Turks as to the Emperor's intentions, and so buy time for his troops to take the field and achieve a surprise attack. Vienna sorely needed time. It was by now the middle of March and in a few weeks the campaigning season would begin, but no Commander-in-Chief had been appointed and no plan of operations drawn up.

The Austrian army possessed 275 officers of the rank of General and above, of whom no less than twenty were Field-Marshals. In selecting his Commander-in-Chief Charles therefore had a wide if not altogether promising field to draw on. Amongst them Prince Hildburghausen, charming, witty and an accomplished courtier, stood high in his favour, but the Emperor was reluctantly bound to admit that he was too young and inexperienced to be given supreme command. After some hesitation his choice fell on the man who Prince Eugen in the last years of his life had regarded as his most able general. In April an Imperial rescript appointed Field-Marshal Seckendorf Commander-in-Chief of the army in Hungary.

Seckendorf was sixty-three, a small man, devoid of either grace or charm, but intelligent, tough and endowed with an immense capacity for work. His knowledge of the area in which he would have to fight dated from 1717, when he had distinguished himself in the battle for Belgrade, and it was to him that Charles, earlier in the year, had entrusted the task of inspecting and reporting on the state of the army in Hungary. Seckendorf was the obvious choice for the post of Commander-in-Chief, but his appointment was not popular. All the generals were jealous of him and disliked his blunt manner, and the Catholics amongst them also resented being under the command of a Protestant. Königsegg and his colleagues in the Hofkriegsrat detested the Field-Marshal. Seckendorf had not concealed his opinion of them in his report to the Emperor earlier in the year. 'It is impossible', he wrote, 'that the Hofkriegsrat at Vienna can issue proper decrees and resolutions on subjects which they neither see nor understand.'9 It was a scathing criticism of their capabilities for which they never forgave him and, while they were forced to acquiesce in the appointment, they were prepared neither to support nor to co-operate with Seckendorf.

A Commander-in-Chief had been appointed, but the plan of campaign had still to be agreed, the point at issue being whether the army should advance from Belgrade to capture the fortress of Vidin about 200 miles lower down the Danube, or strike south-east along the Morava valley towards Nish. Eventually, after much discussion and wrangling, Vidin was designated as the main objective, Prince Eugen, twenty years earlier, when the Turks were in full flight after his capture of Belgrade, had refused to pursue them, on the grounds that to do so would mean advancing into sparsely inhabited territory, and that his supply lines would be dangerously extended. Had he been alive he would have viewed the decision to attack Vidin with deep concern, and insisted that at least the basic precept of all his campaigns against the Turks was followed, and the entire strength of the army concentrated against this one objective. But apparently the Emperor and his advisers had forgotten everything which Eugen had ever advocated, for they decided to detach two corps from the main army, one of which was to advance from Siebenburgen to the north of the Danube into Wallachia, while the other under the command of Prince Hildburghausen overran and conquered Bosnia.

Now that it had been decided to go to war, Charles and his ministers were afflicted by yet another bout of wishful thinking. They optimistically assumed that their armies would be victorious by the end of the summer, and they planned to conclude peace on the basis of *uti posseditis*. This term can be translated as 'What I have I hold'. If peace was concluded on this basis the victor retained all the territory which his army had managed to conquer in the war which had preceded it. It was therefore desirable to overrun and occupy as much territory as possible. Charles VI and the Imperial Privy Council considered that a slice of Wallachia would form a very useful barrier between Hungary and Russia, and that Bosnia would be a valuable addition to the Habsburg possessions. There were of course risks attached to attempting so much at once, but they were covered by the built-in insurance afforded by the great fortress of Belgrade.

Thanks to the contributions of the Holy Catholic Church, Belgrade by the end of 1736 was even stronger than it had been in Eugen's day. It was now surrounded by no less than three defence lines; nine great bastions had been constructed (each appropriately named after a saint); the fortifications of the citadel had been reinforced; there were new barracks and armouries; a harbour had been built and a well 108 feet deep sunk to supply the garrison with water in the event of a siege. Should the unexpected happen and anything go wrong with the campaign, the Imperial armies could always retreat and take refuge under the protection of the fortress. As the Emperor and his ministers saw it, possessing Belgrade, they could lose nothing and might gain much. The plan appeared to be admirable, and once the details had been worked out Charles, well satisfied, resumed his normal hunting programme and Königsegg, Sinzendorf and their colleagues relapsed comfortably into the agreeable pattern of life—for the rich, powerful, and well placed—in baroque Vienna.

Meanwhile Seckendorf, on whom the success or failure of everything depended, rode through Hungary to take up his command. Before leaving Vienna he had received an Imperial rescript calculated to discourage initiative in any leader. It ordered him to consult his generals when contemplating any variation in the operational plan which had been agreed by the Hofkriegs-rat and, having ascertained their views, to obtain final approval from Vienna before taking action. In cases of extreme urgency he could use his own initiative, but he must on no account hazard the army. Finally he was required to make continual reports both to the Hofkriegsrat and to the Emperor.

There had been no time to argue about the terms of the rescript, for the campaigning season was already well advanced, but the Field-Marshal must have brooded on its implications as he rode towards his headquarters at Belgrade. It was evident that he was not going to be allowed a free hand to carry out the task with which he had been entrusted. However, it was now too late to draw back. He devoutly hoped that at least his recommendations had been implemented, and that the deficiencies on which he had reported earlier in the year had been made good.

Seckendorf reached Belgrade on June 11th and at once saw that the situation was even worse than he had feared. On paper his army consisted of over 70,000 men, but large forces had been detached to Bosnia and Siebenburgen and, while these corps were nominally still under his orders, communications were so bad that it was impossible for him to exercise any real control over them. He was left with a main army consisting of no more than 26,000 infantry, 15,000 cavalry and 3,000 local irregular troops. The latter preferred stealing to fighting, there were only a few veterans amongst the regulars, the new recruits were poor physical specimens and the cavalry remounts had not arrived. Many of the generals were incompetent, as the Field-Marshal did not hesitate to point out, observing caustically of one of

them, 'He is even more useless at commanding a cavalry detachment than I would be at reading Mass.'[10]

But the supply situation was even more deplorable. Seckendorf
addressed a string of complaints about it to Vienna. Only half the
necessary provision waggons had arrived, there were not enough
draught oxen and horses, two-thirds of such harness as was
available had rotted, flour was short, there was no hay, provision
for the sick and wounded was inadequate, there was not enough
money to pay the troops. It was a long list of deficiencies and on
June 21st while he was adding to it, the Emperor's son-in-law,
Franz Stefan of Lorraine, arrived to take part in the campaign
as a 'volunteer'. He brought with him two chamberlains, a
secretary, a confessor, three doctors, eight cooks, four serving
men, and a baggage train which included twenty-four armchairs,
three large tents and a baldachin, table silver, carpets, quantities
of food and wine, and enough drinking water to last through the
entire campaign.[11] Franz Stefan's arrival did not improve the
Commander-in-Chief's temper as he contemplated the chaotic
supply position of his army.

In addition to everything else, after very heavy rain in the
spring the Danube had overflowed its banks, turning the low-
lying area round Belgrade into a vast lake, and greatly impeding
troop movements. In view of this the Imperial rescript which
the Duke of Lorraine brought with him ordering Seckendorf
to advance at once bore a certain air of unreality and in his reply
to it the Field-Marshal made no attempt to gloss over the situation. The floods, he stated bluntly, made any immediate advance
impossible and, since the line of march to Vidin lay along the
banks of the Danube, no attack on that fortress could be mounted
for the next two months. He therefore proposed to reverse the
decision taken in the spring and to march on Nish. Seckendorf's
proposals were not well received in Vienna, but the situation
was now beyond argument. On July 7th the Emperor signed a
further, and somewhat tart, rescript to the Field-Marshal which
deplored his delay in advancing, urged speedy action, and
grudgingly consented to his proposals. By the time this reached
Belgrade Seckendorf had already set out for Nish.

It was by now July and very hot indeed. The rain had made such tracks as existed nearly impassable, and the Morava, contrary to expectation, proved to be barely navigable. Two thousand extra waggons and 10,000 draught oxen were therefore needed as the army moved away from its supply line on the Danube, but the country was so thinly inhabited that it was impossible to obtain them locally. Water was short, half the bread had gone bad, many of the soldiers, burdened with muskets five feet long, sweating in thick cloth coats and breeches, collapsed by the way from sheer exhaustion, and had to be driven on with blows by their officers.

On July 14th a manifesto was published in Vienna formally declaring war on the Sultan. Orders were given that, as in former wars against the Turks, bells (the *Türkenglocken*) were to be rung at seven o'clock every morning throughout the Empire, and that all its inhabitants would then fall on their knees and pray for victory. The Emperor and the entire Court went in solemn procession to St. Stephen's Cathedral where a service was held invoking the protection of the Almighty for the Imperial cause. On the same day Seckendorf and his troops at last reached the Turkish frontier. An officer, accompanied by an interpreter and a trumpeter, was sent forward with a letter to the Pasha of Nish informing him that any resistance would be overcome by force. He returned with a Turkish Aga who did not attempt to conceal the fact that no attack had been expected, and asked for a ten days respite in order to give the Pasha time to obtain orders from Constantinople as to whether or not he should capitulate. Seckendorf rejected this request and gave orders for the advance to be resumed. It seemed clear that the Imperial Resident at the Porte had succeeded in deceiving the Turks and that a surprise attack had been achieved. Talman, the Field-Marshal very possibly reflected, had done a great deal more to help him than all the members of the Hofkriegsrat put together.

ﾞﾞ

An Abortive Peace Congress

Nemirow, July–October 1737

On the 14th of July 1737, while Seckendorf and his army were still struggling towards Nish, Talman, the Imperial Resident at the Sublime Porte, unaware of this, was sweltering in a tent pitched in the steppe about a day's march from Nemirow, a small town in southern Poland. Together with the Reis Effendi and three other restive, peevish, and suspicious Turks, he had sat there for three weeks, and he was beginning to find that his exhortations to his companions on the subject of the virtue of patience were wearing a little thin. He consoled himself with the thought that it was an achievement to have got them there at all. He had received powers from Vienna to act as mediator nearly a year ago. Four months had then elapsed until, after unending badgering, he had managed, in mid-December, to extract an invitation from the Grand Vizier to come and discuss the matter. His journey to the latter's camp at Babadagh near the mouth of the Danube, over abominable roads, sustained by the ration of bread, rice and mutton which the Kaimakam of Constantinople provided for itinerant foreign envoys, had been most uncomfortable. On arrival he had found the Turks quite unconvinced either that the Czarina wished for peace or that, if she did, she would ever consent to hand back Azov to the Sultan and, as the Kahya had explained to him, the Grand Vizier's head depended on the fate of that fortress.

Talman had spent the next three months attempting to convince the Grand Vizier that a Peace Congress would be advantageous to the Porte. At times he had despaired of success, and throughout he had received no help at all from either St. Petersburg or Vienna. Ostermann announced that he was prepared to send delegates to the Congress, but nothing, it appeared, would induce him to give any indication of the Czarina's peace terms. From Vienna, Königsegg, while exhorting the Imperial Resident to obtain the Porte's agreement to peace discussions, had sent him a series of blustering letters for onward transmission to the Grand Vizier, all of them drafted in terms calculated to arouse suspicion as to the Emperor's real intentions. Talman had exercised his own discretion about the delivery of these letters and had even suppressed one of them altogether, announcing that it had been accidentally burnt and that he was writing to Vienna to ask for a copy. By such subterfuges, combined with the expenditure of a great deal of money and nervous energy, he had by mid-April succeeded in inducing the Grand Vizier to agree to send a delegation to the proposed Congress.

But it was desirable for the opening of the Congress to be delayed in order to give the Austrian and Russian armies time to overrun as much enemy territory as possible, so that peace might be concluded on the most advantageous terms of *uti posseditis*. Talman appreciated this, but he had also realised that any suggestion to the Turks that the start of discussions should be delayed would fatally undermine the confidence of the Porte in the will of the Emperor and the Czarina for peace. It might even result in his personal incarceration in the Seven Towers. He had therefore decided that he must set out with the Turkish delegates from the Grand Vizier's camp to the Congress (which he thanked God was to be held a very long way away), and then take as long as possible getting there.

Talman had succeeded, as he intended, in prolonging the journey, but it had been most unenjoyable. His party had spent a month crossing a bandit-infested wilderness to the frontier village of Soroki on the Dniester. There the Reis Effendi, alarmed by reports of Austrian troop concentrations in the neighbourhood of Belgrade, demanded to know when the Russians were due to arrive at Nemirow, the place appointed for the Congress. The

Imperial Resident had been obliged to exercise all his diplomatic talents to convince the Turks that, once on the far side of the Dniester, it would be possible to obtain more news of the Russian delegation (which he was well aware was deliberately progressing equally slowly towards Nemirow). Once the party was over the river (and to Talman's unbounded personal relief on neutral territory), he had had no alternative but to reveal that it must be some time before the Russians could reach Nemirow. He never-theless managed to persuade his by now extremely disgruntled travelling companions that it would be beneath their dignity to arrive there before their opponents. In consequence, on July 14th, he was still encamped in most uncongenial company in this particularly unattractive part of the Polish Ukraine.

At least he could congratulate himself that he had succeeded where the other envoys had failed. Fawkener, the British Ambassador, had managed to get to the Grand Vizier's camp, but had made absolutely no progress. The Dutch Ambassador, Calkoen, had not arrived by the time Talman left, and the Imperial Resident was confident that he would have no more success than his British colleague. Above all, and this thought gave Talman great pleasure, the French Ambassador had not even been invited to come and see the Grand Vizier. Admittedly Villeneuve's dragoman Delaria and his special emissary, Baron Tott, had been hanging round the camp, but there was no reason to suppose that they had been able to exert any damaging influence on the Turks. When, on July 20th, the delegation from St. Petersburg having at last arrived, the Imperial Resident entered Nemirow, he felt reasonably optimistic about the prospects for the forthcoming negotiations.

Although Nemirow, 'a pretty large and populous town, well fortified and garrisoned',[1] must have seemed to Talman and his Turkish companions a metropolis after the miserable villages and desolation of the surrounding countryside, it was scarcely Vienna or St. Petersburg. King Augustus III of Poland had done his best to provide the necessary amenities for the Congress. A wooden conference hall was being built; the unfortunate Count Potocki, on whose estates Nemirow lay, had been instructed to keep open house for the delegates, and 1,500 Polish soldiers were detailed to guard them from attack by marauding bandits. There was, however, one defect which the King was powerless to remedy. Nemirow was a very long way from anywhere at all; the better part of 1,000 miles from St. Petersburg, and about 500 miles from Vienna and Constantinople. It was therefore impossible for the delegates to the Congress either to communicate rapidly with their home governments, or to keep in close touch with the progress of the war, with the fortunes of which the outcome of their negotiations was inevitably linked. As the events of the next three months were to show, the isolation of Nemirow had a disastrous effect on the Congress.

The conference hall was not ready when the delegates reached Nemirow, and there was no question of starting the formal proceedings before it was completed, for the protocol of the day demanded that these must take place in appropriate surroundings so that the dignity of the monarchs represented there might be maintained. This suited Talman, his colleague Count Ostein and the Russian delegation led by Neplyuev, the former Resident in Constantinople, for so far as they knew the armies of their respective rulers were continuing to advance. Therefore, they reasoned, the longer the formal opening of the Congress was delayed, the more anxious the Turks would become to conclude peace. In the meantime steps could be taken to render them still more amenable.

The Turkish delegates by now knew of the advance of the Imperial army and the fiction that Talman was at Nemirow as a mediator could no longer be maintained. He considered that it was only possible to negotiate with the Turks with, as he put it, 'a sword in one's hand', and together with Ostein and the Russians lost no opportunity of stressing the strength of the allied armies and raising every possible objection to the wording of the credentials of the Reis Effendi and his colleagues. This browbeating and haggling lasted until the beginning of August when news arrived that Seckendorf had captured Nish, and that Ochakov had been stormed by Münnich. The rejoicing with which the announcement of these victories was received in Vienna (where the

The Emperor's Chancellor, Count Sinzendorf, from an engraving by
Claude Drevet after a painting by Rigaud

The Grand Vizier, from a painting by J. B. Vanmour

Emperor went in solemn procession to a Te Deum in St. Stephen's Cathedral), and in St. Petersburg (where there were fireworks and the Czarina gave a ball), was fully shared by the Austrian and Russian delegates at Nemirow, who were now happily convinced that the Turks were reduced to a state where they would accept any peace terms which were put before them.

Whatever had been proclaimed to the world at large, these terms were scarcely moderate. Talman had been instructed by Königsegg to demand the razing of the fortress of Vidin, reparations for the entire cost of the campaign, and retention of all areas occupied by the Emperor's forces since the outbreak of the war. The latter, Königsegg had confidently written before the Imperial army had even begun to advance, would include a great deal of Serbia and Bosnia, and a substantial part of Wallachia and Moldavia. Ostermann's list of peace terms had reached Neplyuev and his colleagues while they were on the way to Nemirow. The Count laid down as the *sine qua non* for any settlement the extension of the Russian frontier to the Dniester and far into Tartar territory in the Kuban, very large compensation for Tartar raids into Russian territory, freedom of navigation for Russian ships through the Black Sea to the Mediterranean and, if the Tartars of the Crimea could not be resettled in some other part of the Ottoman Empire, the ceding to Russia of two fortresses which would enable the Czarina to control the peninsula. If the Turks agreed to these terms the Tartar problem would be finally settled, and with this Ostermann was prepared to be content, but he saw no harm in trying to extract still more. He therefore added that if the Russian armies were continuing their victorious progress by the time the Congress opened, Neplyuev and his colleagues should also demand that Moldavia and Wallachia be made into independent principalities under Russian protection, which would for all practical purposes establish the frontier of the Czarina's dominions on the Danube.

But soon after Ostermann's directive arrived, the Russian delegates learnt to their dismay that the Emperor's armies were advancing deep into Moldavia and Wallachia. Any demand that these provinces should come under Russian protection would therefore be bitterly resisted not only by the Turks but also by the Austrians. Neplyuev drew Ostermann's attention to this, and asked urgently for further instructions. Unfortunately his request reached St. Petersburg when the capture of Ochakov was being celebrated, and the entire capital was convinced that nothing could prevent Münnich from continuing his victorious advance. Ostermann curtly replied that since the war was going so well Neplyuev should certainly insist on the extension of the Russian sphere of influence to the Danube, and added a short but acid homily reminding his delegates that they were not at Nemirow to conclude peace terms which would be agreeable to the Emperor, but to act in the best interests of the Czarina.

Ostermann's letter took some time to reach Nemirow. When it arrived it made no sense at all to Neplyuev and his colleagues, for they had received information from Talman and Ostein which threw a very different light on the progress of Münnich's, campaign. It was derived from a report from Colonel Barenklau, the Austrian liaison officer with the Russian army, who evidently had a very low opinion indeed of the Emperor's allies. According to Barenklau, Münnich and his army of over 60,000 men encumbered by an enormous baggage train had taken over three months to reach Ochakov. By the time they got there the heat was appalling, and for over eight miles around there was not a stick of wood, a scrap of forage or a drop of water. The fortress was garrisoned by over 20,000 of the best troops in the Ottoman army, the ground was too hard to mine, and the Russian siege artillery had not arrived. Nevertheless within forty-eight hours, overriding as usual the opinion of all his generals, and without even conducting a careful reconnaissance of the defences, Münnich had given orders for the fortress to be stormed. At first it had seemed as though the attack must fail. The Field-Marshal had lost his nerve, and flung his sword on the ground declaring that all was lost. Then the main Turkish powder magazine blew up, and in the resulting confusion the Cossacks broke into Ochakov. In the massacre which followed 20,000 Turks perished, and within twenty-four hours the stench of decaying corpses was such that the Russians had to withdraw fifteen miles from the fortress. In defiance of every known rule of warfare, at a cost of over 3,000 dead, and assisted by an astonishing stroke of luck, Münnich had achieved his objective, but Barenklau was not impressed. There was, he observed scornfully, no Russian general at Ochakov fit to be more than a captain, and their losses had been so great that they would be incapable of undertaking any further operations in the present campaigning season.

Talman and Ostein were thoroughly alarmed by Barenklau's report, for it looked as though the Austrians might, if the war continued, be left alone to sustain the whole weight of the Turkish onslaught. Neplyuev and his colleagues were, for their own reasons, equally alarmed, particularly as they had received news that Lacy, after burning and plundering a large part of the peninsula, had run short of supplies and was retreating from the Crimea. They addressed a second appeal to Ostermann summarising the information which they had been given, pointing out that the failure of the Czarina's armies made it quite impossible to advance a claim on her behalf to Moldavia and Wallachia and asking again for further instructions.

Nearly four weeks had now elapsed since the delegates first arrived at Nemirow, and during that time the Russians and Austrians had become increasingly suspicious of one another. In consequence there had been no consultation between them as to a joint line of approach in the forthcoming negotiations and each was totally unaware of the peace terms which the other intended to put forward. This unhappy state of affairs did not augur well for their prospects of success at the Congress the opening of which, the building of the conference hall having been completed, could now no longer be postponed.

The first formal session took place on August 16th. Protocol was strictly observed. At precisely the same moment the Austrian and the Russians entered the hall by one door, and the Turks by another. They sat down at two long tables, and Count Ostein delivered (to the boredom of everyone), a pompous oration in Latin, after which the delegates exchanged credentials. The second meeting, two days later, was devoted to Russian complaints about the Tartars and Turkish counter-complaints about the Cossacks. At the third meeting the Russians, still without further instructions from Ostermann, outlined their terms. The Turks were horrified and rejected them out of hand. The Austrians were outraged. After the meeting was over Talman and Ostein addressed a written protest to Neplyuev pointing out at great length that the Emperor would never admit the Czarina's claim to include Moldavia and Wallachia within her sphere of influence. At the next session, three days later, the Congress came to a grinding halt. Neplyuev made an attempt to be conciliatory which deceived nobody. The atmosphere deteriorated sharply when the Austrians for the first time stated their terms and Talman, acting on the latest instructions which he had received from Vienna, claimed for the Emperor Moldavia and Wallachia (which infuriated the Russians) and, on the grounds of *uti posseditis*, Vidin and large areas of territory which, as the Turks were aware, the Imperial army had not captured. The Reis Effendi replied that he had no authority to agree to the terms of either the Emperor or the Czarina, and forced their delegates to agree a forty-day suspension of negotiations while he referred to the Grand Vizier and the Sultan for fresh instructions.

The next few weeks were extremely trying for Talman, Neplyuev and their colleagues, all of whom were by this time suffering from bouts of fever and felt frequently 'out of order'. A series of depressing reports began to reach Nemirow from the battle-fronts. Münnich had been forced through lack of supplies to give up all idea of any further advance and, leaving a garrison in Ochakov, was retreating with great difficulty to his winter quarters. Lacy, his supply fleet sunk by the Turks, had withdrawn from the Crimea. Hildburghausen had been defeated in Bosnia and the Emperor's troops were withdrawing from Wallachia, Seckendorf, after weeks of indecision at Nish, had left a garrison there and set out to march 150 miles north over appalling country in a belated attempt to come to Hildburghausen's assistance.

This series of disasters in the field did not improve relations between the allied delegations at Nemirow. Each correctly suspected the other of endeavouring to negotiate a separate peace with the Turks—for this was what each was being exhorted by its government to do. Talman and Neplyuev in turn made a secret and quite unsuccessful approach to the Reis Effendi and his colleagues who, delighted by this evidence of the lack of the unity between their enemies, did all they could to foster it. They informed the Russians that they were ready to conclude peace with the Czarina provided she would sever her alliance with the Emperor; they hinted to the Austrians that they would consider peace with the Emperor provided he abandoned the Czarina; but to neither would they reveal the terms on which the Sultan might be prepared to conclude peace. They became increasingly intransigent. Finally they were extremely rude to Talman and Ostein. After citing the Koran, the Bible, and Grotius in proof of their assertion that Russia and Austria had infringed the rights of God and man in starting the war, they went on to recall the crushing defeat which they had inflicted on the Christians at the battle of Mohács in 1526, and ended by grumbling at the cost to the Sultan of Talman's journey to Nemirow. It was only too apparent that nothing more could be done until the Reis Effendi received the instructions which he had requested from Constantinople.

In Constantinople the French Ambassador had learnt with satisfaction of the arrival of the Reis Effendi's emissary from Nemirow. For the past eight months Villeneuve had remained peacefully in the Ottoman capital, apparently uninformed and, so Talman assumed, quite unable to influence the course of events. In fact he was sadly mistaken, for Villeneuve was not only well informed of the progress of the Imperial Resident's negotiations, but had done a great deal to impede them.

When, at the beginning of the year, the Marquis had dispatched his dragoman, Delaria, and Baron Tott to the Grand Vizier's camp, he had instructed them to make every effort to ensure that the Turks should under no circumstances agree to conclude peace on terms damaging to French interests in the Ottoman Empire. Delaria and Tott, well supplied with money to secure influential friends, had carried out their mission exactly as the Ambassador wished and in April, before Talman and the Turkish delegates left for Nemirow, were able to report to him that the attitude

of the Turks at the forthcoming Congress would be all that
France would desire. This, however, was only the beginning
of their achievements. Towards the end of July, before the
Congress had even opened, an exhausted Tott arrived at the
French Embassy in Constantinople. He had ridden hard, for he
had been entrusted by the Grand Vizier with a letter of great
importance. It was addressed to no less a person than His Eminence Cardinal Fleury, to whom it was to be forwarded by the
Marquis de Villeneuve, who was described therein as 'Ambassa-.
dor of France at the Sublime Porte and our special friend'.
Although Charles VI was referred to as 'Our most esteemed
friend the German Emperor', it was clear that the Grand Vizier
neither regarded the Emperor as a friend, nor considered that
his conduct was in any way estimable. The Czarina received
similar treatment. The most biting invective was reserved for
Talman—'this Ambassador who poses as the Ambassador of a
Court which always keeps its word'.[2] After this preamble the
Grand Vizier came to the point, and formally requested His
Most Christian Majesty of France to mediate in the war.

Villeneuve had read that letter with gratification, but with no
illusions, for this was no more than the first step towards the
objective for which he was working. After dispatching Tott to
France to bear the letter to Cardinal Fleury, he had ordered
Delaria to insinuate to the Grand Vizier that the Reis Effendi and
his colleagues should remain at Nemirow until such time as the
Russian and Austrian armies were on the way back to their winter
quarters, after which they should leave for Constantinople under
the pretext of seeking fresh instructions, promising Talman and
Neplyuev that they would return in the spring. This manœuvre,
Delaria was to explain to the Grand Vizier, would give the Turks
time to assemble their troops for an offensive against the Emperor,
and then they could offer to resume negotiations under French
mediation. The Reis Effendi's emissary had arrived from Nemirow
before Delaria had had time to carry out these orders, but while
this was not precisely what the French Ambassador had intended,
he was not displeased, for it was a satisfactory proof that the
attitude of the Porte was stiffening.

Meanwhile Tott had reached Paris to find the capital rejoicing over the first reports of the reverses suffered by the Imperial army. 'One does not see a man here', the British Ambassador informed Whitehall, 'but what seems pleased at any disadvantage on the Emperor's side.'³ In the circumstances Tott was granted an immediate audience by Fleury, and the Cardinal, confident that public opinion would support any policy likely still further to discomfort Charles VI, acted without delay. On the 17th of October he dictated and signed two letters. The first, to the Grand Vizier, stated that, provided the Emperor would give his consent and obtain the Czarina's agreement, His Most Christian Majesty the King of France would graciously accede to the request of the Porte and mediate between the conflicting powers. The second was addressed to the Marquis de Villeneuve and authorised him, once the consent of the Emperor and the Czarina had been obtained, to proceed to Nemirow in the capacity of Plenipotentiary charged with the mediation, for which purpose the necessary credentials were enclosed.

This letter did not reach the French Ambassador until December 7th, and by this time it was out of date in one vital aspect. The Congress of Nemirow, where it was specifically stated in his credentials Villeneuve's mediation should be conducted, had collapsed. At a final stormy session the Reis Effendi on the Grand Vizier's instructions had demanded the return of Ochakov and the razing of Azov and, when Neplyuev refused to entertain this proposal, had stalked out of the conference hall, and within a few hours had left for Constantinople. The Austrian and Russian delegations had no alternative but to follow his example and depart to their respective capitals. The Congress which had been brought into being through a great deal of political dishonesty, had ended on the level of a diplomatic farce.⁴ It was lamentably apparent to Villeneuve that, not only must he obtain revised credentials before he could formally offer himself in the role of mediator, but also that now any suggestion of peace from any quarter whatsoever would be highly suspect to the Porte.

CHAPTER X

The Second Round

Vienna–St. Petersburg–Paris–the Battlefields–
Constantinople, October 1737–December 1738

Early in 1737 Villeneuve had been urged by Versailles to rouse
the Turks from their lethargy into defending themselves against
their enemies. Towards the end of the year, when he was
instructed to use his good offices to bring the war to an end, he
thought a little sardonically of these earlier instructions, for the
pendulum had now swung violently in the other direction. In
Constantinople the population, incited by fanatical preachers,
seethed with hatred against the entire Christian world, and recruits
flocked to the Sultan's standard. Ssubhi the official Ottoman
historian, summarising the prevailing feeling, described the
Austrians and Russians as ravens and crows intent on destroying
with their talons the well-tended rose garden of the Sultan's
dominions, and invoked against them a text from the Koran,
'Kill them, as they killed you, and drive them out as they drove
you out.'[1] Public opinion in the Ottoman capital clamoured for
the continuation of the war; the ministers of the Porte feared a
revolt if they attempted to restrain it, and in any case saw no
reason for doing so. The first attempt to regain Ochakov from
the Russians had failed but a second would no doubt succeed. In
the Balkans the frontier Pashas had recaptured Nish, regained all
the ground which the Imperial forces had overrun in their
surprise attack, and then deprived the Emperor of much of the
territory which he had acquired twenty years earlier at the Peace
of Passarowitz. If the whole weight of the Ottoman army was

thrown against the Austrians, great victories must be won, and it was even possible that the Turkish crescent would once again fly triumphantly over Belgrade.

In December the all-powerful Kizlar Aga, convinced of the necessity for vigorous leadership in the next campaign, contrived the fall of the Grand Vizier, and the appointment in his place of Jegen Mohammed Pasha, the Kaimakam of Constantinople. Jegen is the Turkish word for 'devil'. The new Grand Vizier, notorious for his skill in extorting money for the Imperial Treasury, was rough, overbearing, a fanatical Muslim, and far more inclined to war than peace. No sooner had he assumed office than he turned for advice to Bonneval.

1737 had been a year of great activity for Bonneval. He had produced excellent maps for the Turkish army commanders; 'fed' the Dutch Ambassador with accounts of Turkish successes in Persia designed to impress the Austrians and Russians with the military prowess of the Ottoman army; attempted (unsuccessfully) to decipher intercepted dispatches between foreign envoys and their governments, and composed a number of memorandum on the strategy to be adopted in the war. In these he stressed that the main Turkish military effort should be concentrated against the Emperor, the Tartars and the wastes of the steppe being left to contain the Russians. He had also advised the Porte to take another step likely to embarrass the Emperor, and to summon Josepi Rákóczi to Constantinople.

Joseph Rákóczi was the eldest son of the exiled Hungarian rebel leader Prince Franz Rákóczi II who had died two years earlier. He was in France at the time of his father's death, where he was more notorious for his love affairs and debts than for either intelligence or good sense. Bonneval nevertheless considered that Rákóczi might be a useful additional pawn in the struggle with the Emperor, and therefore urged Jegen Mohammed Pasha to exploit the young Prince's arrival to the utmost. The new Grand Vizier accepted the renegade's advice. Joseph Rákóczi was allowed to make a state entry into Constantinople, after which he was received with great ceremony by the Sultan, who formally recognised him as Prince of Siebenburgen. The provision of an army corps to operate with Rákóczi against Hungary was an important feature of the plan of campaign which Bonneval submitted to a Council of War presided over by the Grand Vizier.

From the French Embassy on the heights of Pera, Villeneuve had an excellent view of the brilliantly illuminated ship bringing Rákóczi and his suite of exiled Hungarians as it dropped anchor in the Bosphorus. He found the sight distasteful. The ostentatious reception given to yet another enemy of the Emperor seemed to him to be a further sign that the new Grand Vizier, advised by Bonneval, was determined to continue the war regardless of hazards, and from this course the French Ambassador was at that time powerless to deter him. Until he received revised credentials from Versailles he could not formally assume the role of mediator; neither the Emperor nor the Czarina had yet authorised him to act on their behalf, and he had no idea of the terms on which any of the contending parties might now be prepared to end the conflict.

The more Villeneuve considered the situation the more worried he became. A great deal had to be co-ordinated between Paris, Vienna and St. Petersburg before the real work of mediation could begin, and this co-ordination could not be done speedily. Since France had no diplomatic relations with Russia, all communication between Fleury and Ostermann had to be conducted through the intermediary of Vienna. The fastest courier might take a week to ride from Paris to Vienna, and from there, after the Imperial Chancery (which was notoriously dilatory) had prepared the necessary documents, be another fourteen days on the road to St. Petersburg. On the most optimistic calculation it seemed unlikely that the Cardinal could extract the necessary assurances and authorisations from the Emperor and the Czarina and, in the short time which remained before the next campaigning season, forward them to Constantinople. And to wait till they arrived before taking action could, the French Ambassador was gloomily aware, be disastrous, for in the meantime the Grand Vizier might decide to withdraw his predecessor's request for French mediation, take the field, and be defeated. The Sultan had

200,000 men under arms, but, in spite of Bonneval's efforts, few of them were trained in modern tactics and, should it come to a pitched battle against a better-led army, they would probably be beaten. Villeneuve preferred not to think of the peace terms which the Russians and Austrians would then impose on the Porte, for they would undoubtedly be such as to endanger if not destroy the whole French position in the Ottoman Empire. He decided that, his lack of credentials notwithstanding, he must at once endeavour to obtain an assurance from the Grand Vizier that French mediation was still acceptable to the Porte, and then try to persuade him to do no more than remain on the defensive in the forthcoming campaign.

Villeneuve knew from past experience that when things went badly Jegen Mohammed was apt to lose his nerve and would then listen to advice, but that otherwise he was obstinate and self-opinionated. It soon became apparent that he was in one of his worst moods. At first he refused to see the French Ambassador at all. When the Marquis eventually succeeded in obtaining an audience and stressed that the good offices of King Louis XV remained at the Sultan's disposal, he was met with the discouraging reply that while these would no doubt be acceptable at some future date, at present the state of public opinion was such that the war must continue.

At the end of this depressing and useless interview it seemed to Villeneuve that deadlock had been reached. However, a few weeks later a courier arrived with the revised credentials which he had requested from Fleury and a letter from Count Sinzendorf containing the Emperor's and the Czarina's agreement to French mediation and enumerating their peace terms. The Emperor, the Count wrote, would be content with a return to the frontiers agreed at the Peace of Passarowitz in 1718 after Prince Eugen's victories, and the Czarina would graciously restore Ochakov to the Sultan provided she retained Azov. The French Ambassador had little hope that these terms would be in any way acceptable to the Porte, but at least they provided him with an excuse for a further interview with the Grand Vizier. This took place a few days later, and was again entirely unproductive.

Jegen Mohammed demanded from the Czarina the return of Azov and Kinburn as well as Ochakov, and from the Emperor the fortress of Belgrade and Temesvár, as well as an acknowledgement of Joseph Rákóczi as ruler of Siebenburgen. These were terms which Villeneuve had no authorisation to negotiate and which he knew neither Vienna nor St. Petersburg would consider. After pointing this out, he expatiated on the dangers of continuing the war and the risks of campaigning in the wastes of the Ukraine or in the defiles of Serbia, but the Grand Vizier remained unmoved. The Turks, he said, were ready to make peace and to make war. With this unprofitable observation the audience ended. Villeneuve, who had only been able to induce Jegen Mohammed to agree in principle that it was undesirable to have more than one mediator, later said with some exasperation to a colleague that he found the ministers of the Porte 'difficult and backward'.[2]

The French Ambassador next discovered that, although the Czarina had nominally accepted the mediation of France, Ostermann, no doubt in the hope that better terms might be obtained for Russia, had suggested to the Porte firstly that the captured Pasha of Ochakov, secondly that the Persian Nadir Shah might be drawn in to the negotiations of a peace. Both these proposals came to nothing, and so were no more than irritating to Villeneuve, but he was infuriated when the British and Dutch Ambassadors announced that, at the request of the Czarina, they had been instructed by their respective governments to mediate jointly with France. The French Ambassador had no great opinion of either of his colleagues (whom he had described in the previous year as following Talman round the Grand Vizier's camp like a couple of poodles), and he was determined that France must at all costs retain the sole mediation. He therefore took refuge in polite evasiveness, explained that delighted as he would be to act with them, he had no instructions to do anything of the sort, and suggested that they should make an approach to the Porte on their own initiative.

Fawkener and Calkoen spent the next six weeks endeavouring, quite without success, to gain audience of the Grand Vizier. This was gratifying to Villeneuve, but by the end of March he was bound to admit that he had done no better. His efforts to persuade Jegen Mohammed Pasha to modify the terms on which he would be prepared to conclude peace had failed. Nothing, it appeared, could make the Grand Vizier comprehend that the Russians were as determined to keep Azov as the Emperor was adamant in his refusal to recognise Joseph Rákóczi's claim to Siebenburgen. Neither, it seemed, could anyone dissuade the Porte from continuing the war.

At the beginning of April Jegen Mohammed left for the headquarters of the army at Adrianople. Villeneuve repeated his tactics of the previous year and dispatched Delaria to the Grand Vizier's camp accompanied by Peysonnel, a newly arrived member of the French Embassy staff, who was instructed to impress on the Grand Vizier that Villeneuve could at any time come to Adrianople to negotiate at least a preliminary peace. Peysonnel contrived to have a number of discussions with Jegen Mohammed, but they all foundered on the subject of Azov, and the question of the recognition of Rákóczi.

By the middle of May Villeneuve was reluctantly coming to the conclusion that he had exhausted all possible means of diplomatic action when he received a most important letter from Versailles. It authorised him to declare solemnly to the Porte that the King of France would guarantee any treaty concluded under his mediation. This was the first time that any Christian power had offered to protect the existence and security of the Ottoman Empire, and was the strongest card which Cardinal Fleury was able at that stage to give his Ambassador. Villeneuve immediately proceeded to play it, and sent an urgent courier to Peysonnel instructing him to impress the significance of this guarantee on the Grand Vizier. Peysonnel did so with such effect that Jegen Mohammed wrote to the Sultan recommending the negotiation of a preliminary peace under French mediation. For a short time Villeneuve permitted himself to think that his efforts might at the eleventh hour be crowned with success. His hopes were dashed when on June 26th Peysonnel returned to Constantinople. He reported that the Sultan had replied to the Grand Vizier that he must consult with his advisers and do what he thought best. The outcome of that consultation had been totally negative and Jegen Mohammed's reply, which Peysonnel brought with him, reiterated all the previous Turkish demands.

A few months earlier the Reis Effendi had explained to Villeneuve, 'Our government is more democratic than you realise; in St. Petersburg and in Vienna decisions depend on one or two people who are responsible to no one. With us, on the contrary, however absolute a ruler the Sultan may be he cannot conclude peace without the advice of the Mufti and the consent of the men of the Law.'³ The French Ambassador now had bitter proof of the truth of that statement and he was at last compelled to inform both Fleury and Sinzendorf that he had failed. Peace, it now seemed, could only be decided by force of arms, and unless the gap could be narrowed between the terms on which the opposing sides were prepared to conclude it, it might be long delayed. Without fresh instructions which must embody concessions by both the Emperor and the Czarina, he could make no progress with the Porte. When (or whether) he received these instructions must, Villeneuve realised as he dictated his letters to Versailles and Vienna, depend on the degree to which the Cardinal could persuade (or frighten) the Austrians and Russians into some sort of sense. Altogether the Marquis did not feel optimistic as he resigned himself to enduring his tenth successive summer in Constantinople.

The problem of dealing with the Emperor and the Czarina had been one of Fleury's principal concerns ever since the beginning of 1737, when King Louis XV had dismissed Chauvelin, the Keeper of the Seals and *ipso facto* Minister of Foreign Affairs, appointing in his place on the Cardinal's advice M. Amelot de Chaillou, one of the Intendants of Finance. The change delighted His Eminence. Chauvelin had latterly only too often failed to defer to his views. Amelot by contrast was a colourless career civil servant, meticulous in the execution of detail and anxious to please his superiors. He was totally ignorant of foreign affairs and it was rumoured that on assuming office he had to be taught the relative positions of the North Sea and the Mediterranean,⁴ but this did not matter in the least to Fleury for, after Chauvelin's dismissal, the Cardinal assumed personal direction of the foreign policy of France. He was then eighty-four, but appeared to find this no burden, indeed as he shortly afterwards informed the British Ambassador, business 'which had sunk him before was now an amusement to him'.⁵ In pursuit of this 'amusement' he was much concerned with the question of containing the growing power of Russia which he feared might become a grave danger to the position of France, not only in the Levant, but in Europe as a whole. If Russia was to be held in check both the Habsburg and the Ottoman Empire must be preserved, for the collapse of either would leave a vacuum which could only be to the Czarina's advantage. The Cardinal, therefore, neither wished to see the Russians and the Austrians on the Bosphorus nor the Turks once again at the gates of Vienna, and considered that an early end to the war and a peace concluded under French mediation was imperative.

Towards the end of 1737 Fleury had hoped that the situation was improving. The Porte had accepted the mediation of France and there seemed to be every reason to think that the Emperor would soon do likewise. All reports from Vienna described the consternation in the Imperial capital over the disasters of the last campaign. 'Things are very bad . . . everybody laments, and nobody seems inclined to give any advice, or to put any resolution into execution.'⁶ Nobody lamented more than Charles VI who was alleged to have wailed, 'The pain inflicted on us by the waste of money, the loss of Nish, the foregoing of easily obtainable advantages, are as nothing compared with the wound caused by this blow to the honour of our arms.'⁷ General Doxat, the defender of Nish was beheaded; Seckendorf was dismissed and put under house arrest pending trial; from the pulpits of Vienna Jesuit preachers proclaimed that the failure of the campaign was due to the fact that the command of the Imperial army had been entrusted to a Protestant. All observers agreed that the dearest wish of the Emperor was to abandon his ally and get out of the war if this could be done with the slightest vestige of honour.

Fleury calculated that if the Emperor made a separate peace the

Austro–Russian alliance might collapse and, even if the Czarina decided to continue the war alone, the threat to the Ottoman Empire would be greatly reduced. It was essential to increase the Emperor's misgivings so, having instructed the French envoy in Vienna to lose no opportunity of representing to Sinzendorf and his colleagues the risks attached to another campaign, the Cardinal opened a correspondence with Charles VI. In this he protested his sympathy for the Austrian predicament, proclaimed his belief in the importance of Christian solidarity and endeavoured to convey the impression that France would mediate in the war, not only as an honest broker, but also as a sincere friend. At intervals he interspersed these expressions of goodwill with acid comments on the unfriendly behaviour of Austrian diplomats, and did not hesitate to remind the Emperor (rather sharply) that the forbearance of His Majesty King Louis XV had saved him a great deal of trouble in the Imperial possessions in Italy. Any sensible ruler, he assumed, should be convinced by what he had written of the desirability of getting out of the war and concluding a peace under French mediation.

Fleury was too optimistic, Charles VI was not a sensible ruler. In the cast list of an anonymous satire on the Court of Vienna, written in the form of a contemporary French comedy, he was designated 'Le Capricieux',[8] while the Turkish war was entitled 'Le Naufrage',[9] and the funds for the next campaign as 'L'Inconnu'.[10] The author of this satire was probably a member of the staff of the French Embassy in Vienna,[11] and it may possibly have come to the notice of the Cardinal. If so, by the spring of 1738 he would wholeheartedly have agreed with these epithets, for by then it was clear that the Emperor and his ministers were preparing with little enthusiasm and not much competence to continue the war.

According to Fleury's information the cash to finance the next campaign was most certainly 'inconnu'; as it was rumoured in Vienna that, since the greater part of the Emperor's revenues had already been pledged for several years ahead, Charles might even be reduced to melting down the Imperial plate. Most regiments were below strength, difficulty was being experienced in finding

A Janissary, from a drawing by Weigel

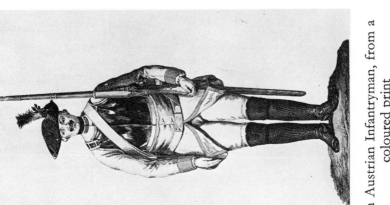

An Austrian Infantryman, from a coloured print

An Ambassador, possibly the Marquis de Villeneuve, received in audience by the Sultan, from a painting by J. B. Vanmour

recruits, and it was unlikely, the Cardinal learnt, that the fighting strength of the army would be above 50,000 men.

His Eminence also heard that, after much indecision, the Emperor had appointed his son-in-law, Franz Stefan Duke of Lorraine who, although courageous, was not a military genius, as Supreme Commander in place of the disgraced Seckendorf with the President of the Hofkriegsrat, Count Königsegg, as his principal lieutenant whose advice the Duke was instructed to seek on all occasions. It was common knowledge in Vienna that Königsegg, who was increasingly troubled by gout, had not the slightest desire to leave the comforts of the capital and had done his best to decline this doubtful honour, protesting that he had little experience of fighting beyond the outer confines of Hungary and did not know the terrain. He had been forced by the Emperor to accept the post, and then obliged to delay his departure to his headquarters while Franz Stefan made a leisurely pilgrimage to Mariazell to invoke the protection of Our Lady of Austria for the forthcoming ordeal. This inevitably meant a late start to the campaign, for which presumably it could only be hoped that the help of Our Lady of Mariazell would compensate. Her assistance was urgently needed, for the Russians had once again refused to contemplate any joint plan of operations with their ally, announcing that Lacy would once again invade the Crimea while (since Biron had not yet been formally invested with the Duchy of Courland, and the Czarina was still anxious to avoid offending the King of Poland) Münnich would once again imitate, as he himself described it, the Children of Israel in the Wilderness, and advance across the southern steppes in the direction of the fortress of Bender on the lower reaches of the Dniester.

Whatever the misgivings of the Emperor, the Russians appeared to be confident of victory and determined to fight on to achieve it. But Fleury thought it possible that by the end of the summer their resolution might have weakened. By then, he calculated, a course of action on which he had embarked should be beginning to show results. The problem of how to render St. Petersburg less intransigent had greatly exercised him, and he had finally reached the conclusion that it could only be done by enlisting Sweden in active support of French policy. Sweden, like Turkey, was a traditional enemy of Russia but, unlike Turkey, not separated from her by hundreds of miles of barren steppe. St. Petersburg was only a few days journey from the Swedish frontier, and a hostile Sweden would confront the Russians, should they persist in the war against the Sultan, with the possibility of having to fight a war on two fronts. Nothing, the Cardinal considered, was more like to make the Czarina and her ministers amenable over the question of concluding peace with the Porte than the possibility of an attack on their northern flank.

Unfortunately, ever since their crushing defeat by Peter the Great at Poltava in 1709, the Swedes, rent by internal strife, had constituted no threat to Russia. Fleury saw only one means of reviving that threat, and that was to bribe the Swedes to conclude a treaty of alliance with France which would be clearly aimed against Russia. There was no doubt that it could be done; there was also no doubt that to do it would cost a great deal of money. The Cardinal was parsimonious, and the sum involved was very large indeed. But, and it was a measure of the importance which he attached to the question of bringing pressure to bear on St. Petersburg, he finally came to the conclusion that it must be expended. He authorised Saint Séverin, the French Ambassador in Stockholm, to buy over the entire Swedish Parliament to the side of France. The project proved to be even more expensive than Fleury had reckoned. There were 700 Swedish Members of Parliament to be bribed and Bestuzhev, the Russian Ambassador in Stockholm, liberally provided with funds by Ostermann, was bidding against Saint Séverin for their support. However, the French Ambassador reported that, whatever the financial inducements offered by Bestuzhev, the Swedes still disliked Russia and, while they happily accepted the Russian Ambassador's money, remained open to a French counter-bid. By the spring of 1738 Fleury, shuddering at the expense which he had authorised, was waiting anxiously for an indication that it had been justified.

In May a letter arrived from Ostermann which the Cardinal found most gratifying. The Russian Foreign Minister protested that the Czarina had no ambition other than to secure her southern frontier against the Tartars, and that the moderation of her war aims was proved by the joy with which she accepted the mediation of France. He denied that his ruler had ever attempted to double-cross the Emperor, or that there had been any failure to keep him informed, and concluded by pressing for an exchange of ambassadors and the immediate resumption of diplomatic relations between France and Russia, which, he observed, would eliminate much misunderstanding. The Cardinal passed this letter to some unidentified person (probably Prince Liechtenstein, the Austrian Ambassador in Paris) for comment. The commentator's note on the question of the interchange of information between St. Petersburg and Vienna was particularly caustic— 'Enough documents', he wrote, 'were sent to the Czarina's ministers in St. Petersburg for their information to fill an entire archive—in return for only a few scraps of paper of no consequence', and, he added, there would never have been so many misunderstandings if Ostermann had not been so infernally secretive.[12]

Fleury, who heartily endorsed this opinion of Ostermann, was delighted by the anxiety betrayed by the Count in his letter. It had cost a great deal of money to reduce the Russian Foreign Minister to this state, and would undoubtedly cost a great deal more before the treaty with Sweden was concluded and Russia finally rendered amenable, but it looked as though his plan was succeeding.

The Cardinal did not hurry to answer Ostermann's letter; it would he felt, do no harm to let the Russian Foreign Minister stew for a little. Eventually on May 31st he composed his reply, and it was a masterpiece of smooth diplomatic drafting.[13] France, he explained blandly, had never offered the Porte mediation for she was totally disinterested in the war. She merely wanted to help all parties and, therefore, her behaviour throughout had been 'simple and straightforward'. (This phrase must have infuriated the Russian Foreign Minister.) Fleury then dealt with Ostermann's suggestion that diplomatic relations be resumed and on this subject he was not bland at all. Russia, he observed flatly, had in his view behaved atrociously in the War of the Polish Succession. He personally was prepared, in the interests of the general good, to let bygones be bygones, but Ostermann would appreciate that the honour of His Most Christian Majesty demanded that the Czarina should first designate her representative and then he would in due course appoint his. It was not a point which the Count appreciated in the least, for in the terms of the protocol of the day it was a calculated snub, but he had to accept it. On July 11th he wrote briefly, informing the Cardinal that Prince Cantemir had been instructed to proceed from London to assume the post of Russian Ambassador in Paris.[14] Fleury, when he read this letter, was able to congratulate himself that he was beginning to make the Count climb down.

The correspondence continued throughout the summer. Neither statesman was in the best of health, for Osterman was confined to his house with gout and Fleury appeared to be failing. Foreign envoys found him confused and irritable and there were rumours that he could not live for more than a few months. These caused a heavy fall in shares on the Paris Bourse, but in his letters to Ostermann there was no sign that the Cardinal was failing. In mid-July he expressed himself with devastating clarity on the subject of what he described as the 'ambiguity' in the conflicting instructions sent to Villeneuve by the ministers of the Emperor and the Czarina. This ambiguity was, he wrote, most annoying and had certainly made a most deplorable impression on the Grand Vizier. 'One could not', he concluded in the tones of an elderly governess, 'be too precise and clear where important matters were at stake.'[15] He followed this up with a further letter[16] in which he alleged that Villeneuve's failure to make any progress with the Turks was due to Russian attempts to confuse the issue. In fact if no progress had been made Ostermann had only himself to blame. The Russian Foreign Minister, when replying to this barrage, was evasive and attempted to give away as little as possible, but by the end of September when it was evident that a Franco-Swedish treaty could not be long delayed, he was pushed into protesting to the Cardinal that Russia was only waiting for the appropriate moment to give Villeneuve full powers to negotiate a peace on her behalf.[17] While final success had still to be achieved, the Cardinal was not altogether dissatisfied with his work.

In Constantinople the summer of 1738 was most unpleasant. Food was short, extremely expensive and the foreign envoys had to get a special order from the Porte to enable them to buy flour. A smallpox epidemic, followed by the plague, forced Villeneuve to follow the example of the rest of the diplomatic corps and to leave the city for his country villa where, condemned to enforced inaction, he could only follow with such patience as he could muster the progress of the war from the reports which filtered through to the capital.

By the end of September the French Ambassador, in common with everyone in Constantinople, knew that the cause of the Russians and the Austrians had not prospered. Lacy, compelled once again to invade the Crimea for, it seemed, no better reason than that, as a subsequent historian put it, 'the journey to the Crimea having become fashionable, it had to be undertaken',[18] had once again been beaten by lack of supplies and forced to retreat to his winter quarters.

Münnich had fared no better for, since he knew after three years of war that the steppes through which he must advance had been reduced to a wilderness, he had encumbered himself with a baggage train so large that his army of 50,000 men was virtually immobilised. The generals each had 300 cartloads of personal possessions and provisions. The sergeants were each allowed sixteen, loaded with every kind of provision—salted oxen and pigs, casks of brandy, cases of biscuits, kegs of butter and vinegar, coffee, tea and sugar. As luck would have it the summer was exceptionally hot, the spring grass had withered in the scorching sun, and there was no rain. It was therefore extremely difficult to find enough forage to feed the enormous number of draught oxen, and it took about four hours to strike camp each day. Münnich 'who' (as Lord Crawford, who was serving as a volunteer under his command, reported) 'to do him justice is everywhere',[19] drove his soldiers on, beating off continual Tartar raids, offering a rouble for every enemy head brought to him, and leaving the sick to die where they fell, but in spite of all his efforts the Russians took thirty hours to march a distance which any other army would have covered in four. In consequence the Field-Marshal did not reach the Dniester till the beginning of August, and there found 60,000 Turks awaiting him on the far bank. Even Münnich realised that it would be suicidal to attempt to cross the river in the face of such opposition, but shortage of forage and water made it impossible for him to remain where he was, nor, if the army was to be saved at all, could he retreat over the route by which he had come. There was no alternative but to violate Polish neutrality and take the shortest and easiest route back to his winter quarters, and this he did having achieved nothing.

Finally, before the winter set in one further disaster, which caused great rejoicing in Constantinople, overtook the Russians. The garrisons of Ochakov and Kinburn had been decimated by plague. Reinforcements died as fast as they arrived, and St. Petersburg was compelled to order the razing and evacuation of both fortresses. By the time this grim operation was completed it was estimated that Ochakov alone had cost 60,000 lives.

The 1738 campaign, it was clear to Villeneuve, had been no more successful for the Austrians than it was for the Russians. As usual supplies were inadequate and it had been impossible to assemble enough waggons and draught oxen. River transport was in a deplorable state and, for want of guns and sailors, ships were laid up at Belgrade. When Königsegg reached his headquarters he was no more pleased by the supply position than Seckendorf had been in the previous year, but he had no time to remedy it, for he was confronted by the news that the Turks were already besieging Orsova. This fortress, built at the point downstream from Belgrade where the Danube flows through a narrow defile known today as the Iron Gate, commanded an approach route to Hungary of great strategic importance. Königsegg decided that at all costs Orsova must be relieved. Within ten days of arriving at Belgrade he crossed the Danube with the greater part of the army, and started on the 100-mile march through narrow mountain defiles to the fortress. At first all went well. The Turks were defeated at Kornia thirty miles from Orsova, and it seemed to the delighted Emperor that the honour of the House of Habsburg was redeemed. But then the enemy reappeared in force and Königsegg, short of supplies and forage, beat a hasty retreat. Shortly afterwards Orsova fell and by September 9th, exhausted by the effort to find the Turks rather than by their one battle with them, the Imperial army was encamped under the walls of Belgrade. Men were dying at the rate of 80–100 a day from the plague, malaria and dysentery. Due to the Emperor's false economy in allowing only 40,000 ducats a year for intelligence, the whereabouts of the Grand Vizier and his army was quite unknown, and all ranks from the Commander-in-Chief downwards were extremely frightened. No reinforcements were available, for Königsegg considered it necessary to keep a large force in Siebenburgen to crush any revolt which might be stirred up by Joseph Rákóczi, who was known to have been sent by the Porte to the frontier for this purpose. The Field-Marshal, in indifferent health and exhausted, was determined to preserve the remnants of his army. He therefore disregarded all the Hofkriegrat's exhortations to take some sort of action, and refused to move from the shelter of Belgrade where he remained until he retreated to winter quarters.

When, in the early autumn, Villeneuve returned to Constantinople, it seemed to him that the moment for concluding peace might be slightly nearer. His own position had been strengthened by the arrival of a further set of powers from Fleury authorising him to extend the French guarantee of any treaty which might be concluded to the Russians and the Austrians, as well as to the Turks. He had received credentials from Vienna stating that the Emperor accepted him as mediator and he possessed a document which, if unsatisfactorily worded, indicated that the Czarina, too, would accept him in this capacity. Admittedly, the terms on which Austria and Russia were prepared to conclude peace were still unrealistic, but the French Ambassador considered that after their recent military disasters these must soon be scaled down. In addition, so far as the Emperor was concerned, two major obstacles to the negotiation of peace were no longer operative.

Bonneval through his outspokenness and lack of tact had fallen
out with the Porte, and young Joseph Rákóczi was reported to be
dying. But, as he awaited the return of the Grand Vizier from the
battlefield, Villeneuve remembered uneasily that, before setting
out for the army, Jegen Mohammed Pasha had told him, 'When
we shall know, and have measured, the Emperor's forces, your
good offices will be more or less efficacious.'[20] That 'measure' had
been such that it was possible that his good offices would not be
efficacious at all.

The Marquis' worst fears were realised when, at the end of
October, the Grand Vizier returned in triumph to Constantinople.
The mood of his army was later summed up by their Kadi who
wrote, 'We set out without money, troops, strategy or cohesion,
and we have returned victorious. Clearly our cause is righteous
and Heaven is on our side.'[21] The atmosphere did not seem at all
propitious to the resumption of any form of peace negotiations,
but eventually the French Ambassador managed to persuade
Jegen Mohammed Pasha to agree that further discussions should
be held. On November 24th he had a secret meeting with a
delegation led by the Reis Effendi in a house in the suburbs of
of Constantinople. Villeneuve came to it with the minimum
of attendants and, after coffee and a meal had been served, the
conference began. It could scarcely have got off to a worse start.
The Turkish envoys immediately expressed their dissatisfaction
with the terminology of such authorisation as the Marquis held
from the Czarina, and were incensed when they saw that by a
disastrous clerical error his credentials from the Emperor referred
not to Sultan Mahmoud, but to his deposed predecessor Sultan
Ahmed. The French Ambassador (not for the first time) inwardly
cursed the incompetence of Vienna; it took all his tact to soothe
the Turks down and to persuade them to discuss the terms on
which peace might be concluded. He was so far successful that
five meetings took place, but nothing was achieved. The Reis
Effendi and his colleagues maintained that the Porte would only
contemplate peace with the Emperor if he ceded them both
Temesvár and Belgrade. They also did not hesitate to point out
that the Czarina's offer of Ochakov and Kinburn was useless as

both fortresses had already been razed and evacuated and demanded the razing of Azov which the Reis Effendi described as 'the apple of discord . . . a prostitute who has had too many lovers to be worthy of marrying an honest man'.[22]

The gap between what Villeneuve was authorised to offer and what the Turks demanded was still unbridged and, as he had done the year before, the Ambassador could only write to Vienna and Versailles pointing out that he could make no progress without fresh instructions, and wait, without much hope, for these instructions to arrive before a further campaign began. A year earlier his British colleague had commented in a dispatch to London: 'It is a particular misfortune attending this unhappy War that the parties are so remote and the general commerce of letters so far broken; that it seems difficult to find time for an overture. While the armies are in the field these operations are to decide everything, and the winter is not long enough for a friendly power to make respectively a proposal and receive an answer to it.'[23] It was a telling summary of Villeneuve's predicament which, at the end of 1738, it looked as though nothing short of a miracle or Divine intervention would solve.

CHAPTER XI

꣒꣒꣒꣒꣒꣒꣒꣒꣒꣒꣒꣒꣒꣒꣒꣒꣒꣒꣒꣒꣒꣒꣒꣒꣒꣒꣒꣒꣒

A Mediator is Appointed

Paris–Constantinople–Belgrade, January–August 1739

While Cardinal Fleury as a Prince of the Church did not deny the possibility of Divine intervention, as a practical statesman he was not prepared to rely on it. Therefore, at the end of the summer of 1738 when, to the astonishment of all Paris, his health miraculously improved, he pursued his diplomatic offensive against the Austrians and the Russians with undiminished vigour.

The Cardinal was reasonably certain that, however much he disliked it, the Emperor now had no alternative but to hold to his acceptance of the good offices of France, and would in time, however reluctantly, become very much less demanding over the terms on which he was prepared to conclude peace. Every report from Mirepoix, the French Ambassador in Vienna, indicated that the softening up of Charles and his ministers was proceeding satisfactorily; an opinion which, Fleury would have been gratified to learn, was endorsed by the British envoy in the Imperial capital who reported to his Government: 'This court dares not yet do anything to disoblige M. de Mirepoix, much less M. de Villeneuve, and still less of all the Court of France.'[1]

Softening up the Russians was a tougher proposition, and through the winter of 1738–9 the Cardinal continued to hammer at Ostermann. On November 8th he dictated a stiff letter to the Russian Foreign Minister.[2] The first part of it was devoted to an exposition of the technique of negotiating with the Porte, 'so subject to revolutions that the possibility of obtaining a settlement on reasonable terms during the forthcoming winter must not be despaired of—it is not always the wisest motives which sway the Turks, and the intrigues of the Serail have a great deal more influence on affairs than practical considerations of policy.' Ostermann, whose experience of negotiating with the Turks went back to the Peace of the Pruth in 1711, must have found this lecture exasperating. He cannot have been any more pleased with what followed. If Villeneuve was to be successful, wrote Fleury, he must be given precise instructions as to the ultimate limit of the concessions which the Czarina was prepared to make, and absolute *carte-blanche* to negotiate within those limits. Constantinople was so far away that if the French Ambassador was not allowed to use his own judgement, the moment for concluding peace might be lost. This statement of the obvious was most unpalatable to Ostermann who was still endeavouring to avoid committing the Czarina to any precise definition of her peace terms. Over the next four months he endeavoured to hedge. [3] He urged the early appointment of a French Ambassador to St. Petersburg; wrote in the most flattering terms of the ability with which Villeneuve was conducting this 'thorny' negotiation; endeavoured to place the blame for lack of progress in it on the Emperor, and invoked the Almighty to witness that Russia was merely acting in the defence of Christianity. He tried going over to the attack and, he was careful to point out more in sorrow than in anger, drew attention to the danger of a Turkish–Swedish rapprochement supported by France which he feared, from the presence of two Swedish emissaries in Constantinople, might be imminent. He fully agreed, he assured the Cardinal, that it was a sad fact that lying and lack of sincerity were much in vogue.

Ostermann got nowhere. Fleury replied that he was making every endeavour to speed up the appointment of a French Ambassador to St. Petersburg—and did nothing whatsoever about it. He denied that Villeneuve had any contact with the Swedish emissaries in Constantinople. This was a flat lie, but in the Cardinal's view well worth telling in a good cause.[4] He simply ignored the rest of the Russian Foreign Minister's points, and waited with interest to see what would happen next.

By this time he was in possession of a good deal of information which suggested that the Austro-Russian alliance was strained to the breaking-point. The Russians had endeavoured to put the best face they could on their failure in 1738, and Münnich proclaimed that it was the hand of God which had prevented him from crossing the Dniester for, had he done so, his army would have been decimated not by the Turks but by the plague raging on the far side of the river. Nobody in Europe believed this story, least of all the Austrians who did not attempt to put anything like such a bold face on the situation. The Emperor concealed neither his disappointment at the failure of his army nor his conviction that the campaign had been thoroughly mismanaged. Königsegg, who had been dismissed both from his post as Commander-in-Chief and from his position as President of the Hofkriegsrat, commented with disarming frankness: 'At the end of the campaign the Turks were in retreat and we were still in possession of Belgrade, Temesvár, Slavonia and Siebenburgen, which was more than we had a right to hope for.'5

Candour was all very well—it did not mollify the Russians, who were not slow to express their view that Austrian military ineptitude was to blame for the parlous state of affairs. Vienna promptly riposted with some most unflattering remarks about Münnich. In St. Petersburg the Imperial envoy, Count Ostein, had a blazing row with Biron and finished by telling him that Russia had done nothing during the war 'but making a great noise and killing three Tartars'.6 A few weeks later, and to the scandal of all onlookers, the two of them came to blows in public. The diplomatic corps in St. Petersburg were therefore not unduly surprised when they heard that the Emperor had decided to withdraw Ostein and to replace him by the Marquis de Botta. But the mistrust between the two Governments had by then gone so deep that it could not be remedied by a change of personalities. Each was convinced that the other would conclude a separate peace if the opportunity arose, and their respective ministers did not hesitate to voice their extremely low opinion of their opposite numbers. In St. Petersburg Biron publicly proclaimed that 'he wished no more hurt to his greatest enemy than to be obliged to negotiate with the court of Vienna'.7 In Vienna Bartenstein, the Secretary of the Imperial Privy Council, made no attempt to disguise his dislike of the Russians who, as he told the British envoy, quite apart from being entirely uncommunicative, 'cavilled at every single word or expression'.[8]

The *tu quoques* and mutual recriminations of the allies, reverberated around Europe, effectively conveying the impression that the alliance had never been in worse shape. In addition, as all informed observers agreed, the state of each partner in this alliance left a great deal to be desired. Outwardly the Courts of St. Petersburg and Vienna were as magnificent as ever, for the military failure of 1738 made no difference to either ruler's expenditure. The Czarina ordered new liveries of yellow cloth laced with silver and black velvet for all her personal servants, and her balls and entertainments were if possible more splendid than before. The Emperor continued to hunt, and the round of ceremonial and festivities at his Court continued unaltered. But in fact both rulers were very hard pressed for cash. Money was said to be 'as rare in Russia as learning and manners'.[9] It was well known that the Imperial Treasury was empty. Moreover both rulers were in indifferent health; the Czarina had gout and scurvy; Charles VI was described as being 'more and more embittered, his passions higher, and his resolutions more sudden and violent'.[10] The condition of their respective ministers was not much better. Ostermann was at loggerheads with Biron. Sinzendorf was losing his memory, and the Hofkriegsrat was in a state of chaos which Count Harrach, who succeeded Königsegg as President, had neither the will nor the ability to disentangle. Finally both the Emperor and the Czarina were experiencing great difficulty in raising the necessary recruits to bring their armies up to strength. Recruiting in Russia was proceeding slowly, in spite of an edict ordering every thirty families to provide one man for the army. The Habsburg hereditary territories had already been bled white, and after the disasters of 1737 and 1738 such men as were available were unwilling to come forward to serve in Hungary. Imperial emissaries were scouring the Empire in an endeavour to hire at least 20,000 men to make good the deficiencies in the Emperor's forces.

Fleury deduced from the information which reached him that the Austro-Russian alliance was now mainly held together by the fact that the Grand Vizier's demands were so excessive that neither the Emperor nor the Czarina could accept them as they stood, and therefore had no alternative but to embark on another campaign. But, if the Porte could only be induced to make some concessions, and to agree to the commencement of peace negotiations, Fleury felt confident that it would be possible to end the war. Everything therefore turned on the situation in Constantinople, and from none of his envoys did the Cardinal await news more anxiously than from Villeneuve.

For the first two months of 1739 Villeneuve had little definite to report. Jegen Mohammed Pasha was still in power and making every preparation for the next campaign which, he proudly asserted, would bring the Emperor yapping like a small dog to his heels. The French Ambassador, however, informed Fleury that the Grand Vizier did not lack enemies. His arrogant and overbearing manner was widely resented. He had been criticised for failing to advance to Belgrade, and for paying no attention to the internal situation in the Ottoman Empire. A revolt was simmering in Asia, taxation on account of the war was unbearably high, the granary of the Crimea had been destroyed by the Russians, and starvation was increasing. There were indications that some at least of the ministers of the Porte were anxious for peace, and that, if they could only win over the Kizlar Aga, the fall of the Grand Vizier might not be long delayed.

At the beginning of March the situation was brought to a head by the arrival of the Tartar Khan in Constantinople. For three consecutive years his country had been laid waste by the Russians, and he urged the necessity of an early peace even at the price of sacrificing Azov. His arguments prevailed on the Kizlar Aga who once again exerted his influence with the Sultan. On March 22nd Villeneuve at last had some definite news for Fleury. Jegen Mohammed had been dismissed and Elvias Mohammed appointed to succeed him. The new Grand Vizier was reputed to be less obstinate and far more inclined for peace than his predecessor but, as the French Ambassador noted in his dispatch to Versailles, preparations for the next campaign were already so far advanced that it was probably too late for Elvias Mohammed to halt them.

His estimate of the situation proved to be correct when, three weeks later, the new Grand Vizier set out from Constantinople to assume the leadership of the army. Villeneuve, however, had an excuse for keeping in touch with him, for a few days later a courier arrived with Sinzendorf's reply to his request for fresh instructions. It was not very satisfactory, for while the Emperor was prepared to make a few concessions, he demanded the return of Orsova, and Sinzendorf stipulated that these terms must be accepted by the Porte by the end of May. The Marquis, without much hope, forwarded this unpromising offer to the Grand Vizier, explaining at the same time that he had so far received absolutely no new instructions from the Russians. The Grand Vizier replied inviting the French Ambassador to join him in his camp at Adrianople.

It seemed that the Turks were now prepared to consider peace negotiations, and Villeneuve allowed himself to believe that the moment for which he had waited so long had at last arrived. As far back as 1736 Chauvelin had advised him that, should it come, he should make every effort to underline to the Porte the importance of the role which, as the representative of France, he was summoned to assume in this supreme effort to conclude a peace. Announcing his imminent departure for the Grand Vizier's camp, the Marquis demanded a solemn audience of the Sultan in order to present his credentials as Ambassador Extraordinary appointed by His Most Christian Majesty King Louis XV of France to mediate in the war. His request was immediately granted, and the audience arranged for May 17th, 1739. In the meantime Villeneuve, who was making preparations to appear at it with 'great lustre and magnificence', was left in no doubt of the changed attitude of the Porte. A stream of visitors bearing presents arrived at the French Embassy, in the forecourt of which one of the Sultan's bands played incessantly (which must have been extremely trying), and a corps of Janissaries was appointed as a guard of honour to escort him wherever he went.

Trial of Strength

On May 17th, the Marquis rose before dawn and, saluted by all the French ships moored off the Golden Horn, crossed to Stamboul and rode in solemn procession up the hill to the Serail. He was preceded by Janissaries wearing their plumed ceremonial headdress, by the members of his household, the Greek valets and Hungarian couriers in their national dress and the lackeys wearing his personal blue and yellow livery, and by a dozen led horses, their harness glittering with jewels and gold. The Embassy staff surrounded the Ambassador who was escorted by the Çavuş Başi and another high official of the Porte. Behind them rode the entire French community.

When the procession reached the Serail the customary ceremonial was observed. The Janissaries were paid, the Kaimakam acting for the Grand Vizier heard petitions, and a meal was served. Finally the crowning moment arrived. Wearing a rose coloured robe trimmed with sable, followed by his nine-year-old son and by the senior members of the staff which had served him so well, one of them holding high the velvet case containing the letter from King Louis XV to his 'dear and perfect friend the Ottoman Emperor', Louis-Sauveur Marquis de Villeneuve, Ambassador of France at the Sublime Porte, entered for the first time the presence of the Sultan Mahmoud I to whom he had been accredited for nine years. He advanced between the close packed ranks of the highest dignitaries of the Serail, in a silence broken only by the sound made by the Çavuşes who preceded him striking the butts of their staffs of office on the paving of the audience chamber. The outward ceremonial of his reception resembled that accorded to every envoy who presented his credentials to the Shadow of God on Earth, but, unlike them, Villeneuve was not received with condescension. On that morning of May 17th, 1739 there was a subtle difference in the atmosphere of the Sultan's audience chamber, for the personality of that ugly little Provençal, the French Ambassador, dominated the whole assembly. As, very slowly, he approached the Sultan's throne, every eye was fixed upon him, for all the onlookers were well aware that their future might lie in his hands. Once arrived in front of Mahmoud I Villeneuve bowed three times and made a short speech, after which the King's letter was delivered to the Kaimakam who laid it at his ruler's feet. The audience was concluded, and, again bowing low, the Ambassador and his suite withdrew. The ceremony was over. The real work, as the Marquis knew, was now about to begin.

A fortnight later, on June 3rd, accompanied by 600 people, and with the equipment for his camp loaded on to 200 waggons, he left the capital on the first stage of his journey to join the Grand Vizier at Adrianople.

On the road Villeneuve was overtaken by an emissary from St. Petersburg who brought with him a letter from Count Ostermann. In this the Russian Foreign Minister at last enumerated the revised terms on which the Czarina would be prepared to conclude peace. In these he laid down a return to the frontiers of 1700 lost by Peter the Great when he was defeated by the Turks on the Pruth as a *sine qua non*, and insisted that the Porte must at the same time make peace with the Emperor. He dealt at great length with the question of Azov, stressing that while Villeneuve should make every effort to secure its retention by Russia he could, if this was the one point on which the Turks were adamant, agree to its being razed provided the Russians were permitted to build a new fort higher up the Don. Ostermann concluded by explaining that, in order to eliminate the inevitable time lag which must ensue if Villeneuve had to seek further instructions from St. Petersburg, Cagnoni the bearer of his letter had been invested with Full Powers to sign a peace treaty. But, he added, during the negotiations he would be subordinate to the French Ambassador, and merely there to enlighten him on the Russian point of view. This apparently sensible arrangement was not entirely agreeable to Villeneuve. Cagnoni was one of those shadowy figures in the background of eighteenth-century politics who, acting as a combination of tool and spy, and owing allegiance only to the statesman who paid them, were extremely useful for the furtherance of intrigues. The Marquis found Ostermann's emissary personally antipathetic and suspected that he had a number of instructions from the Russian Foreign Minister which he was keeping strictly to himself, but the terms of the Count's letter were such that he was unavoidably compelled to attach Cagnoni to his suite.

As he bumped slowly in his coach along the road to Adrianople Villeneuve had plenty of time to review the situation. The mediation of France had been accepted by all three contending parties, and he was invested with the necessary powers to exercise it. The position with regard to the terms on which they were prepared to conclude peace was less satisfactory. The conditions laid down by Ostermann were likely to prove the easiest to handle, for, although they would not be immediately acceptable to the Turks, they were at least clear and provided a basis for negotiation. Fleury, the French Ambassador reflected with gratitude, had evidently at last succeeded in instilling some sense into the Russians.

Sinzendorf's latest set of instructions by contrast were confused and bore not the slightest relation to the realities of the situation. Villeneuve once again permitted himself some most uncharitable thoughts about the incompetence and stupidity of the Court of Vienna.

And the Porte? Although the indications were that that the new Grand Vizier was far more inclined to consider the possibility of concluding a peace than his predecessor, the Marquis had no idea as to what his terms for this would be. Would he be prepared to abandon Jegen Mohammed's demand for Belgrade? If not, and if the Emperor, whatever his reverses, refused to surrender the fortress, would Elvias Mohammed be so foolish as to try to take it by force? This was the possibility which most alarmed the French Ambassador. During his eleven years in Constantinople Villeneuve had learnt too much about the military weakness of the Turks to have any confidence that they could storm and capture one of the strongest fortresses in Europe. If the Ottoman army was shattered on the walls of Belgrade, it would flee as it had done from Vienna in 1683, from Peterwardein in 1716, from Belgrade itself in 1717. The Porte would make peace on whatever terms the Austrians and the Russians dictated and, whatever his powers as mediator, he would then be quite unable to safeguard the interests of France in the Sultan's dominions.

A Mediator is Appointed

Cardinal Fleury had left him in no doubt of the importance to France of the preservation of the Ottoman Empire which, he had indicated, could best be ensured if the Turks regained Belgrade, and so were once again in possession of the keystone of their defence line against the Emperor. Villeneuve, who had a great respect for Fleury's judgement, fully agreed that the return of the fortress to the Sultan would be in the best interests of France, and feared that if this did not occur, the duration of any peace which he succeeded in negotiating might be short. But his anxiety increased with every hour of his journey to Adrianople. He could only pray that he might arrive in time to dissuade the Grand Vizier from taking any rash action.

Towards the end of the third week in June the French Ambassador made a state entry into Adrianople, to find that the Grand Vizier and the Ottoman army had already advanced to Nish. To add to his exasperation he was handed a letter from Sinzendorf asking him to inform the Turks that, since the time limit had expired, the Emperor's last set of proposals were withdrawn, but that peace could still be negotiated on the basis of a return to the terms laid down at Passarowitz in 1718. If rumours of Sinzendorf's increasing decrepitude had reached the Marquis he must have considered them finally proven as he read this letter, for the proposal stood not the slightest chance of being accepted. He dispatched Delaria to communicate it to the Grand Vizier who, as he had anticipated, rejected it out of hand. Villeneuve wrote to inform Sinzendorf of this, and then set out to follow Elvias Mohammed Pasha to Nish.

His large suite and baggage train slowed down his progress and it took him a month to reach Nish, by which time the Grand Vizier had already moved up to Belgrade. A few days later the Marquis received news which made the Austrian proposal appear more impractical than ever. The Grand Vizier, it was reported, had defeated the Imperial army at Groczka a few miles to the south-east of Belgrade.

Villeneuve was by this time virtually cut off from the outside world, and obliged to piece together an account of what had occurred from such information as the Turks saw fit to pass to him. He knew from experience that this information was unlikely to be wholly accurate, for the Turks were always apt to magnify their victories but, even allowing for Oriental exaggeration, it seemed probable that a disaster had befallen the Emperor which must effect the whole outcome of the war. While he was still engaged in trying to assess the situation, the Marquis received a letter from the Grand Vizier instructing him to remain at Nish until further notice.

So Villeneuve was compelled to stay in considerable discomfort for the better part of three weeks in Nish which was hot, dusty and fly-ridden. It was a time of waiting which tried his patience to the limit. The Grand Vizier's refusal to allow him to proceed to Belgrade was very ominous indeed, for it suggested that, rendered over-confident by his victory at Groczka, he was going to attempt to storm the fortress before peace negotiations could be opened. As day succeeded day the French Ambassador was haunted by the thought of what might be occurring.

At last the period of waiting came to an end. On August 11th Villeneuve received a letter from the Grand Vizier summoning him to his camp before Belgrade. The moment for standing on ceremony was past and, leaving most of his suite and the greater part of his baggage to follow him, the Marquis accompanied by a few members of his staff, set out at once. The heat was intense, and the road no more than a rough track winding through narrow defiles and woods across a sparsely inhabited countryside. On the last day of the journey the party passed the battlefield of Groczka where, as a traveller who visited it a year later found, it was impossible to walk for more than ten paces without stumbling over a pile of dead bodies. Villeneuve arrived there on August 15th a little more than three weeks after the battle when, in the torrid heat of the Serbian summer, the stench of decaying corpses must have been indescribable. It was a grim reminder of the horrors of war; it brought home to him that not only the position of France in the Ottoman Empire but also a great many lives depended on the outcome of the negotiations which he had come to conduct. There was now no time to be lost; he could allow himself no rest to recover from the fatigue of the journey but must see the Grand Vizier without delay.

Many younger and stronger men would have been exhausted by riding 150 miles in four days, in great heat and over rough country. But although Villeneuve was sixty-four, and had served for eleven years without leave in the arduous climate and conditions of Constantinople, he appeared to be quite untired. He was a very tough and indomitable man and, whatever his fatigue or inward misgivings, no trace of either was apparent to his companions. He rode calmly on from Groczka on the last stage of his journey to the Grand Vizier's camp, to face what he well knew would be one of the most exacting negotiations ever undertaken by any Ambassador of the King of France.

Towards evening the Marquis and his companions reached the brow of a low hill and saw the Grand Vizier's camp spread out below them. Gaily coloured tents and standards, pitched on the site of Prince Eugen's siege lines of 1717, sprawled across the base of the triangle formed by the junction of the Save and the Danube. But, as he reigned in his horse at the top of the hill Villeneuve barely looked at them. His whole attention was focused on the apex of the triangle beyond the Turkish camp, where a complex of walls and bastions crowned by a citadel riding high above the two rivers dominated the horizon. On the fate of this forbidding mass of masonry the whole of the forthcoming negotiations would turn.

The French Ambassador had heard of the strength of Belgrade for many years and, although he lacked military experience, it seemed to him as he gazed at this imposing array of fortifications, that Prince Eugen's proud assertion that the fortress would never again fall into the hands of the infidel might well be correct. From a distance it looked impregnable. Villeneuve studied it until the outlines of the battlements softened into the evening sky, and then spurred his horse down the hill and rode into the Grand Vizier's camp.

The Marquis was received by the Turks with the ceremonial appropriate to his status, and presented by the Grand Vizier with a magnificent saluki. The initial courtesies having been observed he was left, to his very great relief, to have his evening meal in peace. As he ate he listened to the Turkish guns pounding at Belgrade.

Before long Delaria, who had preceded him to the camp, arrived bringing with him two letters, neither of which pleased the Ambassador at all. One, dated August 5th, was from Sinzendorf and instructed Villeneuve to agree with the Grand Vizier a neutral place for the holding of a peace conference from which couriers could come and go in safety. Once this was done and when negotiations had commenced Villeneuve might offer the Turks the whole of Austrian Wallachia, and Orsova and its surrounding forts with their defences intact. The second letter was from Mirepoix, the French Ambassador in Vienna, who wrote he said at the express request of the Emperor, to inform his colleague that, since the Russians had failed to carry their share of the war, Charles VI considered himself released from all obligations towards his ally and at liberty to conclude a separate peace.

Villeneuve was appalled by these letters. Even the defeat of Groczka had failed to instil any sense into Sinzendorf. His proposals, the Ambassador wearily reflected, with their total omission of any mention of Belgrade, bore once again not the slightest relation to the military situation, and would once again be rejected by the Grand Vizier. Mirepoix's communication of the Emperor's desire to conclude a separate peace regardless of his ally was frankly embarrassing, for Fleury had been emphatic that, since Villeneuve had also been appointed mediator by the Czarina, this was something which he must under no circumstances promote.

Villeneuve's depression was increased by the estimate of the military situation which Delaria then proceeded to give him. The Turkish siege artillery were only just beginning to arrive and the lighter guns, which had been pounding at the walls of Belgrade for the better part of a fortnight, had not yet made any significant breach in them. Nevertheless siege ladders had been prepared, the Grand Vizier's already formidable army had been reinforced by the arrival of Ali Pasha, the former Grand Vizier and now Governor of Bosnia, with 30,000 confident and eager troops, and all information suggested that, whether or not the walls had been breached, the Turks were determined to storm the fortress. As Villeneuve went to bed that night he realised that he must somehow restrain the entire Ottoman army from committing suicide on the walls of Belgrade. Altogether he did not relish the prospect of his forthcoming interview with Elvias Mohammed Pasha.

He was right to be apprehensive. The interview, which took place on the following day, was disheartening. The Grand Vizier opened with a discourse on the manner in which, as Villeneuve subsequently reported to Versailles, 'the infidels were being punished by the hand of God'.[11] He then asked whether the French Ambassador had received any fresh instructions from Vienna, and Villeneuve was obliged to enumerate the proposals contained in Sinzendorf's latest letter. The Porte Dragoman turned pale at the mere idea of having to interpret anything so totally unacceptable to his master, and the Grand Vizier replied brusquely that he had recently seen an Austrian officer called Gross who had been a great deal more forthcoming. Nothing, said Elvias Mohammed, less than the immediate handing over of Belgrade was of the slightest interest to him, and with that ultimatum he ended the interview.

As the French Ambassador returned to his tent, he heard the Turkish batteries increase their fire. The sound formed a dis-agreeable background to his disquieting thoughts.

Sinzendorf's last letter made no mention of Gross, neither did it contain any indication that the Emperor was considering the abandonment of Belgrade. Who then had sent Gross to the Grand Vizier? What offer had he been authorised to make to Elvias Mohammed, and on whose authority? There appeared to be only two possibilities. Either Gross had gone to the Grand Vizier on instructions from Vienna, which could only mean that the Emperor was trying to make peace with the Turks without French mediation. Or Field-Marshal Wallis, the new Imperial Commander-in-Chief, empowered to conclude a preliminary peace in the field, had made an overture to the Grand Vizier without prior consultation with Vienna, in which case, should Charles VI not approve his action, the situation would be more confused than ever. It was a most unsatisfactory state of affairs. The more Villeneuve considered it the more certain he became that he could make no progress in his task of mediation without further enlightenment.

The Marquis was therefore greatly relieved when, a few hours later, he was informed by the Grand Vizier that an Imperial Plenipotentiary was soon expected to arrive in the camp. It was to be hoped that this envoy would bring with him a sensible and up-to-date statement of the terms on which the Emperor was prepared to conclude peace and a clear assessment of the position in Belgrade, both of which were vital to the negotiation of a settlement, not only with Austria but also with Russia. But until this envoy arrived Villeneuve could do no more than wait.

CHAPTER XII

ᘏᘏᘏᘏᘏᘏᘏᘏᘏᘏᘏᘏᘏᘏᘏᘏᘏᘏᘏᘏᘏᘏᘏᘏᘏᘏᘏᘏᘏ

Deadlock

Belgrade, July–August 1739

Villeneuve was unaware that nobody on the Austrian side was capable of making a dispassionate estimate of the position in the fortress of Belgrade, or that by August 18th the Imperial Commander-in-Chief, Field-Marshal Oliver Wallis, was indeed incapable of making a dispassionate estimate of anything at all.

Wallis had been appointed by the Emperor in the spring of 1739 to command the Imperial army in Hungary because, after Seckendorf's disgrace and Königsegg's failure, he was the only remaining senior General remotely qualified for this post. He had served in Prince Eugen's Turkish campaigns and was well acquainted both with the terrain over which he would have to fight, and with the methods of the enemy. If he had never achieved any outstanding distinction, at least he had never made any glaring blunder. Charles, although he did not like the Field-Marshal and knew him to be detested throughout the army, hoped that when in supreme command he would develop hitherto unrevealed qualities of leadership.

The Emperor authorised Wallis to override his Council of Generals should he consider that the situation so demanded, invested him with powers to conclude a preliminary peace in the field, and ordered that the Imperial troops should be assembled by the middle of May so that the campaign could begin before the Turks had time to bring up reinforcements from Asia. A satisfactory operational plan had been concerted with the Russians who, fearful of being attacked by Sweden if peace was not soon concluded, and afraid of being left to carry the whole burden of the war if the Austrians collapsed, had at last agreed to advance, by the shortest route through southern Poland, on the key Turkish fortress of Choczim with the object of linking up with the Imperial forces in Moldavia. The Field-Marshal assumed command with a number of advantages denied to his predecessors, but he was not enthusiastic about his appointment. 'The Emperor has entrusted me with the command of his army', he wrote to the King of Prussia, 'the first of my predecessors in this post is in prison, the second has been demoted to the status of a palace eunuch; it only remains for me to have my head cut off at the end of the campaign.'[1]

This comment was characteristic. Although outwardly overbearing, obstinate and intolerant of criticism, Wallis lacked self-confidence and was all too frequently morose. He had one of his recurrent bouts of fever on the way to his headquarters, and when he arrived there early in May he was feeling extremely ill. He was therefore in no mood to be helpful to General Suckow, the garrison commander of Belgrade, who he disliked and considered to be cowardly and incompetent, or to deal with the problems of shortages of supplies and delay in the assembly of the troops with which he was immediately confronted. When, a few days later, he received a report that the Grand Vizier with a very large army was advancing on Belgrade, his sole reaction was to write to Vienna for a directive as to the strategy which he should adopt.

Two months passed. During this time Wallis supplied Suckow with all the food, guns and ammunition which he could spare, and which he considered should be ample to enable the fortress and its garrison of 15,000 men to withstand an indefinite siege, and inundated Vienna with complaints about the lack of supplies. Apart from this he achieved nothing, as the Hofkriegsrat did not fail to point out, instructing him in the sharpest terms, which he greatly resented, to engage the Turks in battle as soon as a suitable occasion arose. When therefore the Field-Marshal heard that an enemy force, estimated at 4,000 men and apparently an advance column of the main Ottoman army, had been sighted on the south bank of the Danube a few miles downstream from Belgrade, he ordered his troops to advance to attack them at 1 a.m. on the following morning, July 22nd.

A disastrous twenty-four hours followed. When dawn broke the Imperial advance guard, boxed up in rolling hills covered with vineyards and without room to manœuvre, came under heavy fire and, as the sun rose and enemy pressure increased Wallis found that, far from merely having engaged the enemy vanguard, he was confronted by the Grand Vizier's entire army. A savage struggle followed in which all ranks of the Imperial troops, from the Commander-in-Chief downwards, fought with great courage. They managed to stand their ground until dusk when the Turks retreated and left them nominally masters of the field.

As Villeneuve saw when, three weeks later, he passed Groczka on his way to Belgrade, it had been a grim battle. But the most serious casualty of all occurred when it was over, for then Wallis lost both his power of judgement and his nerve. He refused to listen to any suggestion that he should group his forces either to re-engage the enemy or to support Belgrade. Thereafter he was concerned only to preserve the remnants of the army and to use the powers with which he had been invested by the Emperor to negotiate a peace in the field. On July 26th, having dispatched Count Gross to the Grand Vizier's camp with instructions to ascertain the terms on which the Turks would be prepared to conclude peace, the Field-Marshal crossed to the north bank of the Danube with the ultimate objective of withdrawing to the safety of the fortress of Peterwardein fifty miles up the river. On the same day the Grand Vizier, now in command of the whole area to the south of the fortress between the Danube and the Save, began the siege of Belgrade.

Wallis spent the next fortnight marching aimlessly to and fro in intense heat in the unhealthy marshes on the north bank of the Danube. By August 15th (the day on which Villeneuve reached the Grand Vizier's camp), he had arrived, by a circuitous route through seventy miles of swamp, at a point twenty miles upstream from Belgrade. He was in low spirits after another bout of fever,

2,000 of his men were sick, and Gross had reported that the Grand Vizier would be content with nothing less than the immediate surrender of the fortress. The peace overture had done nothing to improve the situation for Suckow who, it was now clear, could only be helped if the main army advanced. But this the Field-Marshal was not prepared to contemplate. He had sent five battalions to reinforce the garrison, and posted a detachment to hold the Borcza redoubt opposite it on the far side of the river which protected its lines of communication with Peterwardein. He was adamant that he could do no more and must now withdraw the main army out of reach of the enemy, abandoning Suckow to his fate.

During the first few days of the siege of Belgrade Suckow had been optimistic about the prospects of holding the fortress. Although the Turks kept up a steady bombardment they made no breach in the defences. Communications across the Danube were still open, and there was no difficulty in bringing in supplies. He rejected the Grand Vizier's demand for the keys of Belgrade and erected three gallows on which he announced he would hang anyone who talked of surrender.

But, when he realised that Wallis was making not the slightest attempt to come to his assistance, the garrison commander's mood altered. This was understandable, for he was being besieged by nearly 150,000 Turks, and the only army from which he might expect help was marching away from him. It was a situation which even the most courageous general might have found unattractive. Suckow was not naturally courageous, and he was greatly concerned about his future standing at Court, which was likely to be seriously impaired should Belgrade fall, and irreparably damaged if the disaster was ascribed to him. He therefore sent a series of reports to Wallis complaining of the shortage of essential supplies, asking for reinforcements, and finally informing the Commander-in-Chief that he had been compelled to abandon the Borcza redoubt because that position had become untenable. He was emphatic that whatever happened Belgrade must be held, and added that this could be done if only Wallis would stop retreating and come to his assistance.

In addition to reporting to the Commander-in-Chief and urging him to take some action, Suckow continued the correspondence which for some time he had been conducting with Vienna. He wrote both to the Emperor with whom, as one of his favourite generals, he had the privilege of corresponding direct—and to the Hofkriegsrat. To both he asserted that the defence was being robustly conducted and that, if Wallis would advance, Belgrade could certainly be held. These letters would, he hoped, successfully convey the impression that so far as his own command was concerned everything was in order and, if there was a disaster, only Wallis was to blame.

In Vienna at the beginning of August the Emperor and his ministers found it difficult to arrive at any assessment of the military situation. While they had received the news of Groczka with consternation, they had remained confident that Belgrade was strong enough to withstand an indefinite siege, a conclusion which seemed to be borne out by Suckow's optimistic reports. But if the fortress was to hold out the pressure on it must be relieved by the main army and this, it seemed, was something which Wallis was not prepared to attempt. On the contrary he went so far as to contend that a well-conducted retreat was worth as much as a victory, and complained in every dispatch about his lack of supplies which, he said, when danger was imminent arrived too late, and when it was past did not arrive at all. The Hofkriegsrat did not appreciate the complaints about supplies, for these reflected on their competence; the Emperor was angered by the reference to the desirability of retreat which impugned the honour of the House of Habsburg. Neither he nor his ministers were reassured by the Field-Marshal's account of his abortive peace overture to the Grand Vizier, or by his assertion that despite his ill health he would stand by the army to his last breath.

The whole position was most unsatisfactory and, as Hofrat Bartenstein who had no love for Sinzendorf and his colleagues, no doubt did not hesitate to point out to his ruler, none of Charles's elderly ministers were capable of dealing with it. The Emperor himself must intervene if the military situation was to be restored and a satisfactory peace concluded. Charles, still convinced in spite of everything, that he was the appointed instrument of the Almighty whose wishes fully coincided with his own and who would therefore guide and support him, fully agreed with this. On August 4th he wrote a long letter to his Commander-in-Chief.

The Emperor ordered Wallis to obtain his general's views on the state of the army, and to forward them with his own comments, adding that they should all remember that it was their duty to concern themselves more with war than with a possible peace. He next turned to Belgrade, and after observing petulantly that he wished Wallis would be more definite about the position in the fortress, insisted that it must be held. At the same time peace negotiations must be kept open until a proper evaluation had been made of the military situation, after which appropriate terms for a settlement could be drawn up. Wallis had made two practical suggestions in his recent dispatches, one being that General Schmettau, whose military ability he considered to be outstanding, should be summoned urgently to reorganise the defence of Belgrade, and the other that, if another emissary was required to go to the Grand Vizier's camp to discuss terms, Count Neipperg should be entrusted with this mission. Charles informed the Field-Marshal that he accepted both these suggestions. He had sent an urgent summons to Schmettau and would personally brief him as to his duties before he left for Belgrade. Neipperg should henceforward undertake all peace negotiations and, to prepare him for this Wallis must show his subordinate general all the instructions which he had received, and provide him with the necessary credentials to enable him to negotiate as the Imperial Plenipotentiary.

Charles in fact no longer trusted either Wallis' military judgement or his capacity to negotiate a peace. When, a few days later, he learnt that the Field-Marshal had written privately to a member of the Court, imploring him to urge upon the Emperor the necessity of handing over Belgrade at once to the Grand Vizier in order to save part at least of the Banat and retain the line of the Save as the frontier of the Imperial possessions, he was outraged, and considered that this confirmed all his misgivings. Henceforward, he decided, he must have a subordinate on the spot who would keep him fully informed as to what was occurring, and on whose unquestioning obedience he could rely. Count Neipperg, who he had already nominated as his Plenipotentiary in any peace negotiations, was one of his most trusted officers. On August 11th Charles wrote two letters to Neipperg.

In the first of these he asked the Count to provide him with a full report on the state of Belgrade and the army. Wallis, he explained, could not be relied on to keep anything secret, and the accuracy of his reports to the Hofkriegsrat was open to question. Therefore Neipperg was to furnish a clear assessment of the situation which, the Emperor emphasised, was to be forwarded to him direct and not through the Commander-in-Chief.

In his second letter, after having expressed his horror at the Field-Marshal's proposal for the immediate handing over of Belgrade, Charles enumerated the terms on which he would be prepared to make peace. Ideally these should not include any mention of Belgrade but, if it seemed likely that the fortress would be captured before an agreement could be reached, then an offer could be made to hand it over, but with its defences razed, in exchange for a razed Orsova and certain strongpoints in Wallachia. If even this offer would not satisfy the Turks, as a last resort, only to be employed when everything else had failed, he would agree to the handing over of Belgrade with its fortifications intact, in return for the retention of everything on the Austrian side of the Save and the Danube together with Orsova. But, the Emperor commanded, these concessions must be offered stage by stage, and only if to do so was quite unavoidable. Then, having given his negotiator scope for a certain amount of oriental bargaining, he proceeded to restrict the flexibility of timing essential for such a transaction by stating that peace negotiations must be speeded up. He further complicated the issue by laying down certain rules as to how Neipperg should conduct the negotiations. He forbade the Count to go to the Grand Vizier's camp, and emphasised that he must only deal with the Turks through Villeneuve until such time as a preliminary agreement had been reached, after which he should demand to meet Elvias Mohammed Pasha in a neutral place. Finally he instructed Neipperg that, if possible, he was not to inform Villeneuve that he was empowered to offer the Turks Belgrade.

When he had signed these letters the Emperor, attended by all his ministers, migrated to Neustadt, leaving in Vienna no one with authority to take any decision. Neither the threat to Belgrade nor the defeat suffered by the army could be permitted to interfere with His Imperial Majesty's hunting programme. In any case, by the time Charles left for Neustadt he was convinced that he had done all that was necessary to assume control of the situation. Within a few days he would be fully informed as to the military position, for the comments on it from Wallis and his generals could be cross-checked against the report which he had secretly requested from Neipperg; he had improved the prospects of peace by transferring the powers to conclude it from Wallis to Neipperg, and he had ensured that there should be no recurrence of past mistakes by making it clear to both that they must report directly to him. Unfortunately he failed to realise that it was impossible to control a rapidly deteriorating situation from a distance, and that authority can only be satisfactorily transferred from a superior to a subordinate if the position is simultaneously made clear to both of them. The Emperor apparently still believed that the best way to rule was to play off his servants against each other.

Wallis was the first to learn of the Emperor's decision when he received the Imperial rescript of August 4th, ordering him to transfer his powers to conclude peace to Neipperg. This was a severe blow to the Field-Marshal who had only proposed that Neipperg should act as his emissary in the negotiations, and had never envisaged a transfer of powers. It made him bitterly jealous of the Count and he disobeyed orders, did not inform Neipperg of the Emperor's decree and, on August 12th, in a last minute endeavour to achieve a coup which would cut out his rival, sent Gross, accompanied by the Imperial interpreter, von Schwacheim, on a second mission to the Turkish camp. Accounts of what occurred when they were received in audience by the Grand Vizier are contradictory. Von Schwacheim later alleged that in the course of

Field-Marshal Oliver Wallis, from an engraving in the Exercitium des löblichen General Graf Wallischer Regiments zu Fuss

Count Neipperg, from a portrait by an unknown artist

it Gross offered Elvias Mohammed Belgrade; Gross insinuated that he had made this offer on Wallis' instructions. Wallis flatly denied having given any such instructions. No mention of the offer can be traced in the Turkish archives.[2] Whatever was said during the discussion the subsequent attitude of the Grand Vizier suggests that he believed, as he later made clear to Villeneuve, that Wallis, and so he assumed the Emperor, was ready to consider the abandonment of Belgrade. The only result of Gross's second mission to the Grand Vizier was therefore greatly to increase the difficulties which were to confront Neipperg.

The Count's only previous experience of negotiating with the Turks had been in 1718 when Prince Eugen, who considered him a great deal more intelligent than the average officer, obtained for him an appointment as Frontier Commissioner at the Peace of Passarowitz. Although able, he lacked the capacity to take sole responsibility, was obstinate, and inclined all too easily to pessimism. He first learnt of his new appointment of which Wallis had known for four days when, on August 16th, he received the Emperor's letters of August 11th. He showed them to no one, and simply informed the Field-Marshal that, having received instructions from the Emperor to negotiate a peace, he must go to the enemy camp to discuss the situation with Villeneueve.

Leaving Wallis, who was in an abominable temper, to arrange the necessary safe conduct for him with the Grand Vizier, Neipperg then drafted his report on the state of the army. As a jeremiad it was well up to the Commander-in-Chief's standard. There were, he assured Charles VI, only about 21,000 men fit to fight, and they were going sick at the rate of a hundred a day; the officers were two-thirds below strength; all ranks had lost faith in Wallis and their morale was abysmal. At the time when he composed this report the Count was in the Austrian camp at Surdock some miles from Belgrade, and he had no immediate first-hand knowledge of the situation there; but he omitted to mention this when he stated that the garrison was down to 9,000 men, the fortifications full of defects, and the fortress could not be held.

After having summed up the military situation in these gloomy terms, the Count then outlined the action which he proposed to take with regard to the peace negotiations. He considered it essential, he explained, to have a personal discussion with Villeneuve and for this purpose had requested Wallis to obtain a safe conduct for him to visit the Grand Vizier's camp. Neipperg laid particular emphasis on the need for secrecy, and asked that this report should be shown to nobody but the Duke of Lorraine and Bartenstein, for otherwise his position would be hopelessly compromised. He also asked for a copyist to be assigned to him, for it might be necessary to conceal what he had to say from Wallis. It was only too clear that he and his Commander-in-Chief no longer trusted one another.

On the following day the Grand Vizier agreed that Neipperg should come to his camp to 'confer on certain matters', and a letter arrived from Villeneuve urging that the conference should take place immediately. It was now necessary to obtain the appropriate credentials. Wallis was once again ill, but a document was drafted by some of his generals which he signed in their presence. Neipperg then signed a statement, also witnessed by the generals, whereby he accepted sole responsibility for the future course of the negotiations. Early on August 18th he left Surdock on the first stage of his journey to the Turkish camp.

Neipperg, who was no longer young, had taken part in an exhausting and disastrous campaign. It was an extremely hot morning. He was not feeling well as he rode along the dusty track towards Belgrade. His lack of physical well-being fostered his natural tendency to pessimism, and he found the whole situation extremely dispiriting. He could expect no co-operation from Wallis who was both jealous and resentful of him; the Emperor—as the fate which had befallen Seckendorf, Königsegg and a number of others demonstrated—did not hesitate to punish anyone whom he considered had failed him; Villeneuve, on whom much depended, was an unknown quantity, and the Count had already made up his mind that the French Ambassador would not be agreeable to work with. By the time he rode into Belgrade, hot, dusty, and tired, at two o'clock on a torrid August afternoon, Neipperg had reduced himself to such a state of gloom that he was quite incapable of forming a balanced estimate of the situation in the fortress. When therefore Suckow, having listed his shortages of men and supplies, and complained about the state of the fortifications, said flatly that if Wallis and the main army advanced to its assistance Belgrade might hold out till the end of September, but that if no such advance was made, it might fall within a few days, he accepted the garrison commander's opinion without question. He stayed in the fortress for only four hours which gave him no time to verify Suckow's statements, and then, convinced that there was no hope of saving Belgrade, left by a small side gate and made his way under intermittent fire from the Turkish guns along a path to the Grand Vizier's camp.

CHAPTER XIII

꿏꿏꿏꿏꿏꿏꿏꿏꿏꿏꿏꿏꿏꿏꿏꿏꿏꿏꿏꿏꿏꿏꿏꿏꿏꿏꿏꿏

'This Thorny Negotiation'

Belgrade, August–September 1739

Neipperg took with him to the enemy camp Momarz, the Secretary and Chief Interpreter to the Hofkriegsrat, Count Gross, and two or three servants; his luggage consisted of a few small valises. It was a suite inappropriate to his status as Imperial Plenipotentiary, and it was not calculated to impress the Turks with the power and majesty of the Holy Roman Emperor; possibly the Count thought that it would be best to come without ostentation, in order to sound out the ground before starting formal negotiations.[1]

When he entered the camp he was conducted to the Janissary Aga with whom he had a short unsatisfactory conversation. After this he was escorted by a guard of Janissaries through the camp to two tents pitched in the place of honour between those of the Grand Vizier and the Reis Effendi. On the way there Neipperg was alarmed to see a great many guns, about a thousand siege ladders and impressive supplies of other kinds of siege equipment. He was not pleased by the position of his tents which, while they commanded an excellent view of the approaches to Belgrade and of both the Save and the Danube, were at least a quarter of an hour's ride from the enclave allocated to the French Ambassador. This suggested that the Turks proposed to keep him under close surveillance, an impression which was enhanced by the arrival of another escort of Janissaries which, he was told, would accompany him wherever he went. He immediately complained to the Porte Dragoman, and demanded that he should be lodged closer to Villeneuve with whom, he pointed out, he must be in constant consultation. The Porte Dragoman replied that of course the Count was at liberty to see the French Ambassador whenever he wished; his tent had only been pitched beside that of the Grand Vizier as a mark of honour and esteem. The Turks, as Neipperg was to discover, were adepts at getting their own way by a display of courtesy which meant absolutely nothing.

As he sat in his tent with the contents of his meagre luggage unpacked around him, Neipperg considered the contrast between his present position and that at his only other diplomatic assignment twenty-one years earlier at the Peace Conference of Passarowitz, a conference held in a neutral place, and conducted with the ceremony and regard for protocol which he understood and considered to be right and fitting. Then he had been a member of the delegation from the winning side, its position further strengthened by the presence of Prince Eugen with a large army ready to bring pressure to bear on the Turks should they prove recalcitrant. Now he was alone in the enemy camp, the sole plenipotentiary of a ruler whose army had suffered a crushing defeat, entrusted with a mission the execution of which would tax the resources of the most experienced diplomat. To carry this out successfully he must depend on an unknown and no doubt unreliable Frenchman. It was a most humiliating position.

Villeneuve had awaited the arrival of the Imperial Plenipotentiary with the utmost impatience. During the three days which he had spent in the Grand Vizier's camp he had watched the situation rapidly deteriorating. If Belgrade was not handed over to the Turks within the next few days, nothing, he was certain, would restrain them from courting disaster by attempting to storm it. He devoutly hoped therefore that Neipperg's instructions would permit him to negotiate the surrender of the fortress, and that he would be reasonable and agree to do this without delay. Negotiations, the French Ambassador was sure, must be started at once, and shortly after the Count reached his tent, he came with Delaria and Peysonnel to call on him.

At this first meeting all the advantages were on Villeneuve's side. He had over ten years experience of diplomacy and of dealing with the Turks, possessed in Delaria and Peysonnel two highly competent subordinates and, more than any other European, was *persona grata* with the Grand Vizier. Within the first few minutes he summed up Neipperg as an elderly General who attached great importance to correct procedure, and was quite out of his depth in his present situation. If frightened enough he should, Villeneuve thought, prove easy to handle.

He therefore gave the Count an alarming picture of the strength of the Turks. The Grand Vizier, he explained, had a well supplied army of 150,000 men at his immediate disposal and an additional force 25,000 strong on the far side of the Danube. He could not abandon the siege, for if he did the Sultan would cut off his head, and he had stated quite plainly that he would consider no peace proposals until he had been handed the keys of Belgrade. The Marquis made no attempt to hide his poor opinion either of the military performance of the Austrians—who, he said bluntly, should never have allowed their enemies to reach Belgrade—or of the inept and tardy instructions which he had received from Vienna. The latter, he asserted, had made his task impossible, and without a directive corresponding to the realities of the situation he was at a loss as to what to do next.

As Neipperg listened to Villeneuve's estimate of the military strength of the Turks, which coincided only too closely with his own observations, he became even more convinced that Belgrade could not be saved. The Emperor had laid great stress on the importance of seizing the most favourable moment for concluding a peace and it was, he reasoned, better to make the Turks an acceptable offer immediately in the hope of thereby saving the Save frontier line, rather than try negotiations during which the Grand Vizier might capture the fortress and then be in a position to dictate what terms he chose. He therefore decided to put forward at once the first of the concessions which he was empowered to make, and authorised Villeneuve to make an immediate offer to the Grand Vizier of Belgrade with its fortifications razed.

It was by then late in the evening, but the French Ambassador immediately left to see Elvias Mohammed Pasha. Before long he returned to tell Neipperg that the interview had been exceptionally stormy and that the Grand Vizier, in a rage, had sworn that nothing less than Belgrade with all its fortifications intact would satisfy him. The Turk was, said Villeneuve, a very angry and a very determined man, and with this discouraging observation he bade the Imperial Plenipotentiary good night. Neipperg, convinced that there was nothing more which he could achieve, ordered his horse, and was preparing to leave the camp when a message arrived from the Reis Effendi asking him to stay for further discussions, 'for', said that official, 'great matters cannot be dealt with in a day'.² The Count reluctantly agreed to this, and after an indifferent meal served by the Grand Vizier's servants, settled down to pass a restless night, consoled only by the hope that in the course of the following day there might be some improvement in the situation.

The morning came, and brought with it no comfort for Neipperg. The Reis Effendi called and asked to see his credentials, a most embarrassing request, for the document signed by Wallis was neither impressive in appearance nor particularly well drafted. The Reis Effendi commented after studying it that it seemed to impose no restrictions on Neipperg as to the terms on which he could conclude a peace. The Count, in an endeavour to get round this difficulty, replied that credentials were always qualified by a letter of instruction, and that his did not empower him to make unlimited concessions. The Reis Effendi, who appeared to be unconvinced by this explanation, then departed, and Neipperg was left alone for the rest of the day. No one visited him and the French Ambassador merely sent a message to inquire after his health. He was left to speculate unhappily as to what might be happening, and by the evening he was very uneasy indeed.

Villeneuve by contrast had spent the entire day exchanging calls with the Grand Vizier's subordinates but, although there had been a great deal of talking, he had made no progress, and towards evening he began to sense an increasing evasiveness on the part of the Turks which, he suspected, boded no good either for Neipperg or for the success of his mission. His suspicions were confirmed when, very late that night, Alexander Ghika, the

Porte Dragoman, came secretly to his tent. After explaining that
the Grand Vizier was absolutely determined to have Belgrade
with all its fortifications intact, Ghika offered the French Ambassador a very large bribe to exert his influence to this end. He also
pointed out that if Villeneuve refused to do this there were other
means of achieving what the Grand Vizier wished. Neipperg had
come to the camp without asking, as was customary, for hostages
to be handed over by the Turks as a guarantee for his safety. He
could therefore be held captive, and pressure put on him to break
down his obstinacy, a course which would be fully justified by
the mood of the army who otherwise could not much longer be
restrained from storming Belgrade.

Villeneuve was faced with a critical situation. As mediator he
was responsible for the safety of the Imperial Plenipotentiary and,
as he knew only too well, should the Turks use violence against
Neipperg France, already suspected of conniving with the infidel,
would be discredited throughout Europe. But it was essential
for Neipperg to remain in the Grand Vizier's camp, for if he left
the negotiations would collapse and it would then be impossible
to conclude peace at all. However, he had no intention of revealing
these anxieties, and calmly informed the Porte Dragoman that he
found the manner in which his night's rest had been interrupted
most distasteful. He added that he had too good an opinion of the
Grand Vizier to believe that he would hurt Count Neipperg,
flatly refused the bribe, dismissed Ghika and returned to bed to
review the situation. He realised that he had to deal both with the
impatience of Neipperg, who was not accustomed to oriental
methods, and with the intransigence of the Turks. The Count, he
decided, was likely to be a liability in any discussion, and therefore
he must as far as possible be kept away from the Grand Vizier
and his ministers. Meanwhile he could only hope that something
would occur to render one or other of them more reasonable.

On the following morning, August 20th, emissaries arrived
from the Sultan with presents and congratulations to the Grand
Vizier and his officers for their victory at Groczka. Two days of
feasting and rejoicing followed, and during this time Elvias
Mohammed and his subordinates were inaccessible. Villeneuve,

accustomed to the delays of the Porte, bore this with resignation. Neipperg did not. He sent a curt note to the Reis Effendi asking when he could expect to be informed of the Grand Vizier's intentions. A curt reply telling him that he must wait until the festivities were over put him in a poor frame of mind to endure the following day, which was only enlivened by a visit from the French Ambassador who lectured him on the necessity of patience. These adjurations made no impression on Neipperg who twenty-four hours later lost his temper, informed the Reis Effendi that unless he received an immediate audience of the Grand Vizier he was returning to the Austrian camp, and sent Villeneuve a note to the effect that unless his offer of a razed Belgrade was accepted he would leave. Then, when the Reis Effendi replied that the Grand Vizier was still occupied with the victory celebrations, he announced in public to the Porte Dragoman that he was departing at once, for anything was preferable to remaining where he was.

Neipperg later alleged that he had made this demonstration in order to stir the Turks into some sort of action. All it produced was a soothing message from the Grand Vizier, who regretted that the Imperial Plenipotentiary was displeased, assured him that he was at liberty to leave the camp to hunt should he desire, said that negotiations would shortly be resumed, and added that he could see the French Ambassador whenever he wished. Villeneuve then arrived and spent some time placating him, endeavouring to convince him that there was every hope of a meeting with the Turks before long. Reluctantly the Count once again agreed to postpone his departure.

For the next two days he sat in his tent fuming with rage, universally shunned, and with no news of any kind either from the Turks or the French Ambassador. On August the 25th he could bear it no longer, ordered his horse, and rode over to see Villeneuve. He complained that he had been in the camp for a week without having had a single formal discussion with the Turks. He announced that if he was compelled to remain there any longer he must stay with the Marquis, in order to be in touch with what was going on and, since the Ambassador's enclave was regarded as neutral territory, for his personal safety.

If Villeneuve, who had been carrying the whole burden of the situation for over a week in the heat of the Serbian summer, was exasperated by Neipperg's mixture of panic and tantrums, he betrayed no sign of it. He cordially invited the Imperial Plenipotentiary to stay with him, and gave him a bed in his own tent. If through close contact he could break down his obstinacy, it would be worth while having to suffer an uncongenial guest. He followed up his invitation by telling Neipperg quite flatly that unless he made some further concession nothing could be achieved. He suggested that it might perhaps be possible to hand over Belgrade with at least part of the fortifications intact, an offer which might satisfy the Grand Vizier, who could then report to the Sultan that he had conquered a walled city. Neipperg replied that it would not be possible to do anything of the sort. The fortifications had been paid for by the Holy Catholic Church, and the Holy Roman Emperor could not conceivably hand them over to the infidel. To Villeneuve, the diplomat and realist, this reply redolent of Habsburg Catholic mystique must have been maddening. He left the Count to meditate on the position in the hope that, since reason and argument had no effect on him, possibly time and frustration would. The French Ambassador had a great deal to do, but what this concerned he had not at that moment the slightest intention of revealing to the Imperial Plenipotentiary.

Neipperg spent the rest of the day considering the situation, as a result of which he became obsessed by the fear that the fortress might fall before peace had been concluded. After much hesitation he decided to accept Villeneuve's advice, and the next morning he authorised the Marquis to make a further and immediate offer to the Turks of a partially razed Belgrade with the citadel and the pre-1717 fortifications left intact.

Villeneuve believed (but was careful to give Neipperg no indication of this), that he was at last making progress with the Turks. For the past few days Delaria had been in close contact with Ali Pasha, the influential Governor of Bosnia and former Grand Vizier, to whom, on Villeneuve's orders, he had represented the advantages of a compromise settlement. The Pasha's first reaction to this overture was apparently negative. If the Emperor would not surrender Belgrade unconditionally the Ottoman army would, he said, advance with fire and sword to the gates of Vienna. But the French Ambassador suspected that this might only be a rhetorical threat. He knew the Pasha to be an intelligent man, and was convinced that whatever he might say he appreciated the risks of continuing the campaign. He had instructed Delaria to persist and, twenty-four hours ago, this persistence had been rewarded by a hint from Ali Pasha that the Grand Vizier might consider a partially razed Belgrade an acceptable basis for a peace settlement. Neipperg's further proposal therefore came at a most opportune moment. On the following morning, August 27th, after a further period of intensive negotiation, Villeneuve was able to tell the Imperial Plenipotentiary that for the first time he saw some hope of concluding peace.

The next day the Grand Vizier was ill. The weather was very hot, and since his supply of ice, usually sent from Nish, had not arrived, he asked Neipperg to get him some from Belgrade. The Count at once forwarded this request to Suckow, hoping that the garrison commander when replying would make use of this heaven-sent opportunity to give him some idea of the state of the fortress. Suckow did nothing of the sort; he merely sent a short note demanding the immediate return of a horse which he had lent Neipperg.

To the Count, in a precarious position in the enemy's camp and convinced that Villeneuve was telling him no more than he saw fit, this was the last straw. He returned the horse, and with it sent a letter to be forwarded to Wallis. In this he gave no indication of the state of the negotiations, other than to say that they were proceedingly slowly and that the Grand Vizier's demands were exorbitant. He emphasised that if the army did not advance at once Belgrade would certainly be lost, and concluded 'I am observed from all sides, and want no answer to this as letters are not to be trusted, they can too easily be opened by the Turks. But if it can be done without risk, it would be well if I could know something of the state of the fortress so that I may adjust my negotiations accordingly.'[3] It was the only letter which he wrote while he was in the Grand Vizier's camp; the Field-Marshal did not answer it.

For ten days Neipperg had been without news from the outside world, and there had been no contact of any kind between him and Wallis. Before leaving for the enemy's camp the Count, fearful of angering the Turks, had given instructions that no attempt was to be made to get in touch with him while he was there. Later he alleged that he had only wished to be spared 'insignificant, unnecessary and superfluous correspondence', and maintained that news of any important development could and should have been sent to him by Wallis.[4] But, whatever the truth of this assertion, the Field-Marshal, still bitterly resentful of Neipperg, had no intention of helping him to make a success of his mission. He had been specifically instructed by the Emperor to concern himself exclusively with the army, and to refrain from interfering in the Count's negotiations. It was a humiliating instruction, and he chose to interpret it literally, at the same time not hesitating to complain of Neipperg's failure to give him any news of his progress, a failure which he regarded as a direct personal insult. The most serious result of this unfortunate clash of personalities and confusion of orders was that by August 28th Neipperg had no idea of some highly important developments which had taken place during the past week within the fortress of Belgrade.

These developments dated from the arrival there of General Schmettau, who Wallis had suggested to the Emperor should reorganise the defence of the fortress. The General was a Protestant and a close friend of Seckendorf, both of which made him personally unacceptable to Charles VI and therefore, in spite of his proven military ability, he had been given no command either in 1738 or 1739. When he arrived in Belgrade he was a very angry man. He had travelled post haste from Karlsbad (where the Imperial summons had reached him) to Neustadt. There he had been kept hanging about for twenty-four hours because Charles VI refused to sign his orders before going out to hunt, and then handed a sealed packet addressed to Wallis by whom he was told he would be informed of his duties. Still ignorant of the precise nature of these duties, he had ridden 400 miles in three days to the headquarters of the army, arriving there to find the Commander-in-Chief ill, despondent and still determined to retreat to Peterwardein. After several hours' argument, the General had prevailed on Wallis to alter his decision; the latter had then informed him that the Emperor had ordered that he would be employed in the army or given the command of Peterwardein, and that Suckow would be left in charge of Belgrade. This was a flagrant contradiction of everything which Schmettau had been given to understand when he had been summoned by Charles VI, and his first thought had been to return to once to Vienna to complain about the way in which he had been treated. He had only been dissuaded from this when Wallis, overriding the Emperor's orders, personally appointed him supreme commander in Belgrade.

Schmettau left at once for the fortress where, after a short and far from amicable interview with a resentful Suckow, he lost no time in starting on the task with which he had been entrusted. During the next few days he inspected the fortifications and discovered no serious breach in them, redeployed the garrison which he found to consist of a fighting force of 13,700 men—nearly double the number reported by Suckow—and brought into action seventy guns which on Wallis' orders had been stored for safety in the citadel. By August 28th after an acid interchange of letters with a now convalescent and therefore querulous Wallis, he had completed his plans for a major sortie with the object of recapturing the Borcza redoubt on the far side of the Danube. His arrival had transformed the defence of the fortress and the morale of its garrison which now, instead of waiting to capitulate, was eager to go over to the attack.

Wallis had not informed Schmettau of Neipperg's departure to the Grand Vizier's camp, and the General only learnt of it when he reached Belgrade. When he complained of this omission, the Field-Marshal replied that he had forgotten to mention the matter, but assumed that Suckow would provide him with any information which he might require. He then formally forbade Schmettau to send Neipperg any report of the up-to-date situation in Belgrade.

The position therefore by the late evening of August 28th was that Neipperg was quite unaware of the transformation which had been effected by Schmettau. Equally Schmettau, Wallis, the Emperor and his ministers, had not the least idea that on the following morning a decisive conference which would decide the fate of Belgrade, was due to take place between the French Ambassador, the Imperial Plenipotentiary and the Turks. Villeneuve, better placed than Neipperg to obtain information, may have had his suspicions about what was happening in the fortress. Delaria had no doubt reported to him two days earlier that the massed bands of the garrison had appeared in one of the main gates and had remained there for some time playing loudly in what could be interpreted as a deliberate gesture of defiance. The French Ambassador himself had noticed that within the last forty-eight hours the guns of Belgrade had increased their rate of firing. But he was careful to conceal from Neipperg any deductions which he had drawn from this, for it was essential to his plans that the Count should come to the conference on the following day firmly convinced that the situation was hopeless and that Belgrade could not be held.

The conference, which started early in the morning of August 29th, took place in the large tent where the Grand Vizier held his council meetings, and was attended by all the principal ministers of the Porte, with the exception of Elvias Mohammed himself who was still diplomatically indisposed. When Neipperg and Villeneuve arrived they were greeted with the usual ceremony, seated on stools covered with cloth of gold, and served with coffee. The Imperial Plenipotentiary was nervous, and the French Ambassador preoccupied, for he knew that this meeting would be crucial. He was very near to achieving Cardinal Fleury's optimum requirement, the return of Belgrade to the Sultan, but all his instincts as a diplomat told him that this opportunity might vanish at any moment, never to recur. He could only pray that Neipperg would not be afflicted with another fit of obstinacy.

Ali Pasha, who presided over the conference, opened by pressing Neipperg to hand over Belgrade with all its fortifications intact. Neipperg once again refused to do this. The Pasha then appealed to Villeneuve as mediator to find a way out of the impasse. The Marquis exerted all his powers of persuasion as he put forward Neipperg's compromise offer. 'I impressed on him', he later wrote to Amelot, 'that I had done everything which could be expected of me in devising this compromise of destroying the new fortifications and leaving the old ones standing, and that M. de Neipperg out of regard for the mediation of France had taken upon himself the responsibility of agreeing to this expedient.'⁵ As he finished his speech he watched Ali Pasha closely. He had the impression that, while the Turk was not entirely satisfied, he was not inclined to press the matter further, and that he would consider peace on those terms. After a pause Ali Pasha asked whether, subject to the Grand Vizier's acceptance of Villeneuve's proposal, the new fortifications could be destroyed without damaging the old, and if the destruction could be begun at once so that it could be witnessed by the Turkish troops. The latter proviso, which had not been anticipated by Villeneuve, was of great consequence, for it implied that the terms of the peace would be implemented before the Emperor had had an opportunity of considering whether or not he would accept them. As they withdrew together for consultation Villeneuve felt that Neipperg might well refuse to agree to it. But, possibly out of sheer nervous exhaustion, the Count raised no objections. There was a further pause, which seemed to Villeneuve eternal, in which the Turks retired to confer with the Grand Vizier. At last the Porte Dragoman returned and asked the French Ambassador and the Imperial Plenipotentiary to draft a preliminary peace treaty with the Emperor embodying the terms which they had suggested.

While the drafting was in process, on the far side of the fortress Schmettau reoccupied the Borcza redoubt.

In the Grand Vizier's camp the next two days were spent haggling over the details of the territorial concessions and frontier adjustments to be made in favour of the Sultan. The Grand Vizier maintained that the settlement of these matters to his entire satisfaction concerned his personal honour; Neipperg had further attacks of obstinacy; even Villeneuve's patience was near breaking point. On several occasions the negotiations nearly collapsed. Finally, after bargaining conducted in a manner which, as the Marquis reported to Versailles was 'more appropriate to a transaction between two private individuals than to the conclusion of a treaty between two great empires',[6] agreement was reached late on the evening of August 31st, and Peysonnel and Momarz settled down to complete the final draft of the preliminary peace treaty which sealed the fate of Belgrade. They worked all through the night, and by dawn had finished their task. At nine o'clock Neipperg and Villeneuve, escorted by the Çavuş Başi, rode in procession to the Grand Vizier's tent where they were conducted to stools opposite the sofa on which, surrounded by all his officials, Elvias Mohammed sat between the Pashas of Rumelia and Bosnia. After the usual exchange of compliments and serving of coffee, the French and Turkish versions of the treaty were read aloud and checked. Neipperg then balanced the French copy on his knee and signed it, and the Grand Vizier signed the Turkish copy. Both were then handed to the French Ambassador who affixed and signed the French guarantee, after which sherbert and pipes were served. The Grand Vizier, according to Neipperg, looked more dead than alive and had lost his voice. Neipperg may well have looked even worse, for he had signed a document which not only abandoned to the Turks Orsova, and the whole of Serbia and Austrian Wallachia, but also handed them Belgrade, and stipulated that the razing of its outer fortifications should begin within six days before the Emperor had time to ratify the agreement concluded in his name.

Peace had been made between the Emperor and the Sultan, but peace between the Czarina and the Sultan had to be negotiated, and it was urgent that this should be done soon. Villeneuve knew this only too well; Münnich's army had crossed the Dniester, and he feared that if they continued to advance, the Czarina might once again insist on conditions quite unacceptable to the Porte. In addition, Neipperg had announced that he could

Belgrade in 1739, from a painting by F. N. Sparr

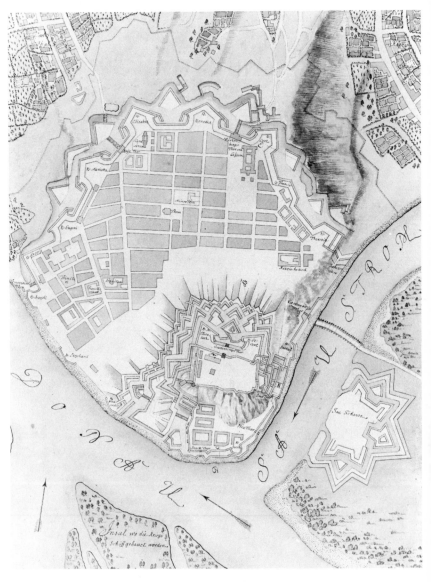

Ground plan of the Fortress of Belgrade, 1739, from a drawing by
F. N. Sparr

not sign a definitive peace treaty on behalf of the Emperor unless a peace with Russia was signed at the same time. Until that definitive treaty was signed the Austrians were entitled to remain in the citadel of Belgrade, and Villeneuve had been warned by the Turkish leaders that if they remained there much longer they could not answer for the consequences. It was therefore essential to conclude peace between the Russians and the Turks as soon as possible, for otherwise everything which had been gained could be lost. Everything hinged on one point—how to induce both sides to come to an agreement about Azov.

At first the Turks were adamant that the Russians must give back Azov. After much argument the French Ambassador managed to cajole them into agreeing to a compromise whereby the fortress would be razed and abandoned, and the area around it declared a neutral zone between the Empires of the Czarina and the Sultan. Villeneuve had been authorised to agree to the razing of Azov at a last resort, but the Russian Foreign Minister had given him no power to agree to the neutral zone. He therefore tried to find out from Cagnoni whether, by virtue of the special powers with which Ostermann had invested him, he was authorised to consent to this. Cagnoni said that he was not. Time was running out. The Grand Vizier announced his imminent departure for Constantinople, and Neipperg made it clear that so far as he was concerned the definitive peace must be signed in Belgrade or nowhere. At this point, when he was balked by the Grand Vizier's impatience and Neipperg's obstinacy, Villeneuve discovered that Cagnoni was distributing very substantial bribes amongst the Turks with the object of making peace with them behind his back. He feared that if Cagnoni succeeded the resulting treaty would include some clause, such as freedom of navigation for Russian ships on the Black Sea, which would be fatal for the interests of France, and that if he failed both the Austrian and Russian treaties might remain in indefinite suspense. It was, as Villeneuve later confessed to Amelot, the one point in all the negotiations where he lay awake throughout the night trying to resolve what to do next.[7] Finally he decided that he must exceed his instructions, and commit the Czarina, not only to the razing of Azov, but also to the neutralisation of the surrounding area, safeguarding himself by reserving the French guarantee until such time as she had ratified the treaty. When he announced this the Reis Effendi instantly objected that it was beneath the Grand Vizier's dignity to sign the treaty unconditionally, while the Czarina's plenipotentiary was only signing subject to her approval. Villeneuve was compelled to embark on yet another round of argument. Eventually his diplomatic skill combined with a 'present' of 5,000 ducats persuaded the Reis Effendi to withdraw his objections.

On September the 18th, without ceremony and at six o'clock in the morning, both the definitive peace with Austria and the peace treaty with Russia were signed. The Grand Vizier departed for Constantinople; Neipperg returned to the Austrian lines; couriers set out for Versailles, Vienna, St. Petersburg and Münnich's headquarters bearing with them dispatches in which Villeneuve with his habitual detachment and lucidity summarised the final outcome of his negotiations.

As he rode out of the camp after the Grand Vizier, the French Ambassador heard a series of explosions from Belgrade where the demolition of the fortifications was in progress, and turned in his saddle to take a last look at the fortress on the fate of which, for thirty-four anxious days, the whole of his mission had depended, During that time it had so often seemed that he must fail. Now he could allow himself the knowledge that he had achieved a settlement which would be applauded by Cardinal Fleury, and had confronted the Emperor and the Czarina with a *fait accompli* which, however reluctantly, they must accept. Villeneuve permitted himself to feel content as he followed the Grand Vizier down the long road to Constantinople.

꒛꒛꒛꒛꒛꒛꒛꒛꒛꒛꒛꒛꒛꒛꒛꒛꒛꒛꒛꒛꒛꒛꒛꒛꒛꒛꒛꒛꒛꒛꒛꒛꒛

CHAPTER XIV

The *Fait Accompli*

October 1739–May 1740

On the Austrian side General Schmettau was the first to learn of the Peace of Belgrade. On the morning of September 1st he had called a meeting of his senior officers in order to inform them of his plans for a sortie in force, which he was confident would transform the whole course of the siege. While the conference was in progress he was handed a note from Neipperg announcing that peace had been concluded and ordering an immediate cease fire. Schmettau, dumbfounded and horrified, ignored it and the bombardment of the Grand Vizier's camp was still in progress when Neipperg came to demand that his order be obeyed. The resulting altercation between the two Generals was only resolved by the arrival of Field-Marshal Wallis who, after listening to Neipperg's account of what had happened, exerted the remnants of his authority as Commander-in-Chief, forced Schmettau to cease hostilities forthwith and, to the garrison commander's astonishment and disgust, embraced the Imperial Plenipotentiary and warmly congratulated him on his achievement.

Wallis commanded Schmettau to draw up an immediate plan for the destruction of the outer fortifications of Belgrade. He then returned to his headquarters from where he spent the next few days corresponding with Neipperg about the execution of the peace terms. The Field-Marshal who had previously complained bitterly about the contempt in which he alleged he was held by the Count, now appeared only to wish to support him in every possible way, and signed himself his most obedient servant. As a result of Wallis' eager collaboration the timetable agreed by Neipperg was strictly adhered to. On September 4th the first Turkish troops entered Belgrade; Schmettau and his men noted with impotent rage that their officers were using the Imperial standards captured at Groczka as saddle cloths. Two days later, on September 6th, the demolition of the outer fortifications began.

In Vienna on that same day the Emperor and his ministers, still quite ignorant that peace had been signed, were anxious about Neipperg, from whom there had been no word since he went to the Grand Vizier's camp on August 18th. They concluded from his silence that he was being treated as a prisoner by the Turks and forced to negotiate under duress, and sent an order to him to return to Belgrade at once.

In a memorandum to Villeneuve sent by the same courier, the Emperor's only expressed fear was, however, that the Russians, might make a separate peace with the Sultan. In spite of Neipperg's silence Charles was still convinced that he was in control of the situation. Over the past two and a half weeks he had received a number of encouraging reports from the generals at Wallis's headquarters and from Schmettau in Belgrade, all of whom appeared to agree, in direct contradiction to the Commander-in-Chief, that the fortress could be held. The Emperor's increasing optimism was reflected in a series of letters which he wrote to Neipperg. The first of these, while piously reminding his pleni-potentiary that it was necessary to bow to the will of the Almighty, went on to say that God helps those who help themselves, and emphasised the importance of the proper timing of the peace negotiations. A few days later Charles wrote again stressing that, while Neipperg was still empowered to hand over a razed Bel-grade, in view of the encouraging reports on the military situation, this might not now be necessary. Finally on August 31st (when the peace agreement was already under draft in the Grand Vizier's camp), he adjured the Count not to proceed too fast with the negotiations, for there was now reason to believe that the Turks would never be able to capture the fortress.

On September 6th the Emperor was quite unaware that, partly

owing to the length of time which letters took to reach Belgrade, and partly because Wallis was both an incompetent and an unwilling intermediary, Neipperg had received no instructions since he left for the Grand Vizier's camp on August 18th, and knew neither of the change in his views, nor of the improvement in the military situation.

Within twenty-four hours the Imperial complacency was rudely shattered. General Mercy d'Argenteau rode into Vienna, requested immediate audience of Charles VI, and broke to him the news that Neipperg had signed a preliminary peace treaty with the Grand Vizier and handed over Belgrade to the Sultan. It was impossible to keep d'Argenteau's arrival secret, but for several days no official announcement was made, and during that time the capital seethed with rumours. When the full extent of the disaster became known all classes of the population were not slow to voice their resentment of such a dishonourable peace, and near riots occurred in some quarters of the city. The Church was at one with citizens of Vienna in condemning the treaty. By an unhappy coincidence, Cardinal Collovitz had recently presented a memorandum to the Emperor on the subject of Belgrade, summarising the reasons why His Imperial Majesty must on no account surrender the 'Principal bulwark of Christendom' to the infidel, on the fortifying of which 'the Church in particular had laid out such considerable sums'.[1]

Charles VI was appalled by what had occurred. He could not sleep, appeared to have aged ten years overnight, and repeated incessantly that since the death of Prince Eugen all good fortune had deserted him. He was considering a repudiation of the treaty when, on September 10th, news reached Vienna that one gate of Belgrade had already been handed over to the Turks, and that the demolition of the fortifications had begun. He was confronted with a *fait accompli*, and thereafter could only attempt to obtain some slight amelioration of the terms imposed by the Grand Vizier; ensure that all Europe knew that Neipperg and Wallis were solely to blame for the disaster, and try to preserve the alliance with Russia.

After much debate the Imperial Privy Council decided to send

Talman to Belgrade in the hope that, with his great experience of the Turks he might be able to do something to remedy the consequences of Neipperg's ineptitude. Unfortunately Talman only left Vienna on September the 17th, and the definitive Treaty was signed on the 18th before he reached Belgrade. Nothing, it seemed could instil a sense of urgency into the Emperor's ministers.

Meanwhile a manifesto was prepared for circulation to all the Imperial ambassadors placing the whole blame for the debacle on Wallis and Neipperg. The Field-Marshal, in an attempt to cover himself, wrote to the Emperor alleging that the responsibility for the loss of Belgrade rested with Neipperg. He also wrote, but in very different terms, to the Count who, he said, he had always regarded as 'his good friend', and to whom, since he had many influential contacts, he appealed for help. It was not a very becoming letter. Neipperg's behaviour was a great deal more dignified. In his petition for mercy to Charles VI while admitting that he had concluded a bad peace, he nevertheless stoutly maintained that in doing so he had averted even greater disasters.[2] He was supported by Villeneuve who informed Sinzendorf that in the circumstances, he considered Neipperg could not have done better, but even this failed to move the Emperor, who refused to differentiate between the Count and Wallis. Both of them were arrested and imprisoned for the rest of his reign.

So far as the Russian alliance was concerned, the only thing to be done was once again to make Wallis and Neipperg the scapegoats. Charles received the Russian Ambassador in audience (it lasted for no more than five minutes), and assured him that everything which had happened had been contrary to his orders. He also wrote to this effect to the Czarina, protesting that in this, the most bitter moment of his life, his sole consolation was that he alone was afflicted by the consequences of this calamity. He could not bring himself to congratulate her on the brilliant victory which on August 28th, four days before Neipperg had signed the fatal preliminary peace, had been won for her by Field-Marshal Münnich.

The Fait Accompli

The Czarina's Commander-in-Chief received the news that her ally had made a separate peace on September 24th at his headquarters in Moldavia. He had forced the crossing of the Dniester, defeated the Turks in a pitched battle at Stavuchankh, captured the important fortress of Choczim and entered Jassy, the Moldavian capital in triumph. He was planning an advance to link up with the Imperial army. The peace of Belgrade therefore enraged him. He made no attempt to disguise his feelings in a letter to Prince Lobkowitz, the Austrian general in the Banat. It was a long letter and in it Münnich compared the Austrian war effort with that of the Russians in the most unflattering terms. He left the Prince in no doubt of his pride in the Russian soldiers (and by implication of his contempt for the Austrians)—'there is not another army in Europe', he declared, 'capable of enduring such fatigues. What', he fulminated, 'is become of that sacred alliance that was to be maintained between the two Courts? The Russians capture fortresses from the enemy; the Austrians demolish or yield them to him. The Russians conquer principalities; the Imperial forces hand over entire kingdoms to the Turks. The Russians press the enemy to the limit of his endurance; the Emperor and his ministers give him everything which he wishes.'[3] Beside this withering invective the comment made by the British envoy in Vienna on the ineptitude of the Imperial commanders—'in the first campaign Seckendorf did nothing against anybody. In the second Königsegg took the advanced guard of the Turks for the whole army, and in the third Wallis took the whole army for the advanced guard'[4]—appears positively benevolent.

St. Petersburg received the news of the peace rather more philosophically. The war had been enormously expensive and, in the course of it, over 100,000 Russians were estimated to have lost their lives. The attitude of Sweden was menacing and, after the Emperor's defection, the Czarina both could not and dared not continue the struggle alone. Orders were sent to Münnich to abandon all his conquests and withdraw to the Ukraine; Ostermann, while protesting that better terms could have been obtained without French mediation, made no attempt to delay the ratification of the treaty which Villeneuve had negotiated. The Czarina distributed orders and estates liberally to her generals and, in celebration of the peace, gave a very grand ball.

Versailles, as was to be expected, had none of the reservations of Vienna or St. Petersburg about the Peace of Belgrade, and when the news of Villeneuve's achievement was received, Louis XV ordered a special medal to be struck, on which an allegorical figure of France was represented with olive branches in her hand, with the motto *'Virtutis et justitiae fama'* subscribed. Cardinal Fleury, while privately sending the warmest congratulations to Villeneuve, was careful to maintain a decently reserved attitude in public. He knew that there would inevitably be criticism of the manner in which French mediation had been conducted, so he instructed the newly appointed French Ambassador to Russia to avoid all discussion of the matter, while consistently maintaining to foreign diplomats that 'M. de Villeneuve had no other hand in the pacification than witnessing in a manner what the Vizier and M. de Neipperg had settled.'[5] However, when summing up the negotiations to Ostermann, Fleury allowed himself one final dig at the Russian Foreign Minister. 'I will not conceal from your Excellency', he wrote, 'that this Minister (Villeneuve) in a letter to me on the second of last month pointed out that if there had been more agreement between the Courts of Vienna and Russia or if he had been given wider powers, he could have obtained better conditions for both your Courts over a year ago.'[6]

The Cardinal was entitled to lecture anyone he chose, for after Villeneuve's success at Belgrade he was the arbiter of Europe. His Eminence would no doubt have been delighted had he known that Bartenstein had commented ruefully to the Emperor on the increased prestige which now accrued to the French Crown, and he would certainly have considered Frederick the Great's subsequent verdict appropriate—'the French owe their most brilliant successes to their diplomacy. The greatest asset of that kingdom is the shrewdness and foresight of its Ministers.'[7]

It now remained for Villeneuve to finalise the treaty which he had concluded on the field, and to exploit his success at Belgrade to the utmost in the interests of his country.

The Fait Accompli

Shortly after his return to Constantinople, preceded by 300 Janissaries and twenty Haiduks, and once again escorted by the entire French community, he rode to the Arsenal where, clad in a magnificent robe of cloth of silver trimmed with ermine presented to him by the Porte, he presided over the solemn exchange of ratifications of the treaty. This ceremony did not mark the end of his work, for throughout the rest of his time at the Porte, he was required to mediate in all the discussions on its detailed implementation. The original text had been drafted in a great hurry in French, because neither Villeneuve nor Neipperg understood much Latin, and confusion arose over the subsequent translations of it into Latin and Turkish. Frontiers had to be demarcated and, since maps were inadequate, there was a great deal of argument about them.

The arrival of Ambassadors Extraordinary to the Sultan from the Emperor, the Czarina, the Persians and the Neapolitans impeded the progress of this work, as the inevitable ceremonial diverted the Grand Vizier and his subordinates from all other business. But, if Villeneuve's work as mediator was then for a time at a standstill he was not idle, for in view of the high regard in which he was held by the Turks he was constantly called upon to smooth out the many difficulties encountered by these envoys.

The French Ambassador's position in Constantinople was now unassailable and, as he had asked to be relieved and was only awaiting the arrival of his successor, he was able to watch the sufferings of his colleagues and their competition for the favours of the Porte with a certain detached amusement. There were the usual grumbles about the monotony and length of the ceremonies and entertainments which they were obliged to attend; and there was the usual competition in gifts to curry favour with the Sultan and his ministers. These included a remarkable range of objects. The Neapolitans presented artificial flowers, brocade, and a tortoiseshell cabinet inlaid with a thousand ounces of gold. The Russians brought furs, china, tea, and rhubarb which was in short supply in Turkey, and always much in demand as a purge. Although this gift gave rise to some adverse comment amongst the diplomatic corps who considered it unsuitable for a solemn occasion, it was rather more practical, and much less inconvenient, than the seven elephants presented (in addition to a quantity of diamonds) by the Persians. A special bridge to enable the elephants to cross from the Asiatic to the European side of the Bosphorus had to be constructed by their reluctant recipients, who then only too quickly discovered that the cost of feeding these creatures was prohibitive.

Perhaps it was to be expected that of all the Ambassadors Extraordinary none would fare worse than the Emperor's envoy. His presents—a very large number of silver ornaments and dishes, and a richly decorated coach—which had been transported from Vienna at great inconvenience and vast expense—did little to ingratiate him with the Porte, and he was subjected to a number of petty humiliations in which he was compelled to appeal for help to the French Ambassador.

From the Austrian envoy and his staff the Marquis no doubt also heard a good deal about the behaviour of the Turkish Ambassador Extraordinary in Vienna, which was most disagreeable for all the officials of the Imperial Court. When, after days of argument about the appropriate etiquette, Prince Auersperg, the Grand Master of the Court came to escort him at his state entry into Vienna, he had announced that he had colic, could not ride, and would therefore make his entry in the coach which he had brought with him from Constantinople. As this coach was so low that its occupants were compelled to squat in it *à la Turque* (it was described as resembling a hen coop), the Imperial Grand Master had been faced by an awkward predicament, not eased by the nature of the Ambassador's indisposition, which made it hardly practicable for the Prince to ride beside him as etiquette demanded.[8]

Listening to these and many similar complaints, Villeneuve thought of all the humiliation and frustration which he himself had endured during his time in the Ottoman Empire. But, had he not done so, the Grand Vizier would never have accepted his mediation at Belgrade and he would not have been able to carry out the mission entrusted to him when he was appointed Ambassador in Constantinople. By the middle of 1740 he could congratulate himself that he had fully exploited the success which he had gained at Belgrade. French influence was once more predominant at the Porte; King Louis XV was once more recognised as the protector of the Latin Christians in the Sultan's dominions; finally, as a direct result of the prestige which he had acquired at Belgrade, Villeneuve had been able to negotiate a renewal of the Capitulations which gave French merchants trading with the Ottoman Empire a decisive advantage over the merchants of all other nations. The proclamation relating to this had been signed by Mahmoud I on the 28th of May 1740. It opened, as was customary, with an enumeration of the places over which the Sultan ruled—'the two illustrious and noble cities of Mecca and Medina . . . Damascus, scent of Paradise . . . Egypt . . . renowned for its delights . . . the whole of Arabia . . . Africa . . . Baghdad the capital of the Caliphs . . . Erzerum the delicious . . . the isles and coasts of the White Sea and the Black Sea . . . Greece . . . Tartary . . . Caucasia.' It was an imposing scroll of names. As he read it Villeneuve noticed with interest that the Sultan had added to them one extra designation—'Lord of the fortress of Belgrade, the place of war.'9

In July 1741, after being accorded the unusual honour of a final audience with the Sultan, 'the paragon of Christian noblemen, the able, discreet, esteemed and honoured Envoy Louis-Sauveur Marquis de Villeneuve' (for so he was described in the Capitulations), set sail for France. Louis XV had nominated him a Counsellor of State and awarded him a handsome pension. Charles VI had given him a portrait of himself set in diamonds. The Czarina had offered him the Order of St. Andrew and when, on the instructions of his Government, he had been obliged to decline it, had presented Madame de Villeneuve with a magnificent diamond ring.

As the ship weighed anchor and began to move slowly down the Bosphorus Villeneuve, gazing for the last time at the city of Constantinople, may have remembered the day of his arrival there in 1728. It had taken thirteen years of struggle and frustration to carry out the instructions which he had been given on his appointment. Now he could depart, secure in the knowledge that his mission was fulfilled and that he had crowned it with a diplomatic coup which denied the Russians access to the Black Sea, deprived the Emperor of his offensive base against the Sultan, and secured a victory for the Turks which masked their internal weakness. The Marquis was entitled to feel that his term as Ambassador, which had started so inauspiciously, had ended with the utmost distinction.

One final recognition of Villeneuve's achievement was still to come. Two years after his return to France Cardinal Fleury died, and Louis XV offered the post of Minister of Foreign Affairs to the man who had represented him so brilliantly at the Sublime Porte. To everyone's astonishment the Marquis declined the offer. He was not in the best of health, and he was well content to let his reputation rest on his achievements in Constantinople. He died a year later.

*   *   *

In September 1717, on the battlefield of Belgrade, an unknown soldier in the Imperial Army composed a song in honour of Prince Eugen of Savoy. *'Der edele Ritter'* passed into Austrian history, and as the years went by successive generations added verses to it. One of these describes the Prince welcoming into Heaven those who had carried on the struggle in which he himself had fought so superbly. It is pleasant to conjecture that among the advancing throng of heroes he may have noticed an ugly little man speaking with a broad Provençal accent and, with his gift for recognising a worthy opponent, have singled him out for a special welcome. The Imperial Field-Marshal and the French Ambassador each in his own manner had triumphed at Belgrade.

Note on Currency

Notes

Bibliography

Index

Note on Currency

By 1730 the conversion rate of the various European currencies mentioned in this book against the pound sterling of the day was approximately:

2 ducats	4 thalers
8 gulden or florins	12 livres
4 crowns	5 roubles

In Constantinople the pound was then worth about six Turkish piastres. The sterling equivalent of the Turkish 'purse' is impossible to determine with any degree of exactitude. The amount of money which it contained appears to have varied and, to confuse the issue still further, many sources omit to state whether they are referring to silver or gold 'purses'. The former seems generally to have been worth about £125, and the latter about £200.

The purchasing power of £1 sterling of 1730 would be equivalent to at least £10 ($28) today.

Notes

PROLOGUE (*pages 1–9*)

THE PIVOT OF THE STRUGGLE

1. Letter from the Empress's mother to her husband (K. St. A. Hanover, Fasc. 3920). Quoted in *Feldzüge des Prinzen Eugen von Savoyen herausgegeben von der Abteilung für Kriegesgeschichte des k.k. Kriegs-Archivs*, Vienna, 1876–92, Vol. 17, p. 183.

2. The Venetian Ambassador in Vienna, December 1699. Quoted in Otto Frass, *Quellenbuch zur Österreichische Geschichte*, Birkenverlag, Vienna, 1959, Vol. 2, p. 188.

3. *See* Janko von Musulin, *Prinz Eugen von Savoyen*, Herold Verlag, Vienna-Munich, 1963, p. 56.

4. Egon Cesare Count Corti, *Der Edele Ritter*, 1941, p. 87.

5. *Hauptbericht Eugens über die Schlacht bei Belgrad*, 25 August 1717. Kretschmayr, *Prinz Eugen*, p. 44. Quoted Frass, op. cit., p. 235.

CHAPTER I (*pages 13–21*)

THE EMPEROR AND HIS MINISTERS

1. Extract from a London broadsheet of 1684 in the British Museum, reproduced in *The Siege of Vienna* by John Stoye, Collins, London, 1964. Opposite p. 287.

2. *See* Anna Coreth, *Pietas Austria*, Munich, 1959.

3. *See* Ann Tizia-Leitich, *Vienna Glorioso* Wilhelm Andermann Verlag, Vienna, 1947, Chapter 1, and Friedrich Heer, *Land im Strom der Zeit*, Vienna, 1958, pp. 109–14.

4. N. William Wraxall, *Memoirs of the Northern Courts*, London, 1806, 3rd edn., Vol. I, p. 359.

5. Abraham a Sancta Clara, quoted Ann Tizia-Leitich, op. cit., p. 39.

6. Lady Mary Wortley Montagu, *Letters written during her Travels in Europe, Asia and Africa*, London, 1727, Vol. I, p. 125.

7. Charles Louis Baron de Pollnitz, *Memoirs*, 2nd edn., London, 1739, Vol. I, p. 251.

8. Lady Mary Wortley Montagu, op. cit., Vol. I, p. 124.

9. Friedrich Förster, *Die Höfe und Cabinette Europas im achtzehnten Jahrhundert*, Potsdam, 1836, Vol. II A, p. 91.

10. Egon Vehse, *Memoirs of the Court and Aristocracy of Austria*, translated by Demmles, London, 1896, pp. 124–5. (Cardinal de Polignac replied: 'After the description you have given me of the measure in which you have fulfilled all the duties of Lent and Holy Week, and of Easter, I believe I can only congratulate you on being quit of it; perhaps you have never done so much of it in your life. Imagine to yourself precisely the same thing of a Cardinal at Rome. It is true that *we* are paid for it.')

11. Frederick the Great, *Histoire de Mon Temps*, Vol. II of *Œuvres Historiques de Frédéric II Roi de Prusse*, Berlin, 1846, p. 3.

12. M. S. Anderson, *Europe in the Eighteenth Century*, Longmans, Green and Co., London, 1961, p. 195.

13. *See* Alfons von Czibulka, *Prinz Eugen. Retter des Abendlandes*, Paul Neff Verlag, Vienna, 1958, p. 112.

14. P.R.O., S.P. 80/113, Vienna, 1735.

15. P.R.O., S.P. 80/115, Vienna, 1735.

16. Alfred Arneth, *Geschichte Maria Theresias*, Vienna, 1863, Vol. I, p. 62.

17. Alfred Arneth, *Prinz Eugen von Savoyen*, Vienna, 1864, Vol. III, p. 38.

18. *See* Ann Tizia-Leitich, op. cit., p. 42.

19. Arneth, *Prinz Eugen*, op. cit., Vol. III, pp. 97–8.

CHAPTER II

THE CZARINA AND HER ADVISERS

1. Robert Nisbet Bain, *The Pupils of Peter the Great*, London, 1897, pp. 170–3.

2. Bain, op. cit., p. 185.

3. Mrs. Ward, *Letters from a Lady who resided some years in Russia to her friend in England*, London, 1775, p. 71.

4. Frederick the Great, op. cit., p. 22.

5. Vehse, op. cit., p. 122.

6. Ward, op. cit., pp. 144–6.

7. Ward, op. cit., pp. 189–205.

8. Mardefelt, quoted Bain, op. cit., pp. 86–7.

9. P.R.O., S.P. 91/19, St. Petersburg, 1736.

10. K. Walizewski, *L'héritage de Pierre-le-Grand, 1725–1741*, Librairie Plon, Paris, 1900, p. 171.

11. Bain, op. cit., pp. 47–51.

12. Christopher Hermann von Manstein, *Contemporary Memoirs of Russia, 1727–1744* (English translation), London, 1856, p. 335.

13. Manstein, op. cit., p. 335.

14. P.R.O., S.P. 91/10, St. Petersburg, 1728.

15. Frederick the Great, *Histoire de mon Temps*, op. cit., p. 22.

16. Francesco, Conte Algarotti, *Letters to Lord Hervey*, London, 1769, p. 75.

17. Ward, op. cit., pp. 9–10.

18. J. Weber, *Das Veränderte Russland*, Frankfurt, 1721, Vol. I, p. 221.

CHAPTER III

THE CARDINAL AND HIS AMBASSADOR

1. *Mémoires du marquis d'Argenson*, published by the Societé de l'histoire de France, Paris, 1859, Vol. I, p. 364.

2. Kretschmayr, *Die Türken vor Wien*, Langen-Müller, 1938. Quoted, Frass, op. cit., Vol. II, p. 149.

3. Kretschmayr, op. cit., *Kaiserliche Gesandtschaftsinstruktion* (February 1677). Quoted Frass, op. cit., p. 149.

4. Kretschmayer, op. cit., *Kaiserliche Gesandtschaftsinstruktion* (March 1683). Quoted Frass, op. cit., p. 150.

5. Albert Vandal, *Une Ambassade Française en Orient sous Louis XV. La Mission du Marquis de Villeneuve, 1728–1741*, Paris, 1887, p. 16.

6. Emile Raunié, *Chansonnier Historique du XVIII siècle*, Paris, 1879–84, Vol. VI, pp. 262–3. Quoted A. Mc. C. Wilson, *French Foreign Policy during the Administration of Cardinal Fleury*, Harvard University Press, 1936, p. 94.

7. St. Simon, *Mémoires*, (ed. de Boislisle), Paris, 1879–1930, Vol., 26, p. 89.

8. H. Carré, *Le régne de Louis XV*, Paris 1909, p. 130, (Vol. VIII, Part 2 of *L'Histoire de France depuis les origines jusqu'a la Révolution*, ed. Larisse.)

9. P.R.O., S.P. 78/213, Paris, 1736.

10. Garrett Mattingly, *Renaissance Diplomacy*, Peregrine Books, 1965, p. 205.

11. Ermolao Barbaro, quoted, Mattingly, op. cit., p. 110.

12. Montagu, op. cit., Vol. I, p. 229.

CHAPTER IV

THE SULTAN, THE PORTE AND THE FOREIGN ENVOYS

1. Count Marsigli. *L'État militaire de l'Empire Ottoman*. Paris 1732, p. 57.

2. *See* H. A. R. Gibb and Harold Bowen, *Islamic Society and the West*, Oxford University Press 1950, Vol. 1., p. 112, footnote 2.

3. *See* Gibb and Bowen, op. cit., Vol., 1, p. 22.

4. Sir George Larpent, *Turkey its history and progress from the Correspondence and journals of Sir James Porter*, London, 1854, p. 291.

5. Larpent, op. cit., p. 292.

6. Larpent, op. cit., p. 293.

7. Baron de Tott, *Mémoires*, 2nd edition, London 1786, Vol. 1, pp. 126–7.

8. P.R.O., S.P., 97/26, Constantinople, 1730.

9. Tott, op. cit., p. 99.

10. Tott, op. cit., p. 98.

11. Vandal, op. cit., p. 378.

12. Shafirov aetat 1713. Quoted, B. H. Summer, *Peter the Great and the Ottoman Empire*, Blackwell, Oxford, 1949, p. 65.

13. 'In Pera there are three evils: plague, fire and dragomen.' M. L. Shay, *The Ottoman Empire from 1720–1734 as revealed in the Despatches of the Venetian Bailo*. University of Illinois, 1944, p. 38.

14. P.R.O., S.P., 97/27, Constantinople, 1730.
15. Larpent, op. cit., p. 229.
16. P.R.O., S.P., 97/25, Constantinople, 1729.
17. Gerhard Fritsch, *Pasches und Pest*, Stiasny Verlag Graz, Vienna 1962, p. 151.
18. Fritsch, op. cit., p. 152.
19. P.R.O., S.P., 97/30. Constantinople 1739.
20. P.R.O., S.P., 97/30. Constantinople 1739.
21. *See* Fritsch, op. cit., pp. 203–6.
22. Shay, op. cit., p. 56.
23. Shay, op. cit., p. 17.
24. Report of the Bailo Dolfin, 1 June 1729. Quoted, Shay, op. cit., p. 25.

CHAPTER V

DIPLOMATIC STALEMATE

1. *See* Basil Williams, *The Whig Supremacy*, Oxford, 1962, p. 78.
2. P.R.O., S.P. 97/27, Constantinople, 1730.
3. D. B. Horn, *The British Diplomatic Service, 1689–1789*. Oxford, Clarendon Press, 1961, p. 86.
4. Vandal, op. cit., p. ii.
5. P.R.O., S.P. 91/10, St. Petersburg, 1729.
6. *See* Czibulka, op. cit., p. 98.
7. P.R.O., S.P. 97/25, Constantinople, 1727.
8. Shay, op. cit., p. 37.
9. P.R.O., S.P. 97/29, Constantinople, 1738.
10. Villeneuve to Chauvelin, 12 October 1730. Quoted, Vandal, op. cit., p. 159.
11. Villeneuve to Chauvelin, 2 January 1732. Quoted, Vandal, op. cit., p. 170.
12. Victorious in all perils.
13. Chauvelin to Villeneuve, 15 October 1729. Quoted, Vandal, Villeneuve, op. cit., p. 138.

CHAPTER VI

THE DISCOMFITURE OF THE FRENCH AMBASSADOR

1. Chauvelin to Villeneuve, 23 May 1733. Quoted, Vandal, op. cit., p. 195.
2. Villeneuve to Chauvelin, 5 November 1733. Quoted, Vandal, op. cit., p. 211.
3. Villeneuve to Chauvelin, 28 July 1734. Quoted, Vandal, op. cit., p. 230.
4. Villeneuve to Chauvelin, 11 September 1734. Quoted, Vandal, op. cit., p. 232.
5. P.R.O., S.P. 91/17, St. Petersburg, 1734.
6. P.R.O., S.P. 78/208, Paris, 1735.

Notes (pages 97–129)

CHAPTER VII

RUSSIA ATTACKS

1. Soloviev, Vol. XV, p. 111. Quoted, Vandal, op. cit., p. 248.
2. *Archiv des Fürsten Voroncov*, Vol. II, p. 509. Quoted, H. Übersberger, *Russlands Orientpolitik in den letzten zwer Jahrhunderten*, Deutsche Verlags-Anstalt, Stuttgart, 1913, p. 171.
3. Bain, *Pupils of Peter the Great*, p. 242.
4. P.R.O., S.P. 97/28, Constantinople, 1736.
5. P.R.O., S.P. 97/28, Constantinople, 1736.
6. P.R.O., S.P. 97/28, Constantinople, 1736.
7. Summer, op. cit., p. 23.
8. *Travels of Eviliya Effendi*, English translation London, 1834–50, Vol. II, p. 76.
9. Alexander Pallis, *In the Days of the Janissaries*, p. 125, Hutchinson, London, 1951. See pp. 119–56 for a detailed description of the Alay.
10. Bailo Contarini, 10 June 1736. Quoted, Vandal, op. cit., p. 263.
11. Soloviev, Vol. XV, p. 111. Quoted, Vandal, op. cit., p. 259.
12. Villeneuve to Chauvelin, 18 June 1736. Quoted, Vandal, op. cit., pp. 267–8.
13. P.R.O., S.P. 97/28, Constantinople, 1736.
14. Chauvelin to Villeneuve, 1 November 1736. Quoted, Va dal, op. cit., pp. 273, 274.

CHAPTER VIII

AUSTRIA GOES TO WAR

1. P.R.O., S.P. 80/140, Vienna, 1740.
2. P.R.O., S.P. 91/20, St. Petersburg.
3. Quoted, Musulin, op. cit., p. 15.
4. Quoted, Musulin, op. cit., p. 70.
5. P.R.O., S.P. 80/122, Vienna, 1736.
6. P.R.O., S.P. 80/121, Vienna, 1736.
7. P.R.O., S.P. 80/123, Vienna, 1736.
8. P.R.O., S.P. 80/123, Vienna, 1736.
9. William Coxe, *History of the House of Austria*, London, 1847, Vol. III, pp. 198, 199.
10. Theresius von Seckendorf, *Versuch einer Lebensbeschreibung des Feldmarschalls Grafen von Seckendorf*, 1792, Vol. 1, Part 2, p. 88.
11. *See* Fred Hennings, *Und Sitzet zur Linken Hand*, Vienna, 1961, p. 189.

CHAPTER IX

AN ABORTIVE PEACE CONGRESS

1. J. Bell, *Travels from St. Petersburg into Russia and various parts of Asia*, Edinburgh, 1806, p. 582.

213

2. M. L'Abbé Laugier, *Histoire des Négociations pour la Paix conclue à Belgrade le 18 Septembre 1739*, Vol. II, pp. 265–71.

3. P.R.O., S.P. 78/216, Paris, 1737.

4. J. W. Zinkeisen, *Geschichte des Osmanisches Reich in Europe*, Hamburg, 1840–63, Vol. V, p. 706.

CHAPTER X

THE SECOND ROUND

1. Joseph von Hammer, *Geschichte des Osmanischen Reiches,* Budapest, 1831, Vol. VII p. 472.

2. P.R.O., S.P. 97/29, Constantinople, 1738.

3. Villeneuve to Amelot, 8 March 1738. Quoted, Vandal, op. cit., p. 315.

4. Carré, op. cit., p. 123.

5. P.R.O., S.P. 78/214, Paris, 1737.

6. P.R.O., S.P. 80/128, Vienna, 1737.

7. Moritz von Angeli, *Der Krieg mit der Pforte, 1736–1739*, Vienna, 1881, p. 335.

8. 'The Capricious'.

9. 'The Shipwreck'.

10. 'The Unknown'.

11. *See* Max Braubach, *Eine Satire auf den Wiener Hof ans den letzten Jahren Kaiser Karls VI*, 1934.

12. *Imperial Russian Historical Society (Sbornik, I.R.I.U.)*, St. Petersburg, 1884–8, Vol. 86, pp. 1–13.

13. Sbornik, op. cit., pp. 14–21.

14. Sbornik, op. cit., pp. 22–4.

15. Sbornik, op. cit., pp. 24–6.

16. Sbornik, op. cit., pp. 32–4.

17. Sbornik, op. cit., pp. 35–41.

18. Charles Joseph Prince de Ligne, *Mémoires et Mélanges Historiques et Littéraires*, Paris, 1829, Vol. VI, p. 10.

19. P.R.O., S.P. 80/130, Vienna, 1738.

20. P.R.O., S.P. 80/130, Vienna, 1738.

21. Villeneuve to Amelot, 17 February 1739. Quoted, Vandal, op. cit., p. 332.

22. Zinkeisen, op. cit., Vol. V, pp. 760–1.

23. P.R.O., S.P. 97/29, Constantinople, 1737.

CHAPTER XI

A MEDIATOR IS APPOINTED

1. P.R.O., SP. 80/135, Vienna, 1739.

2. Sbornik, op. cit., pp. 43–7.

3. Sbornik, op. cit., pp. 47–59, and 63–71.

4. Sbornik, op. cit., pp. 51–63.

5. Angeli, op. cit., p. 436.

6. P.R.O., S.P. 91/22, St. Petersburg, 1738.

7. P.R O., S.P. 91/22, St. Petersburg, 1738.

8. P.R.O., S.P. 80/129, Vienna, 1738.

9. P.R.O., S.P. 80/133, Vienna, 1738.

10. P.R.O., S.P. 80/133, Vienna, 1738.

11. Villeneuve to Amelot, 17 August 1739. Quoted, Vandal, op. cit., p. 376.

CHAPTER XII

DEADLOCK

1. Frederick the Great, *Mémoires de Brandenbourg. Œuvres Historiques de Frédéric II Roi de Prusse*, Berlin, 1846, Vol. 1, p. 172.

2. *See* Oskar Regele, *Die Schuld des Grafen Reinhard Wilhelm von Neipperg am Belgrader Frieden 1739. Mitteilungen des Österreichischen Staatsarchivs*, Vienna, 1954, pp. 386–7.

CHAPTER XIII

'THIS THORNY NEGOTIATION'

1. For accounts of Neipperg's and Villeneuve's negotiations in the Grand Vizier's camp see in particular:
   (*a*) Vandal, op. cit., pp. 369–97.
   (*b*) T. Tupetz, *Der Türkenfeldzug von 1739 und der Friede zu Belgrad,* Munich, *Historische Zeitschrift,* Vol. 40 (1878), pp. 35–50.
   (*c*) Count Neipperg, *Umständliche auf Original Dokumente gegründete Geschichte der sämtlichen und wahren Vorgänge bei der Unterhandlung des zu Belgrad am 18 September 1739 geschlossenen Friedens,* Frankfurt and Leipzig, 1790, pp. 12–82.
   (*d*) Zinkeisen, op. cit., Vol. V, pp. 779–800.
   (*e*) Hammer, op. cit., Vol. VII, pp. 535–41.
   (*f*) Laugier, op. cit., Vol. II, pp. 30–53.

2. Villeneuve to Amelot, 21 August 1739. Quoted, Vandal, p. 377.

3. Neipperg, op. cit., Document XXIII, 28 August 1739, p. 234.

4. Neipperg, op. cit., p. 68.

5. Villeneuve to Amelot, 2 September 1739. Quoted, Vandal, op. cit., p. 387.

6. Villeneuve to Amelot, 2 September 1739. Quoted, Vandal, op. cit., p. 387.

7. Villeneuve to Amelot, 26 September 1739. Quoted, Vandal, op. cit., p. 396.

CHAPTER XIV

THE *FAIT ACCOMPLI*

1. P.R.O., S.P. 80/136, Vienna, 1739.
2. Neipperg, op. cit., p. 389.
3. Manstein, op. cit., pp. 237–43.
4. P.R.O., S.P. 80/130, Vienna, 1739.
5. P.R.O., S.P. 78/221, Paris, 1739.
6. Sbornik, op. cit., pp. 114, 115.
7. Quoted Émile Bourgeois, *Manuel Historique de la Politique Étrangère,* 3rd edn., Paris, 1901, Vol. I, p. 403.
8. P.R.O., S.P. 80/141, Vienna, 1740.
9. M. le Comte de Saint-Priest, *Mémoires sur l'Ambassade de France en Turquie,* Paris, 1877, p. 476.

Bibliography

ALGAROTTI, Francesco. *Letters to Lord Hervey.* London, 1769.

ALLEN, W. E. D. *The Turks in Europe.* London, 1919.

— *The Ukraine.* Cambridge, 1940.

ANDERSON, M. S. *Europe in the Eighteenth Century.* London: Longmans, 1962.

ANGELI, M. von. *Der Krieg mit der Pforte 1736 bis 1739.* Vienna: *Mitteilungen des k.k. Kriegsarchivs. Jahrg. 1881.*

ANONYMOUS, *Feldzüge des Prinzen Eugen in Ungarn.* Vienna, 1788.

ARGENSON, Marquis d'. *Mémoires et Journal du Marquis d'Argenson.* Paris, 1859.

ARNETH, Alfred von. *Prinz Eugen von Savoyen.* Vienna, 1864, Vol. 3.

— *Geschichte Maria Theresias.* Vienna, 1863. Vol. 1.

— *Johann Christoph Bartenstein und seine Zeit.* Vienna: *Archiv für Österreichische Geschichte.* 1871. Vol. 46.

— *Eigenhändige Correspondenz des Königs Karl III von Spanien (nachmals Kaiser Karl VI) mit dem Obersten Kanzler des Königreiches Böhmen Grafen Johann Wenzel Wratislaw.* Vienna: *Archiv für Kunde Österreichs Geschichts-Quellen.* 1856. Vol. 16.

AUBERTIN, Charles. *L'esprit public au dix-huitième Siècle.* Paris, 1873.

BAIN, R. Nisbet. *The Daughter of Peter the Great.* London, 1899.

— *The Pupils of Peter the Great.* London, 1897.

BEER, Adolph. *Zur Geschichte der Politik Karls VI.* Munich: *Historische Zeitschrift.* 1886. New series Vol. 19.

BELL, J. *Travels from St. Petersburg into Russia and Various Parts of Asia.* Edinburgh, 1806. 2 vols.

BENEDIKT, H. *Der Pascha Graf Alexander von Bonneval, 1675-1747.* Graz–Köln: Hermann Böhlau's Nachf., 1959.

— *Bonneval und Prinz Eugen.* Graz: *Mitteilungen des Instituts für Österreichische Geschichtsforschung.* 1953. Vol. 61.

BERNEY, A. *König Friedrich I und das Haus Habsburg (1701-1727).* Munich, 1927.

BITTNER, L. *Chronologisches Verzeichnis der Österreichen Staats Verträge.* Vienna, 1903, Vol. 1.

BITTNER, L. and GROSS, L. *Repertorium der diplomatischen Vertreter aller Lände seit 1698.* Oldenburg, 1936.

BONNAC, Jean Louis Marquis de. *Mémoire Historique sur L'Ambassade de France à Constantinople publié avec un Précis de ses Négociations à la Porte Ottomane par M. Charles Schefer.* Paris, 1894.

BOURGEOIS, Émile. *Manuel Historique de la Politique Étrangère.* Paris, 1901. 3rd edn., Vol. 1.

BOURKE, John. *The Spirit of Baroque.* London: Faber, 1958.

BRAUBACH, Max. *Prinz Eugen von Savoyen.* Vienna: Verlag für Geschichte und Politik, 1964. Vol. 3.

— *Eine Satire auf den Wiener Hof aus den letzten Jahren Kaiser Karls VI.* Innsbruck: *Mitteilungen des Instituts für Österreichische Geschichtsforschung.* 1934. Vol. 53.

Bibliography

BRAUBACH, Max. *Johann Christoph Bartensteins Herkunft und Anfänge*. Graz: Mitteilungen des Instituts für Österreichische Geschichtsforschung. 1953. Vol. 61.

— *Versailles und Wien von Louis XIV bis Kaunitz*. Bonn, 1952.

BRUCE, P. H. *Memoirs*. London, 1782.

CAMBRIDGE MODERN HISTORY. Vol. 3. *The Eighteenth Century*.

CARRÉ, H. *Le Régne de Louis XV*. Vol. 8, Part 2 of the *Histoire de France depuis les origines jusqu'à la Révolution*, edited Lavisse. Paris, 1909.

CORETH, Anna. *Pietas Austriaca*. Munich, 1959.

— *Österreichische Geschichtschreibung in der Barockzeit 1620–1740*. Vienna, 1950.

CORTI, Egon Cesare Conte. *Der Edele Ritter*. Vienna, 1941.

COXE, William. *History of the House of Austria*. London, 1847.

CZIBULKA, Alfons von. *Prinz Eugen. Retter des Abendlandes*. Paul Neff Verlag. Vienna, 1958.

DUMONT, J. *Batailles gagnées par le Sérénissime Prince Fr. Eugen de Savoye*. The Hague, 1723.

— *Le Cérémonial Diplomatique des Cours de l'Europe*. The Hague, 1739. Supplements 4 and 5.

EVLIYA EFFENDI. *Travels in Europe, Asia, Africa in the 17th century*. Translated J. von Hammer. London, 1834–50.

— *Feldzüge des Prinzen Eugen von Savoyen*. Vienna: k.k. *Kriegsarchiv*, 1876, Vol. 1. 1891, Vol. 17.

FILITTI, J. C. *Role diplomatique des Phanariotes de 1700 à 1821*. Paris, 1901.

FLASSAN, G. de. *Histoire de la diplomatie française*. Paris, 1811. Vol. 5.

FÖRSTER, Friedrich. *Die Höfe und Cabinette Europas im achtzehnten Jahrhundert*. Potsdam, 1836.

FRASS, Otto. *Quellenbuch zur Österreichische Geschichte*. Birkenverlag. Vienna, 1959. Vol. 2.

FREDERICK THE GREAT. *Œuvres Historiques de Frédéric II Roi de Prusse*. Berlin, 1848. Vols. 1, 2.

FREYTAG, Rudolf. *Der Nachlass des bei Belgrad gefallenen Prinzen Lamoral von Thurn und Taxis*. Innsbruck: Mitteilungen des Institutes für Österreichische Geschichtsforschung. 1937. Vol. 51.

FRITSCH, Gerhard. *Paschas und Pest*. Graz–Vienna: Stiasny Verlag, 1962.

GAXOTTE, P. *Le siècle de Louis XV*. Paris, 1933.

GIBB, H. A. R. and BOWEN, H. *Islamic Society and the West*. Vol. 1, Parts 1 and 2. Oxford University Press, 1950–7.

GOOCH, G. P. *Louis XV, the Monarchy in Decline*. London: Longmans, 1956.

GREY, Ian. *Peter the Great*. London, 1962.

HALEM, Gerhard Anton von. *Lebensbeschreibung des Feld Marschall. B. C. Grafen von Münnich*. Oldenburg, 1803.

HAMMER, Joseph von. *Geschichte des Osmanischen Reiches*. Budapest, 1827–35. Vol. 7.

HANTSCH, H. *Die Geschichte Österreichs*. Graz–Vienna: Styria Verlag, 1953. 2nd edn., Vol. 2.

— *Reichsvizekanzler Frederick Karl von Schönborn*. Vienna, 1929.

— *Die drei grossen Relationen St Saphorins über die innere Verhältnisse am Wiener Hof zur Zeit Karls VI*. Graz: Mitteilungen des Instituts für Österreichische Geschichtsforschung. 1950. Vol. 58.

Bibliography

HASLUCK, F. W. *Christianity and Islam under the Sultans*. Oxford, 1929.

HEER, Friedrich. *Land im Strom der Zeit*. Vienna, 1958.

HEMPEL, C. F. *Merckwürdiges Leben Des unter dem Namen des Grafen v. Biron weltbekannten Ernst Johann Bürens*. Bremen, 1742.

— *Leben Thaten u. Betrübtes Fall, des Weltberufenen Russischen Grafens Burchard Christoph von Münnich*. Bremen, 1742.

— *Merckwürdiges Leben u. Trauriges Fall des Weltberufenen Russischen Staats-Ministers Andreas Grafen von Ostermann*. Bremen, 1742.

HENDERSON, Nicholas. *Prince Eugen of Savoy*. London: Weidenfeld and Nicolson, 1964.

HENNINGS, Fred. *Und sitzet zur linken Hand*. Vienna–Berlin–Stuttgart: Neff Verlag, 1961.

HORN, D. B. *The British Diplomatic Service, 1689–1789*. Oxford, Clarendon Press, 1961.

JORGA, N. *Geschichte des Osmanischen Reiches*. Gotha, 1908–1913. Vol. 4.

LA LANDE, P. A. *Histoire de l'Empereur Charles VI*. The Hague, 1743.

LAMBERTY, F. *Mémoires pour servir à l'Histoire du XVIII Siècle*. Amsterdam, 1733–40.

LAMY, M. E. *La France du Levant*. Paris, 1900.

LARPENT, Sir George. *Turkey its history and progress from the Correspondence and journals of Sir James Porter*. London, 1854.

LAUGIER, Abbe. *Histoires des Négociations pour la Paix conclue à Belgrade le 18 Septembre 1739*. Paris, 1768.

LERNET-HOLENIA, A. *Prinz Eugen*. Vienna, 1960.

LEWIS, B. *The Emergence of Modern Turkey*. Oxford University Press, 1961.

LEY, Francis. *Le Maréchal de Münnich et la Russie au XVIII siècle*. Paris: Plon, 1959.

LIGNE, Charles Joseph Prince de. *Mémoires et Mélanges Historiques et Littéraires*. Paris, 1829. Vols. 5, 6, 7.

LOCKHART, L. *Nadir Shah*. London: Luczac, 1938.

MANCHIP-WHITE, J. *Marshal of France. The Life and Times of Maurice de Saxe*. London: Hamish Hamilton, 1962.

MANSTEIN, Christoph Hermann von. *Contemporary Memoirs of Russia, 1727–1744*. English translation. London, 1856.

MARSIGLI, Comte de. *L'État Militaire de l'Empire Ottoman*. The Hague and Amsterdam, 1737.

MASSON, P. *Histoire du commerce français dans le Levant au dix-huitième siècle*. Paris, 1911.

MATTINGLY, Garrett. *Renaissance Diplomacy*. London: Peregrine Books, 1965.

MECENSEFFY, G. *Karl VI*. Innsbruck, 1934.

MENSI, F. *Die Finanzen von Österreich, 1701–1740*. Vienna, 1890.

MITTAG, J. *Merkwürdiges Leben und Thaten Annae Ivanownae Kayserin u. Selbsthalterin aller Reussen*. Halle, 1741.

MONTAGU, Lady Mary Wortley. *Letters written during her travels into Europe, Asia and Africa*. London, 1727.

MOSER, Johann Jakob. *Der Belgrader Friedens-Schluss zwischen Ihro Römisch-Kayserl. Majestät und der Ottomanischen Pforte*. Jena, 1740.

MUSULIN, Janko von. *Prinz Eugen von Savoyen*. Herold Verlag. Vienna, Munich, 1963.

NEIPPERG, Count. *Umständliche auf Original Dockumente gegründete Geschichte der sämtlichen und wahren Vorgänge bei der Unterhandlung des zu Belgrad am 18 September 1739 geschlossenen Friedens*. Frankfurt and Leipzig, 1790.

Bibliography

NORADOUNGHIAN, Gabriel. *Recueil d'actes internationaux de l'Empire Ottoman.* Paris, 1897–1903. Vol. 1.

OTTER, M. *Voyage en Turquie et en Perse.* Paris, 1748.

PALLIS, A. *In the Days of the Janissaries.* London: Hutchinson, 1951.

PETRIE, Sir Charles. *Diplomatic History, 1713–1933.* London: Hollis and Carter, 1946.

PICAVET, C. G. *La diplomatie française au temps de Louis XIV.* Paris, 1930.

PICCIONI, C. *Les premiers Commis des affaires étrangères au XVII et au XVIIIe siècles.* Paris, 1928.

POCOCKE, R. *A description of the East and some other Countries.* London, 1743.

POLLNITZ, Charles Louis Baron de. *Memoirs.* London, 1739, 2nd edition.

P.R.O. Public Record Office. London. See note at the end of the Bibliography.

Recueil des Instructions données aux Ambassadeurs et Ministres de France depuis les Traités de Westphalie jusqu'à la Révolution française.

Vol. 2. *Suède.* Paris, 1885.

Vol. 8. *Russie.* Paris, 1890.

REDLICH, Oswald. *Das Werden einer Grossmacht, 1700–1740.* Vienna, 1942.

— *Die Tagebücher Karls VI. Festgabe für H. V. Srbik.* Munich, 1938.

REGELE, O. *Die Schuld des Grafen Reinhold Wilhelm v. Neipperg am Belgrader Frieden 1739.* Vienna: *Mitteilungen der Österreichischen Staatsarchivs.* 1954. Vol. 7

ROUSSET DE MISSY, J. *Supplément au Corps Universal Diplomatique du Droit des Gens. Racueil des Traités.* The Hague, 1739. Vol. 2, Part ii.

— *Mémoires sur le Rang et la Préséance entre les Souverains de l'Europe.* Amsterdam, 1746.

SAINT-PRIEST, Comte de. *Mémoires sur l'Ambassade de France et Turquie.* Paris, 1877

SAINT-SIMON, Duc de. *Mémoires* (ed. de Boislisle). Paris. 1879–1930. Vol. 29.

SAUSSURE, C. de. *Lettres de Turquie, 1730–1739.* Budapest, 1909.

SAX, C. von. *Geschichte des Machtverfalls der Türkei.* Vienna, 1913.

Sbornik Russkago Istoriceskago Obscestva, (Imperial Russian Historical Society). Vol. 86. St. Petersburg, 1884–8.

SCHMETTAU, Comte de. *Mémoires secrets de la Guerre d'Hongrie.* Frankfurt, 1772.

SCHWARZ, H. F. *The Imperial Privy Council in the 17th Century.* Harvard, 1943.

SECKENDORF, Theresius von. *Versuch einer Lebensbeschreibung des Feldmarschalls Grafen von Seckendorff.* 1792.

SEDLMAYR, H. *Die politische Bedeutung der deutsche Barock.* Munich: Festgabe von Srbik, 1938.

SETON-WATSON, R. W. *History of the Roumanians.* Cambridge, 1934.

SHAY, M. L. *The Ottoman Empire from 1720–1734.* Urbania, 1944. University of Illinois.

SPULER, B. *Europäische Diplomatie in Konstantinopel biz zum Frieden von Belgrad 1739.* Breslau: *Jahrbücher für Geschichte Osteuropas.* 1936.

STEFANOVIC-VILOVSKY, T. *Belgrad unter der Regierung Kaiser Karls VI, 1717–1739.* Vienna, 1908.

STERN, Selma. *The Court Jew.* Philadelphia, 1950.

SUMNER, B. H. *Peter the Great and the Ottoman Empire.* Oxford: Blackwells, 1949.

SYVETON, G. *Une Cour et un aventurier au dix-huitieme siècle.* Paris, 1896.

TAESCHNER, Franz. *Alt Stambuler Hof und Volksleben.* Hanover, 1925.

TAVERNIER, J. B. *Nouvelle Relation de l'Intérieur du Serail du Grand Seigneur.* Paris, 1675.

Bibliography

TIZIA-LEITICH, Ann. *Vienna Gloriosa*. Vienna: Willhelm Andermann Verlag, 1947.

TOTT, Baron de. *Mémoires*. London, 1786. 2nd edn.

TUPETZ, T., *Der Türkenfeldzug von 1739 und der Friede zu Belgrad*. Munich: *Historische Zeitschrift*. Vol. 40 (1878).

ÜBERSBERGER, H. *Russlands Orientpolitik in den letzten zwei Jahrhunderten*. Deutsche Verlags-Anstalt. Stuttgart, 1913.

UHLIRZ, Mathilde. *Handbuch der Geschichte Österreichs*. Graz, 1953.

VANDAL, A. *Une Ambassade Française en Orient sous Louis XV*. *La Mission du Marquis de Villeneuve, 1728–1741*. Paris, 1887.

— *Louis XV et Élisabeth de Russie*, Paris, 1882.

VAUCHER, P. *Robert Walpole et la Politique de Fleury*. Paris, 1927.

VEHSE, E. *Memoirs of the Court and Aristocracy of Austria*. Translated Demmles. London, 1896.

VERLAQUE, V. *Histoire du Cardinal de Fleury*. Paris, 1878.

VISCHER, Melchoir. *Münnich. Ingenieur, Feldherr, Hochverräter*. Frankfurt A.M., 1938.

VOLTAIRE. *Précis du Siècle de Louis XV*. Paris, 1888.

WALIZEWSKI, K. *L'héritage de Pierre-le-Grand, 1725–1741*. Paris: Librairie Plon, 1900.

WANDRUSKA, Adam. *Das Haus Habsburg*. Stuttgart, 1956.

WARD, Mrs. *Letters from a Lady who resided some years in Russia to her friend in England*. London, 1775.

WEBER, J. C. *Das Veränderte Russland*. Part 1, Frankfurt, 1721. Part 2, Hanover, 1739. Part 3, Hanover, 1740.

WILLIAMS, Basil. *The Whig Supremacy, 1714–1769*. Oxford, 1962.

WILSON, A. McCandless. *French Foreign Policy during the Administration of Cardinal Fleury*. Harvard, 1936.

WOOD, A. C. *The Levant Co.* London, 1935.

WRAXALL, N. W. *Memoirs of the Northern Courts*. London, 1806. 3rd edn., Vol 1.

WREDE, Alfons von. *Geschichte der k.k. Wehrmacht von 1616 bis Ende des XIX Jahrhunderts*. Vienna, 1903.

WRIGHT, W. L. *Ottoman Statecraft*. Princeton, 1935.

ZALLONY, M. P. *Essai sur les Fanarotes*. Marseilles, 1821.

ZINKEISEN, J. W. *Geschichte des Osmanisches Reich in Europa*. Hamburg, 1840–63. Vol. 5.

PUBLIC RECORD OFFICE LONDON

Dispatches of the British envoys in Constantinople, Vienna, St. Petersburg and Paris:

P.R.O., S.P. 97/25–97/31, *Constantinople*.

P.R.O., S.P. 80/54–80/58 and S.P. 80/113–80/141, *Vienna*.

P.R.O., S.P. 91/10–91/29, *St. Petersburg*.

P.R.O., S.P. 78/207–78/221, *Paris*.

Index

Adrianople, 5, 143, 161, 165
Ahmed III, Sultan, 52, 53, 57, 62–3, 80, 154
Alay, the, 105
Ali Pasha, 84, 90, 92, 106, 168, 188, 193
Amelot de Chaillou, 144, 193, 195
Andrezel, M. d', 50
Anne I, Czarina of Russia (formerly Duchess of Courland), 29–37, 43, 86, 97, 98, 100, 159, 201–2; Court of, 33–6
Argenson, Marquis d', 49
Armies:
  Imperial, 26, 119–21, 124–6, 146, 147, 152, 159
  Ottoman, 3, 56–9, 141
  Russian, 102, 151, 159
Auersperg, Prince, 204
Augesseau, Chancellor d', 51
Augustus II of Poland, 85
Augustus III of Poland (formerly Frederick Augustus, Prince of Saxony), 86, 87, 98, 101, 129
Austro-Russian Treaty 1726, 28, 29, 43, 98
Azov, 101, 104, 109, 110, 127, 137, 141–3, 155, 163, 195–6

Babadagh, 109, 111
Bakchiserai, 110
Baltic, 30, 98
Bánát, 14, 176, 201
Barbary pirates, 74
Barenklau, Colonel, 132, 133
Bartenstein, Hofrat Johann Christoph von, 117, 158–9, 175, 180, 202

Belgrade, 1, 2, 13–15, 26, 27, 47, 73, 87, 98, 122–5, 139, 142, 152–4, 164–6, 197–202, 204–6, capture of (1717), 4–9; siege and Peace of (1739), 167–96
Belvedere Palace (Vienna), 13
Bender, 121, 147
Beshir, Kizlar Aga, 62, 139, 160
Bestuzhev, Count, 148
Biron, Ernst Johann, 32–4, 37, 41–3, 86, 97, 101, 147, 158, 159
Black Sea, 38, 43, 97, 98, 100, 101, 104, 131, 195
Bohn, 89
Bonneval, Count Claude Alexandre de, 81–5, 87, 89, 90, 92–4, 107, 118, 139, 140, 154
Borcza redoubt, 174, 191, 193
Bosnia, 14, 123, 124, 131
Bosphorus, 52, 53, 98, 145, 205
Bossuet, Jacques Bénigne, 47
Botta, Marquis de, 158
Brunswick, Prince of, 35
Budapest, 2
Bug, river, 101
Buhren, see Biron, Ernst Johann
Burgundy, Duke of, 48
Byzantine Empire, 28

Cabinet Noir, 74
Cagnoni, 163, 195
Calkoen, Cornelius, 76, 108, 129, 142
Capitulations, 45, 46, 60, 205
Caroline, Queen, 76
Caspian Sea, 40, 79
Catherine I, Czarina of Russia, 28, 29, 40

Index

Caucasus, 58, 98, 104
Chancellery of Secret Investigation (St. Petersburg), 37
Charles V, Emperor, 44
Charles VI, Emperor, 1, 5, 13–29, 32, 33, 43, 94, 98, 115–23 136, 137, 145, 146, 156, 158–9, 168–70, 171, 175–9, 190–1, 198–200, 205; and Pragmatic Sanction, 27–8, 86; Court of, 16–21, 25–6, 34
Chauvelin, Germain-Louis de, 52, 84, 88, 92, 111, 144, 161
Choczim, 172, 201
Colbert, Jean Baptiste, 45
Collovitz, Cardinal, 199
Constantinople, the city and its inhabitants, 52–3, 63–5
Cossacks, 78, 101, 102, 132
Courland, Duchy of, 30, 31, 33, 36, 86, 101, 147
Crawford, Lord (quoted), 151
Crimea, 46, 78, 98–104, 109, 110, 121, 131, 133, 134, 147, 151

Daghestan, 79
Danube, river, 1, 2, 4, 5, 6, 8, 107, 108, 120, 121, 122, 123, 125, 126, 131, 152, 167, 173, 174, 177, 182, 184
Danzig, 30, 87, 91, 92
Daoud Pasha, 105, 107
Delaria, 67, 89, 129, 135, 136, 143, 165, 168, 183, 184, 188, 189, 192
Denain, battle of, 40
Djanum Khoda, 80
Dnieper, river, 78, 101, 110, 121
Dniester, river, 121, 128, 131, 147, 152, 158, 194, 201
Don, river, 78, 101, 163
Doxat, General, 145

Edle Ritter, song, 206
Elvias Mohammed Pasha, Grand Vizier, 160, 161, 164, 169, 177, 179, 184–6, 192, 194
Erlach, Fischer von, 18

Favorita Palace (Vienna), 1, 17, 19
Fawkener, Sir Everard, 108, 129, 142
Ferdinand, Duke of Courland, 30
Ferriol, M. de, 61

Fleury, André Hercule, Cardinal, 47–52, 69, 87, 88, 91–2, 94–6, 107, 111, 136, 137, 140, 141, 143–51, 153, 156, 157, 160, 165, 168, 192, 196, 202, 206
Francis I, King of France, 44
Franz Stefan, Duke of Lorraine, 125, 147, 180
Frederick Augustus, Prince of Saxony, see Augustus III of Poland
Frederick the Great (quoted), 22, 32, 41, 202
Frederick William, Duke of Courland, 30
Fréjus, 47

Geheime Konferenz, see Imperial Privy Council
Genghis Khan, 78
George I of England, 27
George II of England, 75
Georgia, 79
Ghika, Alexander, 185, 186
Golden Horde, 78
Golden Horn, 53, 162
Golitsuin, Prince, 29, 30
Gran, Daniel, 16
Groczka, battle of, 165–7, 173, 186, 198
Gross, Count, 169, 173–4, 178–9, 182

Hakimouglou Ali Pasha, Grand Vizier, see Ali Pasha
Halbthurn, Schloss, 17
Hamilton, Count, 1
Harrach, Count Joseph, 116, 159
Herrenhausen, League of, 27
Hildburghausen, Prince, 121, 123, 134
Hildebrandt, Lukas von, 13
Hofburg Palace (Vienna), 17, 19
Hofkammer, 24, 120
Hofkriegsrat, 4, 6, 15, 24, 120, 122, 124, 126, 153, 159, 172
Holy Roman Empire, 13, 15, 23
Hungary, 2, 5, 9, 14, 89, 118, 123, 140, 152

Ibrahim Pasha, Grand Vizier, 52, 60, 62, 63, 80
Imperial Library (Vienna), 16
Imperial Ostend Company, 47
Imperial Privy Council, 15, 24, 116, 123, 199
Imperial Riding School (Vienna), 15, 16
Imperial Treasury (Vienna), see Hofkammer

Imperial War Council (Vienna), *see* Hofkriegsrat
Inner Council of Three (Russia), 38
Iron Gate, 152
Issy, 49

Janissaries, *see* Armies, Ottoman
Jassy, 201
Jegen Mohammed Pasha, Grand Vizier, 139–44, 154, 160, 164
Joseph I, Emperor, 27

Kahlenberg, 13
Karlskirche (Vienna), 15, 16
Khalil, Grand Vizier, 6, 7
Kinburn, 110, 142, 152, 154
Kinnoull, Lord, 76
Königsegg, Count Lothar Joseph Dominic, 116, 120, 122, 124, 128, 131, 147, 152, 153, 158, 201
Kornia, 153
Kuban, 131

Lacy, General, 101, 121, 133, 134, 151
Ladoga, Lake, 40
Laxenburg Palace (Vienna), 17, 19
Leopoldsberg, 13
Leopoldstadt, 2
Leszczynski, Stanislas, 86, 87, 90, 92, 94
Levant Company, 75
Liechtenstein, Prince, 149
Lobkowitz, Prince, 201
Louis XIV, 45, 47, 48
Louis XV, 47, 48, 86, 90, 91, 95, 141, 144, 146, 202, 205, 206

Mahmoud I, Sultan, 80, 90, 154, 162
Marly, 63
Maria Theresa (as Archduchess), 27
Mariazell, 27, 147
Marseilles, 45, 73, 92; Chamber of Commerce, 45
Max Emmanuel, Elector of Bavaria, 2
Mazarin, Cardinal, 48
Mediterranean, 74, 92, 131
Mehmet II, the Conquerer, 53
Mercy d'Argenteau, General, 199
Metastasio, 18
Mirepoix, Marquis de, 156, 168
Mittau, 30, 33
Mohács (1687), 2; (1526), 44, 135

Moldavia, 65, 100, 121, 131, 133, 134, 172, 201
Momarz, 182, 194
Montagu, Lady Mary Wortley (quoted), 20, 53
Morava, river, 122, 126
Moscow, 78
Münnich, Field-Marshal Burchard Christoph, 37, 39–42, 43, 97, 99–103, 104, 110, 121, 130, 132–4, 147, 151–2, 158, 194, 200–1

Nadir Shah, 79–80, 84, 142
Neipperg, Count Reinhold Wilhelm, 176–200, 202, 203
Nemirow, Congress of, 127–37
Neplyuev, Ivan Ivanovich, 76–7, 79, 80, 89, 99, 130, 132–5, 137
Neustadt, 178, 190
Nish, 2, 73, 122, 125, 130, 134, 138, 145, 165, 166, 189
Nointel, M. de, 61
Nystedt, Peace of, 37

Ochakov, 121, 130, 132–4, 137, 138, 141, 142, 152, 154
Orsova, 152, 153, 161, 168, 177, 194
Ostein, Count Heinrich, 115, 119, 120, 130, 132–5, 158
Ostermann, Count Andrej Ivanovič, 37–9, 41–3, 49, 77, 87, 88, 96–100, 104, 115, 117, 119, 121, 128, 131–4, 140, 142, 148–50, 156–7, 159, 163, 164, 195, 201, 202

Passarowitz, Treaty of (1718), 14, 47, 138, 141, 183
Pera, 53, 140
Perekop, Isthmus of, 103, 110
Persia, 79, 84, 89, 109
Peter the Great, 27–30, 32, 34, 36–8, 40, 42, 79, 98, 100, 101, 148, 163
Peter II, 29, 40
Peterwardein, 3, 173, 191
Peysonnel, 143, 144, 183
Pietas Austriaca, 13
Poland, 45, 86–8, 90–1, 100–1, 120, 172
Polignac, Cardinal de, 21
Poltava, battle of, 148
Potocki, Count, 129
Preobrezensky Guards, 31
Prussia, 27, 92

Index

Rákóczi, Prince Franz II, 89, 139
Rákóczi, Joseph, 139–40, 142, 143, 153, 154
Reichstag, 23, 119
Revolution of 1730, Constantinople, 80
Richelieu, Cardinal, 48
Richelieu, Duc de (quoted), 21
Rousseau, Jean Baptiste, 81
Rudolf the Founder, 14

Safavid dynasty, 79
St. Petersburg, the city and its inhabitants, 42
Saint Séverin, 148
St. Simon (quoted), 49
St. Stephen's Cathedral (Vienna), 126, 131
Santa Sophia (Constantinople), 53, 100
Sarajevo, 82, 83
Save, river, 1, 5, 6, 167, 173, 176, 177, 182, 184
Savoy, Prince Eugen of, captures Belgrade (1717), 2–9; 13, 14, 25, 26, 81–2, 87, 88, 115–18, 122, 167, 183, 199, 206
Schmettau, General Samuel von, 176, 190–3, 197–8
Schwacheim, von, 178
Schwarzenberg, Prince Adam, 17
Scutari, 80
Seckendorf, Field-Marshal Friedrich Heinrich von, 122, 124–6, 130, 134, 145, 147, 201
Serail, the, 53–5
Serbia, 14, 131, 142, 194
Seven Towers, the, 61, 106, 128
Siebenbürgen, 15, 123, 124, 139, 142, 143, 153
Sinzendorf, Count Philipp Ludwig von, 25, 116–18, 124, 141, 144, 146, 159, 161, 164, 165, 168, 175
Soroki, 128
Ssubhi (quoted), 138
Stamboul, 57, 100, 162
Stanyan, Abraham, 76
Starhemberg, Count Gundaker, 25, 116, 119
Stavuchankh (battle of), 201
Suckow, General, 172, 174–5, 181, 189, 191
Suleiman the Magnificent, Sultan, 44, 53

Supreme Privy Council (St. Petersburg), 29–31, 36
Sweden, and the Swedes, 37, 148, 149, 157, 171, 201
Sweet Waters of Europe, 62
Surdock, 179, 180

Talman, Leopold von, 76, 79, 80–3, 87, 89, 108–9, 118–21, 126, 127–36, 142, 200
Tartar Khan and the Tartars, 78, 90, 95–103, 104, 109, 110, 131, 139, 151
Temesvár, 14, 119, 142, 154
Topal Osman Pasha, 80, 83, 84
Tott, Baron, 90, 110–11, 129, 135–7
Trubetskoy, Prince, 102
Tsaritzinka, 102
Türkenglocken, 126

Ukraine, 78, 91, 110, 142, 201
Uti Posseditis, 123, 128, 134

Vantelac, M. de, 61
Veshniakov, Alexsej, 77, 99–100, 104–6
Vidin, 122, 125, 131, 134
Vienna, the city and its inhabitants, 1, 2, 13, 15–16, 20
Villeneuve, Louis-Saveur, Marquis de; appointed Ambassador in Constantinople 51–3; presents credentials, 57–60; difficulties of 1728–33, 61–70, 73, 76, 80–1, 83–5; discomfiture of 1733–5, 88–94; frustrations of 1736–8, 103, 106–9, 110–11, 135–8, 140–4, 150–7; appointed mediator 1739, 160–3; journey of to Belgrade, 163–70; negotiates Peace of Belgrade, 179–80, 183–9, 192–6; concludes mission, 202–6
Villeneuve, la Marquise de, 52, 205
Volga, river, 40, 78

Waldegrave, Lord (quoted), 49
Wallachia, 14, 26, 65, 121, 123, 131, 133, 134, 168, 177, 194
Wallis, Field-Marshal Georg Oliver, 169, 171–80, 189–92, 197–201
Walpole, Sir Robert, 75

Zenta, battle of, 3